D0963860

FRENCH

PHRASE BOOK & DICTIONARY

CONTENTS

Hi, I'm Rick Steves.

I'm the only monolingual speaker I know who's had the nerve to design a series of European phrase books. But that's one of the things that makes them better.

You see, after more than 30 years of travel through Europe, I've learned firsthand: (1) what's essential for communication in another country; and (2) what's not. I've assembled the most important words and phrases in a logical, no-frills format, and I've worked with native Europeans and seasoned travelers to give you the simplest, clearest translation possible.

But this book is more than just a pocket translator. The words and phrases have been carefully selected to help you have a smarter, smoother trip in France. The key to getting more out of every travel dollar is to get closer to the local people, and to rely less on entertainment, restaurants, and hotels that cater only to foreign tourists. This book will not only help you order a meal at a locals-only Parisian restaurant—but also help you talk with the family who runs the place...about their kids, travel dreams, and favorite ***fromage.*** Long after your memories of châteaux have faded, you'll still treasure the personal encounters you had with your new French friends.

While I've provided plenty of phrases, you'll find it just as effective to use even just a word or two to convey your meaning, and rely on context, gestures, and smiles to help you out. To make harried postal clerks happy, don't say haltingly in French: "I would like to buy three stamps to mail these postcards to the United States." All you really need is ***timbres*** (stamps), ***les Etats-Unis*** (USA), and ***s'il vous plaît*** (please). Smile, point to the postcards, hold up three fingers...and you've got stamps. (For more advice, see Tips for Hurdling the Language Barrier on page 411.)

To get the most out of this book, take the time to internalize and put into practice my French pronunciation tips. But don't worry too much about memorizing grammatical rules, like the gender of a noun—forget about sex, and communicate!

This book has a nifty menu decoder and a handy dictionary. You'll also find tongue twisters, international words, telephone tips, and two handy "cheat sheets." Tear out the sheets and tuck them in your beret, so you can easily memorize key phrases during otherwise idle moments. A good phrase book should help you enjoy your travel experience—not just survive it—so I've added a healthy dose of humor. And as you prepare for your trip, you may want to read the latest editions of my guidebooks on Paris, Provence & the French Riviera, and France.

Adjust those cultural blinders. If you come to France expecting rudeness, you are sure to find it. If you respect the fine points of French culture and make an attempt to use their language, you'll find the French as warm and friendly as anyone in Europe.

Your experience will be enriched by a basic understanding of French etiquette. Here's the situation in a nutshell: The French feel that informality is rude and formality is polite, while Americans feel that informality is friendly and formality is cold. So, ironically, as the Americans and French are both doing their best to be nice, they accidentally offend one another. Remember you're the outsider, so watch the locals and try to incorporate some French-style politeness into your routine. Walk into any shop in France and you will hear a cheery, ***"Bonjour, Monsieur / Madame."*** As you leave, you'll hear a lilting, ***"Au revoir, Monsieur / Madame."*** Always address a man as ***Monsieur,*** a woman as ***Madame,*** and an unmarried young woman or a girl as ***Mademoiselle*** (leaving this out is like addressing a French person as "Hey, you!"). For good measure, toss in ***s'il vous plaît*** (please) whenever you can.

My goal is to help you become a more confident, extroverted traveler. If this phrase book helps make that happen, or if you have suggestions for making it better, I'd love to hear from you at rick@ricksteves.com.

Bon voyage! Have a good trip!

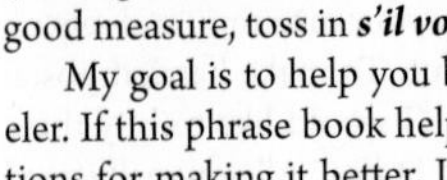

GETTING STARTED

Challenging, Romantic French is spoken throughout Europe and thought to be one of the most beautiful languages in the world. Half of Belgium speaks French, and French rivals English as the handiest second language in Spain, Portugal, and Italy. Even your US passport is translated into French. You're probably already familiar with this poetic language. Consider: ***bonjour, c'est la vie, bon appétit, merci, au revoir,*** and ***bon voyage!*** The most important phrase is ***s'il vous plaît*** (please), pronounced see voo play. Use it liberally—the French will notice and love it.

You can communicate a lot with only a few key French words: ***ça, ça va, je peux,*** and ***voilà***. Here's how:

Ça (pronounced "sah") is a tourist's best friend. Meaning "that" or "this," it conveys worlds of meaning when combined with pointing. At the market, ***fromagerie,*** or ***pâtisserie,*** just point to what you want and say ***Ça, s'il vous plaît,*** with a smile.

Ça va (sah vah), meaning roughly "it goes," can fit almost any situation. As a question, ***Ça va?*** (Does it go?) can mean "Is this OK?" When combined with a gesture, you can use ***Ça va?*** to ask, "Can I sit here?" or "Can I touch this?" or "Can I take a picture?" or "Will this ticket get me into this museum?"...and much more. As a statement, ***Ça va*** (which basically means "Yes, it's OK") is almost as versatile. When the waiter asks if you want anything more, say ***Ça va*** ("I'm good"). If someone's hassling you and you've had enough, you can just say ***Ça va*** ("That's enough.").

Je peux? (zhuh puh, means "Can I?") can be used in many of the ***Ça va?*** situations, and more. Instead of saying, "Can I please sit here?", just gesture toward the seat and say ***Je peux?*** Instead of asking "Do you accept credit cards?" show them your Visa and ask ***Je peux?***

While English speakers use ***Voilà*** (vwah-lah) only for a grand unveiling at a special occasion, the French say it many times each day. It means "Yes" or "Exactly" or "That's it" or "There you go." Unsure of how much your plums cost, you hold a euro coin out to the vendor and say ***Ça va?*** He responds with a cheery ***Voilà***...and you're on your way, plums in hand.

While a number of French people speak fine English, many don't. The language barrier can seem high in France, but locals are happy to give an extra boost to any traveler who makes an effort to communicate. As with any language, the key to communicating is to go for it with a mixture of bravado and humility.

French pronunciation differs from English in some key ways:

Ç sounds like S in sun.
CH sounds like SH in shine.
G usually sounds like G in get.
But G followed by E or I sounds like S in treasure.
GN sounds like NI in onion.
H is always silent.
J sounds like S in treasure.
R sounds like an R being swallowed.
I sounds like EE in seed.
È and **Ê** sound like E in let.
É and **EZ** sound like AY in play.
ER, at the end of a word, sounds like AY in play.
Ô and **EAU** sounds like O in note.

In a Romance language, sex is unavoidable. A man is ***content*** (happy), a woman is ***contente.*** In this book, when you see a pair of words like ***content / contente,*** use the second word when talking about a woman.

French has four accents. The cedilla makes **Ç** sound like "s" ***(façade).*** The circumflex makes Ê sound like "eh" ***(crêpe),*** but has no effect on ***Â, Î, Ô,*** or ***Û.*** The grave accent stifles **È** into "eh" ***(crème),*** but doesn't change the stubborn ***À (à la carte).*** The acute accent opens **É** into "ay" ***(café).***

French is tricky because the spelling and pronunciation seem to have little to do with each other. ***Qu'est-ce que c'est?*** (What is that?) is pronounced: kehs kuh say.

The final letters of many French words are silent, so ***Paris*** sounds like pah-ree. The French tend to stress every syllable evenly: pah-ree. In contrast, Americans say ***Par***-is, emphasizing the first syllable.

In French, if a word that ends in a consonant is followed by a word that starts with a vowel, the consonant is frequently linked with the vowel. ***Mes amis*** (my friends) is pronounced: mayz-ah-mee. Some words are linked with an apostrophe. ***Ce est*** (It is) becomes ***C'est,*** as in ***C'est la vie*** (That's life). ***Le*** and ***la*** (the masculine and feminine "the") are intimately connected to words starting with a vowel. ***La orange*** becomes ***l'orange.***

French has a few sounds that are unusual in English: the French ***u*** and the nasal vowels. To say the French ***u,*** round your lips to say "oh," but say "ee." Vowels combined with either ***n*** or ***m*** are often nasal vowels. As you nasalize a vowel, let the sound come through your nose as well as your mouth. The vowel is the important thing. The ***n*** or ***m,*** represented in this book by n for nasal, is not pronounced.

There are a total of four nasal sounds, all contained in the phrase ***un bon vin blanc*** (a good white wine).

Nasal vowels	Phonetics	To make the sound
un	uhn	nasalize the U in lung
bon	bohn	nasalize the O in bone
vin	van	nasalize the A in sack
blanc	blahn	nasalize the A in want

If you practice saying ***un bon vin blanc,*** you'll learn how to say the nasal vowels...and order a fine white wine.

Here's a guide to the rest of the phonetics in this book:

ah	like A in father
ay	like AY in play
eh	like E in let
ee	like EE in seed
ehr / air	sounds like "air" (in merci and extraordinaire)
ew	pucker your lips and say "ee"
g	like G in go
ī	like I in light

oh	like O in note
oo	like OO in too
s	like S in sun
uh	like U in but
ur	like UR in purr
zh	like S in treasure

FRENCH BASICS

Be creative! You can combine the phrases in this chapter to say "Two, please," or "No, thank you," or "Open tomorrow?" or "Please, where can I buy a ticket?" "Please" is a magic word in any language, especially in French. If you know the word for what you want, such as the bill, simply say ***L'addition, s'il vous plaît*** (The bill, please).

HELLOS AND GOODBYES

Pleasantries

Hello.	Bonjour. bohn-zhoor
Do you speak English?	Parlez-vous anglais? par-lay-voo ahn-glay
Yes. / No.	Oui. / Non. wee / nohn
I don't speak French.	Je ne parle pas français. zhuh nuh parl pah frahn-say
I'm sorry.	Désolé. day-zoh-lay
Please.	S'il vous plaît. see voo play
Thank you (very much).	Merci (beaucoup). mehr-see (boh-koo)
Excuse me. (to get attention)	Excusez-moi. ehk-skew-zay-mwah
Excuse me. (to pass)	Pardon. par-dohn
OK?	Ça va? sah vah
OK. (two ways to say it)	Ça va. / D'accord. sah vah / dah-kor
Good.	Bien. bee-an
Very good.	Très bien. treh bee-an
Excellent.	Excellent. ehk-seh-lahn
You are very kind.	Vous êtes très gentil. vooz eht treh zhahn-tee
It doesn't matter.	Ça m'est égal. sah meht ay-gahl
No problem.	Pas de problème. pah duh proh-blehm

You're welcome.	De rien. duh ree-an
Goodbye.	Au revoir. oh ruh-vwahr

Pardon and ***Excusez-moi*** aren't interchangeable. Say ***Pardon*** to get past someone; use ***Excusez-moi*** to get someone's attention.

Meeting and Greeting

The French begin every interaction with ***Bonjour, Monsieur*** (to a man) or ***Bonjour, Madame*** (to a woman). It's impossible to overstate the importance of this courtesy. To the French, a proper greeting respectfully acknowledges the recipient as a person first, and secondly as a professional. Taking the time to say a polite hello marks you as a conscientious visitor and guarantees a warmer welcome.

Good day.	Bonjour. bohn-zhoor
Good morning.	Bonjour. bohn-zhoor
Good evening.	Bonsoir. bohn-swahr
Good night.	Bonne soirée. buhn swah-ray
Hi / Bye. (informal)	Salut. sah-lew
Welcome!	Bienvenue! bee-an-vuh-new
Mr.	Monsieur muhs-yuh
Mrs.	Madame mah-dahm
Miss	Mademoiselle mahd-mwah-zehl
Good day, gentlemen and ladies.	Bonjour, Messieurs et Madames. bohn-zhoor mays-yuh ay mah-dahm
My name is ____.	Je m'appelle ____. zhuh mah-pehl ____
What's your name?	Quel est votre nom? kehl ay voh-truh nohn
Pleased to meet you.	Enchanté. ahn-shahn-tay
How are you?	Comment allez-vous? koh-mahnt ah-lay-voo
Very well, thank you.	Très bien, merci. treh bee-an mehr-see

Fine.	Bien. bee-an
And you?	Et vous? ay voo
Where are you from?	D'où êtes-vous? doo eht-voo
I am from _____.	Je suis de _____. zhuh swee duh _____
I am / We are...	Je suis / Nous sommes... zhuh swee / noo suhm
Are you...?	Êtes-vous...? eht-voo
...on vacation	...en vacances ahn vah-kahns
...on business	...en voyage d'affaires ahn vwah-yahzh dah-fair

The greeting ***Bonjour*** (Good day) turns to ***Bonsoir*** (Good evening) at dinnertime. If the French see someone they've just greeted recently, they may say ***Rebonjour***.

You might hear locals use the breezy ***Bonjour, Messieurs / Dames*** or even ***Bonjour, tout le monde*** (Hello, everybody) if both men and women are present. But to proper French people, this is too rushed and sloppy. Take the time to say ***Bonjour, Messieurs et Madames*** (Hello, gentlemen and ladies).

Moving On

I'm going to _____.	Je vais à _____. zhuh vay ah _____
How do I go to _____?	Comment aller à _____? koh-mahnt ah-lay ah _____
Let's go.	Allons-y. ah-lohn-zee
See you later.	À bientôt. ah bee-an-toh
See you tomorrow!	A demain! ah duh-man
So long! (informal)	Salut! sah-lew
Goodbye.	Au revoir. oh ruh-vwahr
Good luck!	Bonne chance! buhn shahns
Happy travels!	Bon voyage! bohn vwah-yahzh

STRUGGLING WITH FRENCH

Who Speaks What?

French	français frahn-say
English	anglais ahn-glay
Do you speak English?	Parlez-vous anglais? par-lay-voo ahn-glay
A teeny weeny bit?	Un tout petit peu? uhn too puh-tee puh
Please speak English.	Parlez anglais, s'il vous plaît. par-lay ahn-glay see voo play
Slowly.	Lentement. lahnt-mahn
Repeat?	Répétez? ray-pay-tay
I understand.	Je comprends. zhuh kohn-prahn
I don't understand.	Je ne comprends pas. zhuh nuh kohn-prahn pah
Do you understand?	Vous comprenez? voo kohn-pruh-nay
You speak English well.	Vous parlez bien l'anglais. voo par-lay bee-an lahn-glay
Does somebody nearby speak English?	Quelqu'un près d'ici parle anglais? kehl-kuhn preh dee-see parl ahn-glay
I don't speak French.	Je ne parle pas français. zhuh nuh parl pah frahn-say
I speak a little French.	Je parle un petit peu français. zhuh parl uhn puh-tee puh frahn-say
What does this mean?	Qu'est-ce que ça veut dire? kehs kuh sah vuh deer
How do you say this in French?	Comment dit-on en français? koh-mahn dee-tohn ahn frahn-say
Write it down?	Ecrivez? ay-kree-vay

A French person who is asked "Do you speak English?" assumes you mean "Do you speak English fluently?" and will likely answer no. But if you just keep on struggling in French, you'll bring out the English in most any French person.

Quintessentially French Expressions

Bon appétit! boh<u>n</u> ah-pay-tee	Enjoy your meal!
Ça va? sah vah	How are you? (informal)
Ça va. (response to Ça va?) sah vah	I'm fine.
Sympa. / Pas sympa. sa<u>n</u>-pah / pah sa<u>n</u>-pah	Nice. / Not nice.
C'est chouette. ("That's a female owl.") say shweht	That's cool.
Ce n'est pas vrai! suh nay pah vray	It's not true!
C'est comme ça. say kohm sah	That's the way it is.
Comme ci, comme ça. kohm see kohm sah	So so.
D'accord. dah-kor	OK.
Formidable! for-mee-dah-bluh	Great!
Mon Dieu! moh<u>n</u> dee-uh	My God!
Tout de suite. tood sweet	Right away.
Bonne journée. boh<u>n</u> zhoor-nay	Have a good day.
Voilà. vwah-lah	Here it is.
Oh la la! oo lah lah	Wow!

REQUESTS

The Essentials

Can you help me?	Vous pouvez m'aider? voo poo-vay meh-day
Do you have ____?	Avez-vous ____? ah-vay-voo ____
I'd like...	Je voudrais... zhuh voo-dray
We'd like...	Nous voudrions... noo voo-dree-ohn
...this / that.	...ceci / cela. suh-see / suh-lah
How much does it cost, please?	Combien, s'il vous plaît? kohn-bee-an see voo play
Is it free?	C'est gratuit? say grah-twee
Included?	Inclus? an-klew
Is it possible?	C'est possible? say poh-see-bluh
Yes or no?	Oui ou non? wee oo nohn
Where are the toilets?	Où sont les toilettes? oo sohn lay twah-leht
men	hommes ohm
women	dames dahm

To prompt a simple answer, ask ***Oui ou non***? (Yes or no?). To turn a word or sentence into a question, ask it in a questioning tone. ***C'est bon*** (It's good) becomes ***C'est bon?*** (Is it good?). An easy way to say "Where is the toilet?" is to ask ***Toilette, s'il vous plaît?***

Where?

Where?	Où? oo
Where is...?	Où est...? oo ay
...the tourist information office	...l'office de tourisme loh-fees duh too-reez-muh
...a cash machine	...un distributeur uhn dee-stree-bew-tur
...the train station	...la gare lah gar

Where can I buy _____?	Où puis-je acheter _____? oo pweezh ah-shuh-tay _____
Where can I find _____?	Où puis-je trouver _____? oo pweezh troo-vay _____

French makes it easy if you're looking for a ***pharmacie, hôtel,*** or ***restaurant.***

How Much?

How much does it cost, please?	Combien, s'il vous plaît? kohn-bee-an see voo play
Write it down?	Ecrivez? ay-kree-vay
I'd like...	Je voudrais... zhuh voo-dray
...a ticket.	...un billet. uhn bee-yay
...the bill.	...l'addition. lah-dee-see-ohn
This much. (gesturing)	Comme ça. kohm sah
More. / Less.	Plus. / Moins. plew / mwan
Too much.	Beaucoup trop. boh-koo troh

When?

When?	Quand? kahn
What time is it?	Quelle heure est-il? kehl ur ay-teel
At what time?	À quelle heure? ah kehl ur
_____ o'clock	_____ heures _____ ur
opening times	horaires d'ouverture oh-rair doo-vehr-tewr
open / closed	ouvert / fermé oo-vehr / fehr-may
What time does this open / close?	À quelle heure c'est ouvert / fermé? ah kehl ur say oo-vehr / fehr-may
Is this open daily?	C'est ouvert tous les jours? say oo-vehr too lay zhoor

What day is this closed?	C'est fermé quel jour? say fehr-may kehl zhoor
On time?	A l'heure? ah lur
Late?	En retard? ahn ruh-tar
Just a moment.	Un moment. uhn moh-mahn
now / soon / later	maintenant / bientôt / plus tard man-tuh-nahn / bee-an-toh / plew tar
today / tomorrow	aujourd'hui / demain oh-zhoor-dwee / duh-man

For tips on telling time, see "Time and Dates" on page 34.

How Long?

How long does it take?	Ça prend combien de temps? sah prahn kohn-bee-an duh tahn
How many minutes / hours?	Combien de minutes / d'heures? kohn-bee-an duh mee-newt / dur
How far?	C'est loin? say lwan

Just Ask

Why?	Pourquoi? poor-kwah
Why not?	Pourquoi pas? poor-kwah pah
Is it necessary?	C'est nécessaire? say nay-suh-sair
Can I...?	Je peux...? zhuh puh
Can we...?	Nous pouvons...? noo poo-vohn
...borrow that for a moment	...emprunter ça pour un moment ahn-pruhn-tay sah poor uhn moh-mahn
...use the toilet	...utiliser les toilettes ew-tee-lee-zay lay twah-leht
Next? (in line)	Le prochain? luh proh-shan

The last? (in line)	Le dernier? luh dehrn-yay
What? (didn't hear)	Comment? koh-mahn
What is this?	Qu'est-ce que c'est? kehs kuh say
What's going on?	Qu'est-ce qui se passe? kehs kee suh pahs

SIMPLY IMPORTANT WORDS

Numbers

0	zéro zay-roh
1	un uhn
2	deux duh
3	trois trwah
4	quatre kah-truh
5	cinq sank
6	six sees
7	sept seht
8	huit weet
9	neuf nuhf
10	dix dees
11	onze ohnz
12	douze dooz
13	treize trehz
14	quatorze kah-torz
15	quinze kanz
16	seize sehz
17	dix-sept dee-seht
18	dix-huit deez-weet
19	dix-neuf deez-nuhf
20	vingt van

You'll find more to count on in the "Numbers" section (page 26).

The Alphabet

If you're spelling your name over the phone, you can use the nouns in the third column to help make yourself understood. I'd say my name as: ***R...Raoul, I...Irma, C...Célestin, K...Kléber.***

A	ah	Anatole	ahn-ah-tohl
B	bay	Berthe	behrt
C	say	Célestin	say-luh-stan
D	day	Désiré	day-zee-ray
E	uh	Emile	eh-meel
F	"f"	François	frahn-swah
G	zhay	Gaston	gah-stohn
H	ahsh	Henri	ahn-ree
I	ee	Irma	eer-mah
J	zhee	Joseph	zhoh-zuhf
K	kah	Kléber	klay-behr
L	"l"	Louis	loo-ee
M	"m"	Marcel	mar-sehl
N	"n"	Nicolas	nee-koh-lahs
O	"o"	Oscar	ohs-kar
P	pay	Pierre	pee-yehr
Q	kew	Quintal	kween-tahl
R	ehr	Raoul	rah-ool
S	"s"	Suzanne	sew-zahn
T	tay	Thérèse	tay-rehs
U	ew	Ursule	ewr-sewl
V	vay	Victor	veek-tor
W	doo-bluh-vay	William	weel-yahm
X	"x"	Xavier	zhahv-yehr
Y	ee-grehk	Yvonne	ee-vohn
Z	zehd	Zoé	zoh-ay

Days and Months

Sunday	dimanche dee-mahnsh
Monday	lundi luhn-dee
Tuesday	mardi mar-dee
Wednesday	mercredi mehr-kruh-dee
Thursday	jeudi zhuh-dee
Friday	vendredi vahn-druh-dee
Saturday	samedi sahm-dee
January	janvier zhahn-vee-yay
February	février fay-vree-yay
March	mars mars
April	avril ahv-reel
May	mai may
June	juin zhwan
July	juillet zhwee-yay
August	août oot
September	septembre sehp-tahn-bruh
October	octobre ohk-toh-bruh
November	novembre noh-vahn-bruh
December	décembre day-sahn-bruh

Big Little Words

I	je zhuh
you (for formal use or a group)	vous voo
you (informal)	tu tew
we	nous noo
he	il eel
she	elle ehl
it (m / f; varies by gender of noun)	le / la luh / lah

they (m / f)	ils / elles eel / ehl
and	et ay
at	à ah
because	parce que pars kuh
but	mais may
by (train, car, etc.)	par par
for	pour poor
from	de duh
here	ici ee-see
if	si see
in	en ahn
not	pas pah
now	maintenant man-tuh-nahn
of	de / du duh / dew
only	seulement suhl-mahn
or	ou oo
out	dehors / à l'extérieur duh-or / ah lehk-stay-ree-ur
this	ceci suh-see
that	cela suh-lah
to	à ah
too	aussi oh-see
very	très treh

Opposites

good / bad	bon / mauvais bohn / moh-vay
best / worst	le meilleur / le pire luh meh-yur / luh peer
a little / lots	un peu / beaucoup uhn puh / boh-koo
more / less	plus / moins plew / mwan

cheap / expensive	bon marché / cher bohn mar-shay / shehr
big / small	grand / petit grahn / puh-tee
hot / cold	chaud / froid shoh / frwah
warm / cool	tiède / frais tee-ehd / fray
cool (nice) / not cool	sympa / pas sympa san-pah / pah san-pah
open / closed	ouvert / fermé oo-vehr / fehr-may
entrance / exit	entrée / sortie ahn-tray / sor-tee
push / pull	pousser / tirer poo-say / tee-ray
arrive / depart	arriver / partir ah-ree-vay / par-teer
early / late	tôt / tard toh / tar
soon / later	bientôt / plus tard bee-an-toh / plew tar
fast / slow	vite / lent veet / lahn
here / there	ici / là-bas ee-see / lah-bah
near / far	près / loin preh / lwan
inside / outside	l'intérieur / dehors lan-tay-ree-ur / duh-or
mine / yours	le mien / le vôtre luh mee-an / luh voh-truh
this / that	ceci / cela. suh-see / suh-lah
easy / difficult	facile / difficile fah-seel / dee-fee-seel
left / right	à gauche / à droite ah gohsh / ah drwaht
up / down	en haut / en bas ahn oh / ahn bah
above / below	au-dessus / en-dessous oh-duh-sew / ahn-duh-soo
young / old	jeune / vieux zhuhn / vee-uh
new / old	neuf / vieux nuhf / vee-uh
heavy / light	lourd / léger loor / lay-zhay
dark / light	sombre / clair sohn-bruh / klair
happy / sad	content / triste kohn-tahn / treest

beautiful / ugly	beau / laid boh / lay
nice / mean	gentil / méchant zhahn-tee / may-shahn
intelligent / stupid	intelligent / stupide an-teh-lee-zhahn / stew-peed
vacant / occupied	libre / occupé lee-bruh / oh-kew-pay
with / without	avec / sans ah-vehk / sahn

SIGN LANGUAGE

Here are common signs you'll see in your travels.

À disposition ici	Available here
À louer	For rent or for hire
À ne pas utiliser en cas d'urgence	Do not use in case of emergency
À vendre	For sale
À vos risques et périls	At your own risk
Accès réservé au personnel	Authorized personnel only
Alarme incendie	Fire alarm
Appel d'urgence	Emergency call
Appuyer sur l'interrupteur svp	Please press button (to change light)
Arrivées	Arrivals
Attendez	Wait
Attention	Caution
Attention à la marche	Watch your step
Caisse	Cashier
Carte Bancaire (CB) à partir de €_____	Credit cards accepted for purchases over €_____
Centre-ville	Town center
Chambre libre	Vacancy
Chien méchant	Mean dog
Complet	No vacancy
Compostage de billets	Validate tickets here

Composter avant de voyager	Validate tickets before traveling
Compostez ici	Validate tickets here
Dames	Women
Danger	Danger
Défense de fumer	No smoking
Défense de toucher	Do not touch
Défense d'entrer	Keep out
Départs	Departures
Eau non potable	Undrinkable water
Eau potable	Drinking water
En cas d'urgence	In case of emergency
En panne	Out of service
Entrée	Entrance
Entrée interdite	No entry
Entrée libre	Free admission
Étage	Floor
Faites l'appoint	Exact change only
Femmes ("F" on bathroom door)	Women
Fermé	Closed
Fermé pour restauration	Closed for restoration
Fermeture annuelle	Closed for vacation
Guichet	Ticket window
Hommes ("H" on bathroom door)	Men
Horaire	Timetable
Horaires d'ouverture	Opening times
Hors service	Out of service
Interdit	Forbidden
La file commence par la gauche / droite	The line begins at the left / right
Midi / Heure du déjeuner	Midday / Lunch break
Ne pas déranger	Do not disturb
Niveau	Level (of a building)
Nous avons...	We have...

Nous n'acceptons pas les paiements par cartes bancaires (CB)	We do not accept credit cards
Occupé	Occupied
Office de tourisme	Tourist information office
Ouvert	Open
Ouvert de ____ à ____	Open from ____ to ____
Pas de monnaie	No change given
Passage interdit	Do not enter
Passage piéton	Crosswalk / School crossing
Pelouse interdite	Keep off the grass
Poussez	Push
Poussez ici	Push here
Prenez un ticket	Take a ticket
Prudence	Be careful
Réduction	Special offer
Réservé	Reserved
Réservé aux piétons	Pedestrians only
Sens de la file	Direction of the line
Sens de la visite	Direction of the tour
Sens unique	One-way street
Solde	Sale
Sortie	Exit
Sortie de secours	Emergency exit
Stationnement interdit	No parking
Tirez	Pull
Toilettes	Toilets
Veuillez attendre ici	Please wait here
Veuillez prendre un numéro	Please take a number
Voie piétonne	Pedestrian zone
WC	Toilet
Zone piétonne	Pedestrian zone

NUMBERS, MONEY & TIME

You can count on this chapter to cover French numbers, currency, credit and debit cards, time, dates, and major holidays and celebrations.

NUMBERS

0	zéro zay-roh
1	un uhn
2	deux duh
3	trois trwah
4	quatre kah-truh
5	cinq sank
6	six sees
7	sept seht
8	huit weet
9	neuf nuhf
10	dix dees
11	onze ohnz
12	douze dooz
13	treize trehz
14	quatorze kah-torz
15	quinze kanz
16	seize sehz
17	dix-sept dee-seht
18	dix-huit deez-weet
19	dix-neuf deez-nuhf
20	vingt van
21	vingt et un vant ay uhn
22	vingt-deux vant-duh
23	vingt-trois vant-trwah
30	trente trahnt
31	trente et un trahnt ay uhn
40	quarante kah-rahnt

41	quarante et un kah-rahnt ay uhn
50	cinquante san-kahnt
51	cinquante et un san-kahnt ay uhn
60	soixante swah-sahnt
61	soixante et un swah-sahnt ay uhn
70	soixante-dix swah-sahnt-dees
71	soixante et onze swah-sahnt ay ohnz
72	soixante-douze swah-sahnt-dooz
73	soixante-treize swah-sahnt-trehz
74	soixante-quatorze swah-sahnt-kah-torz
75	soixante-quinze swah-sahnt-kanz
76	soixante-seize swah-sahnt-sehz
77	soixante-dix-sept swah-sahnt-dee-seht
78	soixante-dix-huit swah-sahnt-deez-weet
79	soixante-dix-neuf swah-sahnt-deez-nuhf
80	quatre-vingts kah-truh-van
81	quatre-vingt-un kah-truh-van-uhn
82	quatre-vingt-deux kah-truh-van-duh
83	quatre-vingt-trois kah-truh-van-trwah
84	quatre-vingt-quatre kah-truh-van-kah-truh
85	quatre-vingt-cinq kah-truh-van-sank
86	quatre-vingt-six kah-truh-van-sees
87	quatre-vingt-sept kah-truh-van-seht
88	quatre-vingt-huit kah-truh-van-weet
89	quatre-vingt-neuf kah-truh-van-nuhf
90	quatre-vingt-dix kah-truh-van-dees
91	quatre-vingt-onze kah-truh-van-ohnz
92	quatre-vingt-douze kah-truh-van-dooz
93	quatre-vingt-treize kah-truh-van-trehz
94	quatre-vingt-quatorze kah-truh-van-kah-torz
95	quatre-vingt-quinze kah-truh-van-kanz
96	quatre-vingt-seize kah-truh-van-sehz

97	quatre-vingt-dix-sept kah-truh-van-dee-seht
98	quatre-vingt-dix-huit kah-truh-van-deez-weet
99	quatre-vingt-dix-neuf kah-truh-van-deez-nuhf
100	cent sahn
101	cent un sahnt uhn
102	cent deux sahn duh
200	deux cents duh sahn
300	trois cents trwah sahn
400	quatre cents kah-truh sahn
500	cinq cents sank sahn
600	six cents sees sahn
700	sept cents seht sahn
800	huit cents weet sahn
900	neuf cents nuhf sahn
1000	mille meel
2000	deux mille duh meel
2010	deux mille dix duh meel dees
2011	deux mille onze duh meel ohnz
2012	deux mille douze duh meel dooz
2013	deux mille treize duh meel trehz
2014	deux mille quatorze duh meel kah-torz
2015	deux mille quinze duh meel kanz
2016	deux mille seize duh meel sehz
2017	deux mille dix-sept duh meel dee-seht
2018	deux mille dix-huit duh meel deez-weet
2019	deux mille dix-neuf duh meel deez-nuhf
2020	deux mille vingt duh meel van
million	million meel-yohn
billion	milliard meel-yar
number one	numéro un new-may-roh uhn
first	premier pruhm-yay

second	deuxième duhz-yehm
third	troisième trwahz-yehm
once	une fois ewn fwah
twice	deux fois duh fwah
a quarter	un quart uhn kar
a third	un tiers uhn tee-ehr
half	demi duh-mee
this much	comme ça kohm sah
a dozen	une douzaine ewn doo-zehn
a handful	une poignée ewn pwahn-yay
enough	suffisament sew-fee-zah-mahn
not enough	pas assez pah ah-say
too much	trop troh
more	plus plew
less	moins mwan
50%	cinquante pour cent san-kahnt poor sahn
100%	cent pour cent sahn poor sahn

French numbers are a little quirky from the seventies through the nineties. Let's pretend momentarily that the French speak English. Instead of saying 70, 71, 72, up to 79, the French say "sixty ten," "sixty eleven," "sixty twelve" up to "sixty nineteen." Instead of saying 80, the French say "four twenties." The numbers 81 and 82 are literally "four twenty one" and "four twenty two." It gets stranger. The number 90 is "four twenty ten." To say 91, 92, up to 99, the French say "four twenty eleven," "four twenty twelve" on up to "four twenty nineteen." But take heart. If little French children can learn these numbers, so can you. Besides, didn't Abe Lincoln say "Four score and seven..."?

Learning how to say your hotel room number is a good way to practice French numbers. You'll likely be asked for the number frequently (at breakfast, or to claim your key when you return to the room).

MONEY

France uses the euro currency. One ***euro*** (€, uh-roh) is divided into 100 cents (***centimes,*** sahn-teem), so "two euros and fifty cents" is ***deux euros et cinquante centimes,*** or simply ***deux-cinquante.***

Use your common cents—cents are like pennies, and the currency has coins like nickels, dimes, and half-dollars. There are also €1 and €2 coins.

Cash Machines (ATMs)

To get cash, ATMs are the way to go. At French banks, you may encounter a security door that allows one person to enter at a time. Push the ***entrez*** (enter) button, then ***attendez*** (wait), and ***voilà!,*** the door opens. Every ***distributeur*** (cash machine; also called a ***point d'argent***) is multilingual, but if you'd like to learn French under pressure, look for these buttons: ***annuler*** or ***annulation*** (cancel), ***modifier*** or ***correction*** (change), ***valider*** or ***validation*** (confirm). Your PIN code is a ***code.***

money	argent ar-zhahn
cash	liquide lee-keed
card	carte kart
PIN code	code "code"
Where is a...?	Oú est...? oo ay
...cash machine	...un distributeur uhn dee-stree-bew-tur
...bank	...une banque ewn bahnk
My debit card has been...	Ma carte de débit a été... mah kart duh day-bee ah ay-tay
...demagnetized.	...démagnétisée. day-mahg-nay-tee-zay
...stolen.	...volée. voh-lay
...eaten by the machine.	...avalée par la machine. ah-vah-lay par lah mah-sheen
My card doesn't work.	Ma carte ne marche pas. mah kart nuh marsh pah

Key Phrases: Money

euro(s) (€)	euro(s) uh-roh
cent(s)	centime(s) sahn-teem
cash	liquide lee-keed
Where is a...?	Oú est...? oo ay
...cash machine	...un distributeur uhn dee-stree-bew-tur
...bank	...une banque ewn bahnk
credit card	carte de crédit kart duh kray-dee
debit card	carte de débit kart duh day-bee
Do you accept credit cards?	Vous prenez les cartes de crédit? voo pruh-nay lay kart duh kray-dee

Credit and Debit Cards

Credit cards are widely accepted at larger businesses, though smaller shops, restaurants, and guest houses might prefer cash. Even if they accept credit cards, some hotels might cut you a discount for paying cash. In France, they often say ***Carte Blue***—the name of the most widely used credit card—as a generic term for any credit card. The abbreviation ***CB*** written on signs usually stands for ***carte bancaire*** (credit card).

credit card	carte de crédit / carte bancaire kart duh kray-dee / kart bahn-kair
debit card	carte de débit kart duh day-bee
receipt	reçu ruh-sew
sign	signer seen-yay
pay	payer pay-yay
cashier	caisse kehs
cash advance	crédit de caisse kray-dee duh kehs

Do you accept credit cards?	Vous prenez les cartes de crédit? voo pruh-nay lay kart duh kray-dee
Is it cheaper if I pay cash?	C'est moins cher si je paye en espèces? say mwan shehr see zhuh pay ahn ehs-pehs
I do not have a PIN.	Je n'ai pas de code PIN. zhuh nay pah duh "code" peen
Can I sign a receipt instead?	Je peux signer un reçu à la place? zhuh puh seen-yay uhn ruh-sew ah lah plahs
Print a receipt?	Imprimer un reçu? an-pree-may uhn ruh-sew
I have another card.	J'ai une autre carte. zhay ewn oh-truh kart

Much of Europe is adopting a "chip-and-PIN" system for credit cards, which are embedded with an electronic chip (called a ***carte à puce***). If an automated payment machine won't take your card, look for a cashier who can swipe it instead, or find a machine that takes cash.

Paying with a Credit Card

If calling to reserve tickets or a hotel room, you may need to convey your credit-card information over the phone. Prepare in advance: To fill in the blanks, use the numbers, alphabet, and months on pages 16-18 and the years on page 28.

The name on the card is _____.	Le nom sur la carte est _____. luh nohn sewr lah kart ay _____
The credit card number is _____.	Le numéro de carte de crédit est _____. luh noo-may-roh duh kart duh kray-dee ay _____
The expiration date is _____.	La date d'expiration est _____. lah daht dehk-spee-rah-see-ohn ay _____
The secret code (on the back) is _____.	Le cryptogramme c'est _____. luh kreep-toh-grahm say _____

Exchanging Money

exchange	bureau de change bew-roh duh shahnzh
change money	changer de l'argent shahn-zhay duh lar-zhahn
exchange rate	taux de change toh duh shahnzh
dollars	dollars doh-lar
traveler's check	cheque de voyage shehk duh voy-yahzh
buy / sell	acheter / vendre ah-shuh-tay / vahn-druh
commission	commission koh-mee-see-ohn
Any extra fee?	Il y a d'autre frais? eel yah doh-truh fray
I would like...	Je voudrais... zhuh voo-dray
...small bills.	...des petits billets. day puh-tee bee-yay
...large bills.	...des gros billets. day groh bee-yay
...a mix of small and large bills.	...un assortiment de petits et gros billets. uhn ah-sor-tee-mahn duh puh-teet ay groh bee-yay
...coins.	...des pieces. day pee-ehs
Can you break this? (large into small bills)	Vous pouvez casser ça? voo poo-vay kah-say sah
Is this a mistake?	C'est une erreur? sayt ewn ehr-ur
This is incorrect.	C'est incorrect. say an-koh-rehkt
Where is the nearest casino?	Oú se trouve le casino le plus proche? oo suh troov luh kah-see-noh luh plew prohsh

French banks don't change currency; you'll need to use a ***bureau de change.*** Traveler's checks are a complete waste of time (French banks won't take them) and money (fees to get them, fees to cash them).

TIME AND DATES

Telling Time

In France, the 24-hour clock (military time) is used for setting formal appointments (for instance, arrival times at a hotel), for the opening and closing hours of museums and shops, and for train, bus, and ferry schedules. Informally, Europeans use the 24-hour clock and our 12-hour clock interchangeably—***17:00*** is also ***5:00 de l'après-midi*** (in the afternoon).

What time is it?	Quelle heure est-il? kehl ur ay-teel
_____ o'clock	_____ heures _____ ur
in the morning	dans le matin dahn luh mah-tan
in the afternoon	dans l'après-midi dahn lah-preh-mee-dee
in the evening	dans le soir dahn luh swahr
at night	la nuit lah nwee
half	la demi lah duh-mee
quarter	le quart luh kar
minute	minute mee-newt
hour	heure ur
It's... / At...	Il est... / À... eel ay / ah
...8:00 in the morning.	...huit heures du matin. weet ur dew mah-tan
...16:00.	...seize heures. sehz ur
...4:00 in the afternoon.	...quatre heures de l'après-midi. kah-truh ur duh lah-preh-mee-dee
...10:30 in the evening.	...dix heures et demi du soir. deez ur ay duh-mee dew swahr
...a quarter past nine.	...neuf heures et quart. nuhv ur ay kar
...a quarter to eleven.	...onze heures moins le quart. ohnz ur mwan luh kar

Key Phrases: Time and Dates

What time is it?	Quelle heure est-il? kehl ur ay-teel
_____ o'clock	_____ heures _____ ur
minute	minute mee-newt
hour	heure ur
It's...	Il est... eel ay
...7:00 in the morning.	...sept heures du matin. seht ur dew mah-tan
...2:00 in the afternoon.	...deux heures de l'après-midi. duhz ur duh lah-preh-mee-dee
At what time does this open / close?	À quelle heuere c'est ouvert / fermé? ah kehl ur say oo-vehr / fehr-may
day	jour zhoor
today	aujourd'hui oh-zhoor-dwee
tomorrow	demain duh-man
(this) week	(cette) semaine (seht) suh-mehn
August 21	le vingt et un août luh vant ay uhn oot

at 6:00 sharp	à six heures précises ah sees ur pray-seez
from 8:00 to 10:00	de huit heures à dix heures duh weet ur ah dees ur
noon	midi mee-dee
midnight	minuit meen-wee
It's my bedtime.	C'est l'heure où je me couche. say lur oo zhuh muh koosh
I'll return / We'll return at 11:20.	Je reviens / Nous revenons à onze heures vingt. zhuh ruh-vee-an / noo ruh-vuh-nohn ah ohnz ur van

I'll be / We'll be there by 18:00.	Je serai / Nous serons là avant dix-huit heures. zhuh suh-ray / noo suh-rohn lah ah-vahn deez-weet ur

The word ***heures*** (roughly meaning "o'clock") is sometimes abbreviated as ***H*** in writing. So ***18 H*** means 18:00, or 6 p.m.

Timely Questions

When?	Quand? kahn
At what time?	À quelle heure? ah kehl ur
opening times	horaires d'ouverture oh-rair doo-vehr-tewr
At what time does this open / close?	À quelle heure c'est ouvert / fermé? ah kehl ur say oo-vehr / fehr-may
Is the train...?	Le train est...? luh tran ay
Is the bus...?	Le bus est...? luh bews ay
...early	...en avance ahn ah-vahns
...late	...en retard ahn ruh-tar
...on time	...à l'heure ah lur
When is checkout time?	À quelle heure on doit libérer la chambre? ah kehl ur ohn dwah lee-bay-ray lah shahn-bruh

It's About Time

now	maintenant man-tuh-nahn
soon	bientôt bee-an-toh
later	plus tard plew tar
in one hour	dans une heure dahnz ewn ur
in half an hour	dans une demi-heure dahnz ewn duh-mee-ur

in three hours	dans trois heures dahn trwahz ur
early / late	tôt / tard toh / tar
on time	à l'heure ah lur
anytime	n'importe quand nan-port kahn
immediately	immédiatement ee-may-dee-aht-mahn
every hour	toutes les heures toot layz ur
every day	tous les jours too lay zhoor
daily	quotidien koh-tee-dee-ahn
last	dernier dehrn-yay
this (m / f)	ce / cette suh / seht
next	prochain proh-shan
before	avant ah-vahn
after	après ah-preh
May 15	le quinze mai luh kanz may
in the future	dans l'avenir dahn lah-vuh-neer
in the past	dans le passé dahn luh pah-say

The Day

day	jour zhoor
today	aujourd'hui oh-zhoor-dwee
sunrise	l'aube lohb
this morning	ce matin suh mah-tan
sunset	le coucher de soleil luh koo-shay duh soh-lay
tonight	ce soir suh swahr
yesterday	hier ee-ehr
tomorrow	demain duh-man
tomorrow morning	demain matin duh-man mah-tan
day after tomorrow	après demain ah-preh duh-man

The Week

Sunday	dimanche dee-mahnsh
Monday	lundi luhn-dee
Tuesday	mardi mar-dee
Wednesday	mercredi mehr-kruh-dee
Thursday	jeudi zhuh-dee
Friday	vendredi vahn-druh-dee
Saturday	samedi sahm-dee
week	semaine suh-mehn
last week	la semaine dernière lah suh-mehn dehrn-yehr
this week	cette semaine seht suh-mehn
next week	la semaine prochaine lah suh-mehn proh-shehn
weekend	weekend "weekend"
this weekend	ce weekend suh "weekend"

The Months

month	mois mwah
January	janvier zhahn-vee-yay
February	février fay-vree-yay
March	mars mars
April	avril ahv-reel
May	mai may
June	juin zhwan
July	juillet zhwee-yay
August	août oot
September	septembre sehp-tahn-bruh
October	octobre ohk-toh-bruh
November	novembre noh-vahn-bruh
December	décembre day-sahn-bruh

For dates, say the number of the day and then the month. June 19 is ***le dix-neuf juin***.

The Year

year	année ah-nay
season	saison say-zohn
spring	printemps pran-tahn
summer	été ay-tay
fall	automne oh-tuhn
winter	hiver ee-vehr

For a list of years, see the "Numbers" section at the beginning of this chapter.

Holidays and Happy Days

holiday	jour férié zhoor fay-ree-ay
festival	festival feh-stee-vahl
Is it a holiday today / tomorrow?	C'est un jour férié aujourd'hui / demain? sayt uhn zhoor fay-ree-ay oh-zhoor-dwee / duh-man
Is a holiday coming up soon?	C'est bientôt un jour férié? say bee-an-toh uhn zhoor fay-ree-ay
When?	Quand? kahn
What is the holiday?	C'est quel jour férié? say kehl zhoor fay-ree-ay
Mardi Gras / Carnival	Mardi Gras / Carnaval mar-dee grah / kar-nah-vahl
Holy Week	Semaine Sainte suh-mehn sant
Easter	Pâques pahk
Ascension	Ascension ah-sahn-see-ohn
Labor Day (May 1)	Fête du Travail (le Premier Mai) feht dew trah-vī (luh pruhm-yay may)

VE Day (Victory in Europe, May 8)	Fête de la Victoire (le Huit Mai) feht duh lah veek-twahr (luh weet may)
Pentecost	Pentecôte pahn-tuh-koht
Corpus Christi	Fête-Dieu feht-dee-uh
Bastille Day (July 14)	Fête Nationale (le Quatorze Juillet) feht nahs-yoh-nahl (luh kah-torz zhwee-yay)
Assumption (Aug 15)	Assomption (le Quinze Août) ah-sohm-see-ohn (luh kanz oot)
All Saints' Day (Nov 1)	Toussaint (le Premier Novembre) too-san (luh pruhm-yay noh-vahn-bruh)
Armistice Day (Nov 11)	Armistice 1918 (le Onze Novembre) ahr-mees-tees meel-nuf-sahn-dees-weet (luh ohnz noh-vahn-bruh)
Christmas Eve	Réveillon de Noël ray-vay-ohn duh noh-ehl
Christmas	Noël noh-ehl
Merry Christmas!	Joyeux Noël! zhwah-yuh noh-ehl
New Year's Eve	La Saint-Sylvestre lah san-seel-vehs-truh
New Year's Day	Jour de l'An zhoor duh lahn
Happy New Year!	Bonne année! buhn ah-nay
wedding anniversary	anniversaire de marriage ah-nee-vehr-sair duh mah-ree-ahzh
Happy anniversary!	Bon anniversaire de mariage! bohn ah-nee-vehr-sair duh mah-ree-ahzh
Best wishes!	Meilleurs vœux! may-ur vuh
birthday	anniversaire ah-nee-vehr-sair
Happy birthday!	Joyeux anniversaire! zhwah-yuh ah-nee-vehr-sair

The French sing "Happy Birthday" to the same tune we do. Here are the words: ***Joyeux anniversaire, joyeux anniversaire, joyeux anniversaire*** (fill in name), ***nos voeux les plus sincères.***

TRANSPORTATION

This chapter will help you buy transit tickets, get around—by train, bus, subway, taxi, rental car, and foot—and generally find your way around.

GETTING AROUND

train	train tran
city bus	bus bews
shuttle bus	navette nah-veht
long-distance bus	car kar
subway	Métro may-troh
taxi	taxi tahk-see
car	voiture vwah-tewr
walk / by foot	marcher / à pied mar-shay / ah pee-ay
Where is the...?	Où est...? oo ay
...train station	...la gare lah gar
...bus station	...la gare routière lah gar root-yehr
...bus stop	...l'arrêt de bus lah-reh duh bews
...subway station	...la station de Métro lah stah-see-ohn duh may-troh
...taxi stand	...la station de taxi lah stah-see-ohn duh tahk-see
I'm going / We're going to ____.	Je vais / Nous allons à ____. zhuh vay / nooz ah-lohn ah ____
What is the cheapest / fastest / easiest way...?	Quel est le moins cher / plus rapide / plus facile...? kehl ay luh mwan shehr / plew rah-peed / plew fah-seel
...to downtown	...au centre-ville oh sahn-truh-veel
...to the train station	...à la gare ah lah gar
...to my / our hotel	...à mon / notre hôtel ah mohn / noh-truh oh-tehl
...to the airport	...à l'aéroport ah lah-ay-roh-por

Getting Tickets

When it comes to buying tickets for the bus, train, or subway, the following phrases will come in handy.

Where can I buy a ticket?	Où puis-je acheter un billet? oo pweezh ah-shuh-tay uhn bee-yay
How much (is a ticket to_____)?	C'est combien (le ticket pour _____)? say kohn-bee-an (luh tee-kay poor_____)
I want to go to _____.	Je veux aller à _____. zhuh vuh ah-lay ah _____
One ticket / Two tickets (to _____).	Un billet / Deux billets (pour _____). uhn bee-yay / duh bee-yay (poor _____)
When is the next train / bus (to _____)?	A quelle heure part le prochain train / bus (pour _____)? ah kehl ur par luh proh-shan tran / bews (poor _____)
What time does it leave?	Il part à quelle heure? eel par ah kehl ur
Is it direct?	C'est direct? say dee-rehkt
Is a reservation required?	Une réservation est obligatoire? ewn ray-zehr-vah-see-ohn ay oh-blee-gah-twahr
I'd like / We'd like to reserve a seat.	Je voudrais / Nous voudrions réserver une place. zhuh voo-dray / noo voo-dree-ohn ray-zehr-vay ewn plahs
Can I buy a ticket on board?	Est-ce que je peux acheter un ticket à bord? ehs kuh zhuh puh ah-shuh-tay uhn tee-kay ah bor
Exact change only?	Montant exact seulement? mohn-tahn ehg-zahkt suhl-mahn

TRAINS

For tips and strategies about rail travel and railpasses in France, see www.ricksteves.com/rail. Note that many of the following train phrases work for bus travel as well.

Ticket Basics

At the train station, you can buy tickets at the ***espace de vente*** (sales area). Choose between the ticket office or window (***guichet***) and the machines (marked ***achat-retrait-échange***). On tickets, ***1ère*** means first class, and ***2ème*** means second class.

ticket	billet bee-yay
reservation	réservation ray-zehr-vah-see-ohn
ticket office	guichet gee-shay
ticket machine	guichet automatique gee-shay oh-toh-mah-teek
validate	composter kohn-poh-stay
Where can I buy a ticket?	Où puis-je acheter un billet? oo pweezh ah-shuh-tay uhn bee-yay
Is this the line for...?	C'est la file pour...? say lah feel poor
...tickets	...les billets lay bee-yay
...reservations	...les réservations lay ray-zehr-vah-see-ohn
...information	...l'accueil lah-kuh-ee
One ticket (to _____).	Un billet (pour _____). uhn bee-yay (poor _____)
Two tickets.	Deux billets. duh bee-yay
I want to go to _____.	Je veux aller à _____. zhuh vuh ah-lay ah _____
How much (is a ticket to _____)?	C'est combien (le ticket pour _____)? say kohn-bee-an (luh tee-kay poor _____)
one-way	aller simple ah-lay san-pluh

round-trip	aller retour ah-lay ruh-toor
today / tomorrow	aujourd'hui / demain oh-zhoor-dwee / duh-man

Ticket Specifics

As trains and buses can sell out, it's smart to buy your tickets at least a day in advance, even for short rides. For phrases related to discounts (such as children, families, or seniors), see page 48.

schedule	horaire oh-rair
When is the next train / bus (to ____)?	A quelle heure part le prochain train / bus (pour ____)? ah kehl ur par luh proh-shan tran / bews (poor ____)
What time does it leave?	Il part à quelle heure? eel par ah kehl ur
I'd like / We'd like to leave...	Je voudrais / Nous voudrions partir... zhuh voo-dray / noo voo-dree-ohn par-teer
I'd like / We'd like to arrive...	Je voudrais / Nous voudrions arriver... zhuh voo-dray / noo voo-dree-ohn ah-ree-vay
...by ____ o'clock.	...avant ____ heures. ah-vahn ____ ur
...at ____ o'clock...	...à ____ heures... ah ____ ur
...in the morning.	...le matin. luh mah-tan
...in the afternoon.	...l'après-midi. lah-preh-mee-dee
...in the evening.	...le soir. luh swahr
Is there a... train / bus?	Il y a un train / bus...? eel yah uhn tran / bews
...earlier	...plus tôt plew toh
...later	...plus tard plew tar
...overnight	...de nuit duh nwee

...cheaper	...moins cher mwahn shehr
...express	...rapide rah-peed
...direct	...direct dee-rehkt
Is it direct?	C'est direct? say dee-rehkt
Is a transfer required?	Un transfert est nécessaire? uhn trahns-fehr ay nay-suh-sair
How many transfers?	Combien de correspondances? kohn-bee-an duh koh-rehs-pohn-dahns
When? Where?	À quelle heure? Où? ah kehl ur / oo
first / second class	première / deuxième classe pruhm-yehr / duhz-yehm klahs
How long is this ticket valid?	Ce billet est bon pour combien de temps? suh bee-yay ay bohn poor kohn-bee-an duh tahn
Can you validate my railpass?	Pouvez-vous valider mon passe Eurail? poo-vay-voo vah-lee-day mohn pahs "eurail"

When buying tickets, you'll either wait in line or take a number (***Prenez un ticket*** or ***Prenez un numéro***). The number readout screen says ***Nous appellons le numéro...*** or simply ***Numéro*** (the number currently being served) and ***Guichet*** (the numbered or lettered window to report to).

Be sure you go to the correct window: ***Départ immédiat*** is for trains departing immediately, ***Autres départs*** is for other trains, ***Ventes internationales*** is international, and ***Toutes ventes*** is for any tickets.

Train Reservations

You're required to pay for a ***réservation*** for any TGV train, for selected other routes, and for couchettes (sleeping berths on night trains). On other trains, reservations aren't required, but are advisable during busy times (e.g., Friday and Sunday afternoons, Saturday mornings, weekday rush hours, and particularly holiday weekends). If you have a railpass, you're still required to reserve a seat for any TGV train (only a limited number of reservations are available for passholders, so book early) and some high-speed international trains as well—look for the Ⓡ symbol in the timetable.

Is a reservation required?	Une réservation est obligatoire? ewn ray-zehr-vah-see-ohn ay oh-blee-gah-twahr
I'd like / We'd like to reserve...	Je voudrais / Nous voudrions réserver... zhuh voo-dray / noo voo-dree-ohn ray-zehr-vay
...a seat.	...une place. ewn plahs
...an aisle seat.	...une place côté couloir. ewn plahs koh-tay kool-wahr
...a window seat.	...une place côté fenêtre. ewn plahs koh-tay fuh-neh-truh
...two seats.	...deux places. duh plahs
...a couchette (sleeping berth).	...une couchette. ewn koo-sheht
...an upper / middle / lower berth.	...une couchette en haut / milieu / en bas. ewn koo-sheht ahn oh / meel-yuh / ahn bah
...two couchettes.	...deux couchettes. duh koo-sheht
...a sleeper (with two beds).	...un compartiment privé (à deux lits). uhn kohn-par-tee-mahn pree-vay (ah duh lee)
...the entire train.	...le train entier. luh tran ahn-tee-ay

Ticket Machines

The ticket machines available at most train stations are great time-savers for short trips when ticket-window lines are long (but plan to use euros, because your American credit card probably won't work in the machines). Some have English instructions, but for those that don't, you'll see the following prompts. The default is usually what you want;

turn the dial or touch the screen to make your choice, and press ***Validez*** to agree to each step.

Quelle est votre destination?	What's your destination?
Billet Plein Tarif	Full-fare ticket (yes for most)
1ère ou 2ème	First or second class
Aller simple ou aller retour?	One-way or round-trip?
Prix en Euro	Price in euros

Discounts

Is there a cheaper option?	Il y a un solution moins cher? eel yah uhn soh-lew-see-ohn mwan shehr
discount	réduction ray-dewk-see-ohn
reduced fare	tarif réduit tah-reef ray-dwee
refund	remboursement rahn-boor-suh-mahn
Is there a discount for...?	Il y a une réduction pour les...? eel yah ewn ray-dewk-see-ohn poor lay
...children	...enfants ahn-fahn
...youths	...jeunes zhuhn
...seniors	...personnes âgées pehr-suhn ah-zhay
...families	...familles fah-mee
...groups	...groupes groop
...advance purchase	...achat à l'avance ah-shaht ah lah-vahns
...weekends	...week-ends "week-end"
Are there any deals for this journey?	Il y a des réductions pour ce voyage? eel yah day ray-dewk-see-ohn poor suh vwah-yahzh

At the Train Station

La gare means train station. Big cities can have several. High-speed, long-distance trains use the ***gare TGV,*** which can be on the outskirts of town; ***gare ville*** or ***gare centre-ville*** is near the city center.

Key Phrases: Trains

train station	gare gar
train	train tran
platform	quai kay
track	voie vwah
What track does the train leave from?	Le train part de quelle voie? luh tran par duh kehl vwah
Is this the train to ____?	C'est le train pour ____? say luh tran poor ____
Which train to ____?	Quel train pour ____? kehl tran poor ____
Tell me when to get off?	Dîtes-moi quand je descends? deet-mwah kahn zhuh day-sahn
transfer (n)	correspondance koh-rehs-pohn-dahns
Change here for ____?	Transfère ici pour ____? trahns-fehr ee-see poor ____

Where is...?	Où est...? oo ay
...the train station	...la gare lah gar
train information	accueil / renseignements SNCF ah-kuh-ee / rahn-sehn-yuh-mahn S N say F
customer service	conseiller clientèle kohn-say-yay klee-ahn-tehl
tickets	billets bee-yay
departures	départs day-par
arrivals	arrivées ah-ree-vay
On time?	À l'heure? ah lur
Late?	En retard? ahn ruh-tar
How late?	Combien de retard? kohn-bee-an duh ruh-tar

platform / track	quai / voie kay / vwah
What track does the train leave from?	Le train part de quelle voie? luh tran par duh kehl vwah
waiting room	salle d'attente sahl dah-tahnt
VIP lounge	salon grand voyageur sah-lohn grahn voy-ah-zhur
locker	consigne automatique kohn-seen-yuh oh-toh-mah-teek
baggage-check room	consigne de bagages / espaces bagages kohn-seen-yuh duh bah-gahzh / ehs-pahs bah-gahzh
tourist info office	office du tourisme oh-fees dew too-reez-muh
lost and found office	bureau des objets trouvés bew-roh dayz ohb-zhay troo-vay
toilets	toilettes twah-leht

In French rail stations, look for the ***Accueil*** office, where you can get information about train schedules without waiting in a long ticket line.

French trains are operated by ***SNCF*** (pronounced "S N say F"). The country is connected by an ever-growing network of high-speed trains called TGV (tay zhay vay, ***train à grande vitesse***). There are also regional and suburban lines that go by various names; for example, around Paris you'll see ***RER, Transilien, banlieue,*** and ***trains Ile-de-France.***

For security reasons, all luggage (including day packs) must carry a tag with the traveler's first and last name and current address. Free tags are available at all train stations in France.

Train and Bus Schedules

European timetables use the 24-hour clock. It's like American time until noon. After that, subtract twelve and add p.m. So 13:00 is 1 p.m., 20:00 is 8 p.m., and 24:00 is midnight.

To ask for a schedule at an information window, say ***Horaire*** (oh-rair) ***pour*** ____, ***s'il vous plaît*** (Schedule for ____ [city], please).

French train schedules show blue (quiet), white (normal), and red (peak and holiday) times. You can save money if you get the blues (travel during off-peak hours).

à	to
à l'heure	on time
accès aux quais / trains	to the trains
arrivée	arrival
aussi	also
avant	before
de	from
départ	departure
dernier passage	last trip
desserte	initial departure time
destination (finale)	(final) destination
dimanche	Sunday
direction	goes
en retard	late
en semaine	weekdays
environ ____ minutes de retard	about ____ minutes late
et	and
heure	time / hour
heures	hours
horaire	timetable
intervalle prévu	during this time
jour férié	holiday
jours	days
jusqu'à	until
minutes	minutes
nature	company and / or type of train
numéro / n°	train number
par	via
parcularités	specific details
pas	not
pour	to
premier passage	first trip
provenance	coming from
régime	major stops en route

retard / retardé	late
samedi	Saturday
sauf	except
seulement	only
terminus	final destination
tous	every
tous les jours	daily
train direct	does not make every stop
train omnibus	makes every stop ("milk run")
vacances	holidays
voie	track number
1ère	first class
2ème	second class
1-5	Monday-Friday
6 / 7	Saturday / Sunday

All Aboard

In the station, ***accès aux quais*** or ***accès aux trains*** signs direct you to the trains. (A sign reading ***voyageurs munis de billets*** means that it's an area only for passengers with tickets in hand.) At the track, you are required to ***composter*** (validate) all train tickets and reservations. Look for the yellow, waist-high boxes marked ***compostage de billets***. (Do not ***composte*** your railpass, but do validate it at a ticket window before the first time you use it.)

platform / track	quai / voie kay / vwah
number	numéro new-may-roh
train	train tran
train car	voiture vwah-tewr
conductor	conducteur kohn-dewk-tur
Is this the train to _____?	C'est le train pour _____? say luh tran poor _____
Which train to _____?	Quel train pour _____? kehl tran poor _____

Which train car to ____?	Quelle voiture pour ____? kehl vwah-tewr poor ____
Where is...?	Où est...? oo ay
Is this...?	C'est...? say
...my seat	...ma place mah plahs
...first / second class	...la première / deuxième classe lah pruhm-yehr / duhz-yehm klahs
...the dining car	...la voiture restaurant lah vwah-tewr rehs-toh-rahn
...the sleeper car	...la voiture-lit lah vwah-tewr-lee
...the toilet	...la toilette lah twah-leht
front / middle / back	à l'avant / au milieu / au fond ah lah-vahn / oh meel-yuh / oh fohn
reserved / occupied / free	réservé / occupé / libre ray-zehr-vay / oh-kew-pay / lee-bruh
aisle / window	couloir / fenêtre kool-wahr / fuh-neh-truh
Is this (seat) free?	C'est libre? say lee-bruh
May I / May we...?	Je peux / Nous pouvon...? zhuh puh / noo poo-vohn
...sit here	...s'asseoir ici sah-swahr ee-see
...open the window	...ouvrir la fenêtre oo-vreer lah fuh-neh-truh
...eat here	...manger ici mahn-zhay ee-see
...eat your meal	...manger votre repas mahn-zhay voh-truh ruh-pah
(I think) that's my seat.	(Je pense) c'est ma place. (zhuh pahns) say mah plahs
These are our seats.	Ce sont nos places. suh sohn noh plahs
Save my place?	Garder ma place? gar-day mah plahs
Save our places?	Garder nos places? gar-day noh plahs
Where are you going?	Où allez-vous? oo ah-lay-voo

I'm going / We're going to ____.	Je vais / Nous allons à ____. zhuh vay / nooz ah-lohn ah ____
Does this train stop in ____?	Ce train s'arrête à ____? suh tran sah-reht ah ____
When will it arrive in ____?	Il va arriver à ____ à quelle heure? eel vah ah-ree-vay ah ____ ah kehl ur
Where is a (handsome) conductor?	Où est un (beau) conducteur? oo ay uhn (boh) kohn-dewk-tur
Tell me when to get off?	Dîtes-moi quand je descends? deet-mwah kahn zhuh day-sahn
I'm getting off.	Je descends. zhuh day-sahn
How do I open the door?	Comment puis-je ouvrir la porte? koh-mahn pweezh oo-vreer lah port

To confirm you're boarding the right train, point to the train, and ask a conductor ***À ____*** [city]***?*** For example, ***À Chartres?*** means "To Chartres?" Some longer trains split cars en route; make sure your train car is continuing to your destination by asking ***Cette voiture va à Chartres?*** (This car goes to Chartres?).

If a non-TGV train seat is reserved, it'll usually be labeled ***réservé,*** with the cities to and from which it is reserved.

As you approach a station on the train, you will hear an announcement such as: ***Mesdames, Messieurs, dans quelques minutes, nous entrons en gare de Paris*** (In a few minutes, we will arrive in Paris).

Changing Trains

Change here for ____?	Transfère ici pour ____? trahns-fehr ee-see poor ____
Where does one change for ____?	Où faut-il changer pour ____? oo foh-teel shahn-zhay poor ____
At what time?	À quelle heure? ah kehl ur

From what track does the connecting train leave?	De quelle voie part le train en correspondance? duh kehl vwah par luh tran ahn koh-rehs-pohn-dahns
How many minutes in ____ (to change trains)?	Combien de minutes à ____ (pour changer de train)? kohn-bee-an duh mee-newt ah ____ (poor shahn-zhay duh tran)

Strikes

If a strike is pending, hoteliers or travel agencies can check for you to see when the strike goes into effect and which trains will continue to run.

strike	grève grehv
Is there a strike?	Il y a une grève? eel yah ewn grehv
Only for today?	Juste pour aujourd'hui? zhewst poor oh-zhoor-dwee
Tomorrow, too?	Demain aussi? duh-man oh-see
Are there some trains today?	Il y a quelques trains aujourd'hui? eel yah kehl-kuh tran oh-zhoor-dwee
I'm going to ____.	Je voyage à ____. zhuh voy-ahzh ah ____

CITY BUSES AND SUBWAYS

Ticket Talk

Most big cities offer deals on transportation, such as one-day tickets or cheaper fares for youths and seniors. In Paris, you'll save money by buying a ***carnet*** (kar-nay, batch of 10 tickets) at virtually any Métro station. The tickets, which are sharable, are valid on the buses, Métro, and RER (suburban railway) within the city limits.

Key Phrases: City Buses and Subways

bus	bus bews
subway	Métro may-troh
How do I get to ____?	Comment je vais à ____? koh-mahn zhuh vay ah ____
Which stop for ____?	Quel arrêt pour ____? kehl ah-reh poor ____
Tell me when to get off?	Dîtes-moi quand je descends? deet-mwah kahn zhuh day-sahn

Where can I buy a ticket?	Où puis-je acheter un ticket? oo pweezh ah-shuh-tay uhn tee-kay
I want to go to ____.	Je veux aller à ____. zhuh vuh ah-lay ah ____
How much (is a ticket to ____)?	C'est combien (le ticket pour ____)? say kohn-bee-an (luh tee-kay poor ____)
single (trip)	aller simple ah-lay san-pluh
batch of 10 tickets	carnet kar-nay
a day pass	un passe à la journée uhn pahs ah lah zhoor-nay
Is this ticket valid (for ____)?	Ce ticket est bon (pour ____)? suh tee-kay ay bohn (poor ____)
Can I buy a ticket on board the bus?	Est-ce que je peux acheter un ticket à bord le bus? ehs kuh zhuh puh ah-shuh-tay uhn tee-kay ah bor luh bews
Exact change only?	Montant exact seulement? mohn-tahn ehg-zahkt suhl-mahn
validate (here)	composter (ici) kohn-poh-stay (ee-see)

To enter the Paris Métro, insert your ticket in the automatic turnstile, reclaim your ticket, pass through, and keep it until you exit the system (some stations require you to pass your ticket through a turnstile to exit). For basic ticket-buying terms, see page 44.

Transit Terms

city bus	bus bews
bus stop	arrêt de bus ah-reh duh bews
bus map	plan de bus plahn duh bews
subway	Métro may-troh
suburban train (Paris)	RER ehr-uh-ehr
subway station	station de Métro stah-see-ohn duh may-troh
subway map	plan du Métro plahn dew may-troh
subway entrance	l'entrée du Métro lahn-tray dew may-troh
subway stop	arrêt de Métro ah-reh duh may-troh
exit	sortie sor-tee
line (bus / subway)	ligne (de bus / de Métro) leen-yuh (duh bews / duh may-troh)
direction	direction dee-rehk-see-ohn
direct	direct dee-rehkt
connection	correspondance koh-rehs-pohn-dahns
public transit map	plan des lignes plahn day leen-yuh
pickpocket	pickpocket / voleur peek-poh-keht / voh-lur

Before entering the Métro system, be very clear on which line you'll be taking, and what direction you're headed toward (i.e., the name of the final station on that line). At major Métro stations, several lines intersect, creating a labyrinth of underground corridors; following signs for your direction is the only way you'll find the right platform.

Once at your platform, look for the digital information board. See the first column below for examples, with the English explanation:

M-1 (or M-2, etc.)	Métro line number
La Défense	end station (direction)
1er train	time until arrival of the next train
2e train	time until arrival of the following train
correspondance	connections to another line, listed by direction

Riding Public Transit

How do I get to _____?	Comment je vais à _____? koh-mahn zhuh vay ah _____
How do we get to _____?	Comment nous allons à _____? koh-mahn nooz ah-lohn ah _____
Which bus to _____?	Quel bus pour _____? kehl bews poor _____
Does it stop at _____?	Il s'arrête à _____? eel sah-reht ah _____
Which bus stop for _____?	Quel arrêt pour _____? kehl ah-reh poor _____
Which subway stop for _____?	Quel arrêt de Métro pour _____? kehl ah-reh duh may-troh poor _____
Which direction for _____?	Quelle direction pour _____? kehl dee-rehk-see-ohn poor _____
Is there a transfer?	Il y a une correspondance? eel yah ewn koh-rehs-pohn-dahns
When is the...?	C'est quand le...? say kahn luh
...first / next / last...	...premier / prochain / dernier... pruhm-yay / proh-shan / dehrn-yay
...bus / subway	...bus / Métro bews / may-troh
How often does it run per hour / day?	Combien de fois par heure / jour? kohn-bee-an duh fwah par ur / zhoor

When does the next one leave?	Quand part le prochain? kahn par luh proh-shan
Where does it leave from?	D'où il part? doo eel par
Tell me when to get off?	Dîtes-moi quand je descends? deet-mwah kahn zhuh day-sahn
I'm getting off.	Je descends. zhuh day-sahn
How do I open the door?	Comment je peux ouvrir la porte? koh-mahn zhuh puh oo-vreer lah port

If you press the button to request a stop on a bus or tram, a sign lights up that says ***Arrêt demandé*** (Stop requested). Upon arrival, you might have to press a green button or pull a lever to open the door—watch locals and imitate.

Before leaving the Métro through the ***sortie*** (exit), check the helpful ***plan du quartier*** (map of the neighborhood) to get your bearings and decide which ***sortie*** you want—this can save lots of walking.

TAXIS

While Paris and other major cities have slick public transportation, taxis are generally affordable, efficient, and worth considering. Taxis can take up to four people, and larger taxis take more. So you'll know what to expect, ask your hotelier about typical taxi fares. Fares go up at night and on Sundays, and drivers always charge for loading baggage in the trunk. Your fare can nearly double if you're taking a short trip with lots of bags.

If you're having a tough time hailing a taxi, ask for the nearest taxi stand ***(station de taxi)*** or seek out a big hotel where they're usually waiting for guests. The simplest way to tell a cabbie where you want to go is by stating your destination followed by "please" ***(Louvre, s'il vous plaît).*** Tipping isn't expected, but it's polite to round up. So if the fare is €19, round up to €20.

Key Phrases: Taxis

Taxi!	Taxi! tahk-see
taxi stand	station de taxi stah-see-ohn duh tahk-see
Are you free?	Vous êtes libre? vooz eht lee-bruh
Occupied.	Occupé. oh-kew-pay
To _____, please.	À _____, s'il vous plaît. ah _____ see voo play
The meter, please.	Le compteur, s'il vous plaît. luh kohn-tur see voo play
Stop here.	Arrêtez-vous ici. ah-reh-tay-voo ee-see
My change, please.	La monnaie, s'il vous plaît. lah moh-nay see voo play
Keep the change.	Gardez la monnaie. gar-day lah moh-nay

Getting a Taxi

Taxi!	Taxi! tahk-see
Can you call a taxi?	Pouvez-vous appeler un taxi? poo-vay-voo ah-puh-lay uhn tahk-see
Where can I get a taxi?	Où puis-je trouver un taxi? oo pweezh troo-vay uhn tahk-see
Where is a taxi stand?	Où est une station de taxi? oo ay ewn stah-see-ohn duh tahk-see
Are you free?	Vous êtes libre? vooz eht lee-bruh
Occupied.	Occupé. oh-kew-pay
To _____, please.	À _____, s'il vous plaît. ah _____ see voo play
To this address.	À cette adresse. ah seht ah-drehs

Approximately how much does it cost to go...?	C'est environ combien pour aller...? say ahn-vee-rohn kohn-bee-an poor ah-lay
...to _____	...à _____ ah _____
...to the airport	...à l'aéroport ah lah-ay-roh-por
...to the train station	...à la gare ah lah gar
...to this address	...à cette adresse ah seht ah-drehs
Is there an extra supplement?	Il y a un supplément? eel yah uhn sew-play-mahn
It's too much.	C'est trop. say troh
Can you take _____ people?	Pouvez-vous prendre _____ passagers? poo-vay-voo prahn-druh _____ pah-sah-zhay
Any extra fee?	Il y a d'autres frais? eel yah doh-truh fray
Do you have an hourly rate?	Avez-vous un taux par heure? ah-vay-voo uhn toh par ur
How much for a one-hour city tour?	Combien pour une visite d'une heure en ville? kohn-bee-an poor ewn vee-zeet dewn ur ahn veel

Before hopping in a taxi, it's smart to ask ***C'est environ combien pour aller à _____?*** (About how much does it cost to go to _____?).

Cabbie Conversation

The meter, please.	Le compteur, s'il vous plaît. luh kohn-tur see voo play
Where is the meter?	Où est le compteur? oo ay luh kohn-tur
I'm / We're in a hurry.	Je suis / Nous sommes pressé. zhuh swee / noo suhm preh-say
Slow down.	Ralentissez. rah-lahn-tee-say

If you don't slow down, I'll throw up.	Si vous ne ralentissez pas, je vais vomir. see voo nuh rah-lahn-tee-say pah zhuh vay voh-meer
Left.	À gauche. ah gohsh
Right.	À droite. ah drwaht
Straight ahead.	Tout droit. too drwah
Please stop here...	S'il vous plaît arrêtez-vous ici... see voo play ah-reh-tay-voo ee-see
...for a moment.	...un instant uhn an-stahn
...for ____ minutes.	...pour ____ minutes. poor ____ mee-newt
Can you wait?	Pouvez-vous attendre? poo-vay voo ah-tahn-druh
Crazy traffic, isn't it?	C'est fou, cette circulation, non? say foo seht seer-kew-lah-see-ohn nohn
You drive like a madman!	Vous conduisez comme un fou! voo kohn-dwee-zay kohm uhn foo
You drive very well.	Vous conduisez très bien. voo kohn-dwee-zay treh bee-an
I can see it from here.	Je peux le voir d'ici. zhuh puh luh vwahr dee-see
Point it out?	Vous pouvez me le montrer? voo poo-vay muh luh mohn-tray
Stop here.	Arrêtez-vous ici. ah-reh-tay-voo ee-see
Here is fine.	Ici c'est bien. ee-see say bee-an
At this corner.	À ce coin. ah suh kwan
The next corner.	Au prochain coin. oh proh-shan kwan
My change, please.	La monnaie, s'il vous plaît. lah moh-nay see voo play
Keep the change.	Gardez la monnaie. gar-day lah moh-nay

This ride is / was more fun than Disneyland.	Ce trajet est / était plus drôle que Disneyland. suh trah-zhay ay / ay-tay plew drohl kuh "Disneyland"

DRIVING

Renting Wheels

I'd like to rent a...	Je voudrais louer... zhuh voo-dray loo-ay
...car.	...une voiture. ewn vwah-tewr
...station wagon.	...un break. uhn brayk
...van.	...un van. uhn vahn
...convertible.	...une décapotable. ewn day-kah-poh-tah-bluh
...motorcycle.	...un moto. uhn moh-toh
...motor scooter.	...un scooteur. uhn skoo-tur
How much per...?	Combien par...? kohn-bee-an par
...hour	...heure ur
...half-day	...demi-journée duh-mee-zhoor-nay
...day	...jour zhoor
...week	...semaine suh-mehn
car rental agency	agence de location de voiture ah-zhahns duh loh-kah-see-ohn duh vwah-tewr
tax / insurance	taxe / assurance tahx / ah-sewr-rahns
Includes taxes and insurance?	Taxes et assurances comprises? tahx ay ah-sewr-ahns kohn-preez
Any extra fees?	Il y a d'autres frais? eel yah doh-truh fray
Unlimited mileage?	Kilométrage illimité? kee-loh-may-trahzh ee-lee-mee-tay

Key Phrases: Driving

car	voiture vwah-tewr
gas station	station service stah-see-ohn sehr-vees
parking lot	parking par-keeng
Where can I park?	Où puis-je me garer? oo pweezh muh gah-ray
downtown	centre-ville sahn-truh-veel
straight ahead	tout droit too drwah
left	à gauche ah gohsh
right	à droite ah drwaht
I'm lost.	Je suis perdu. zhuh swee pehr-dew
How do I get to _____?	Comment je vais à _____? koh-mahn zhuh vay ah _____

manual / automatic transmission	boîte manuelle / boîte automatique bwaht mah-new-ehl / bwaht oh-toh-mah-teek
pick up	prendre prahn-druh
drop off	retour / dépose véhicule ruh-toor / day-pohz vay-ee-kewl
Is there a...?	Est-ce qu'il y a...? ehs keel yah
...discount	...une réduction ewn ray-dewk-see-ohn
...deposit	...une caution ewn koh-see-ohn
...helmet	...un casque uhn kahsk
When must I bring it back?	Je dois le ramener à quelle heure? zhuh dwah luh rah-muh-nay ah kehl ur
Can I drop it off in another city / in _____?	Est-ce que je peux déposer le véhicule dans une autre ville / dans _____? ehs kuh zhuh puh day-poh-zay luh vay-ee-kewl dahnz ewn oh-truh veel / dahn _____

How do I get to the expressway / to ____?	Comment puis-je rejoindre l'autoroute / en direction de ____? koh-mahn pweezh ray-zhwan-druh loh-toh-root / ahn dee-rehk-see-ohn duh ____

Before leaving the car-rental office, get directions to your next destination—or at least to the ***autoroute*** (expressway).

For all the details on the dizzying variety of insurance options, see www.ricksteves.com/cdw.

Getting to Know Your Rental Car

Before driving off, familiarize yourself with your rental car. Examine it to be sure that all damage is already noted on the rental agreement so you won't be held responsible for it later.

It's damaged here.	Il est endommagée ici. eel ay ahn-doh-mah-zhay ee-see
Please add it to the rental agreement.	Veuillez l'ajouter au contrat de location. vuh-yay lah-zhoo-tay oh kohn-trah duh loh-kah-see-ohn
That scratch / dent was already here.	Cette éraflure / bosse était déjà présente ici. seht ay-rah-flewr / bohs ay-tay day-zhah pray-zahnt ee-cee
What kind of fuel does it take?	Quel type de carburant doit-on utiliser? kehl teep duh kar-bewr-ahn dwah-tohn ew-tee-lee-zay
gas	essence eh-sahns
diesel	gazole / gasoil gah-zohl / gah-zwahl
How do I open the gas cap?	Comment puis-je ouvrir le réservoir? koh-mahn pweezh oo-vreer luh ray-zehr-vwahr
How does this work?	Comment ça fonctionne? koh-mahn sah fohnk-see-ohn
key	clé / clef klay / kleh

headlights	phares far
radio	radio rah-dee-oh
windshield wipers	essuies-glace ehs-wee-glahs
alarm / security system	alarme / système de sécurité ah-larm / see-stehm duh say-kew-ree-tay
How do I turn off the security system?	Comment puis-je déconnecter le système de sécurité? koh-mahn pweezh day-koh-nehk-tay luh see-stehm duh say-kew-ree-tay
GPS	GPS zhay pay ehs
How do I change the language to English?	Comment peut-on basculer sur l'anglais? koh-mahn puh-tohn bah-skew-lay sewr lahn-glay

Sometimes you can rent a GPS device with your car. The language for the menus and instructions can be changed to English.

Traffic Troubles

traffic	circulation seer-kew-lah-see-ohn
traffic jam	bouchon boo-shohn
rush hour	heure de pointe ur duh pwant
delay	délai / retard / ralentissement day-lay / ruh-tar / rah-lahn-tees-mahn
construction	travaux trah-voh
accident	accident ahk-see-dahn
detour	déviation day-vee-ah-see-ohn
How long is the delay?	Combien de temps dure le ralentissement? kohn-bee-an duh tahn dewr luh rah-lahn-tees-mahn
Is there another way to go (to _____)?	Il y a un autre itinéraire pour aller (à_____) ? eel yah uhn oh-truh ee-tee-nay-rair poor ah-lay (ah _____)

Along the ***autoroute,*** electronic signs flash messages to let you know what's ahead: ***bouchon*** (traffic jam), ***circulation*** (traffic), and ***fluide*** (no traffic). For more navigational words, see "Finding Your Way," on page 72.

Tolls

The shortest distance between any two points in France is the ***autoroute,*** but the tolls add up. (You'll travel cheaper, but slower, on a ***route nationale.***) You'll usually take a ticket when entering an ***autoroute*** and pay when you leave (plan to pay with cash, since most US credit and debit cards won't work in the machines). Shorter ***autoroute*** sections have periodic toll booths, where you can pay by dropping coins into a basket.

toll road	autoroute oh-toh-root
toll	péage pay-ahzh
tollbooth	poste de péage pohst duh pay-ahzh
toll ticket	ticket de péage tee-kay duh pay-ahzh
cash	espèces / monnaie ehs-pehs / moh-nay
card	carte kart
pay	payer pay-ay

At the Gas Station

Unleaded is ***sans plomb*** (which can be ***normale*** or ***super***), and diesel is ***gazole*** or ***gasoil.*** The cheapest gas in France is sold in ***hypermarché*** (supermarket) parking lots. Prices are listed per liter; there are about four liters in a gallon.

gas station	station service stah-see-oh<u>n</u> sehr-vees
The nearest gas station?	La plus proche station service? lah plew prohsh stah-see-oh<u>n</u> sehr-vees
Self-service?	Libre service? lee-bruh sehr-vees
Fill it up.	Faites le plein. feht luh pla<u>n</u>

I need...	Il me faut... eel muh foh
...gas.	...de l'essence. duh leh-sahns
...unleaded.	...sans plomb. sahn plohn
...regular.	...normale. nor-mahl
...super.	...du super. dew sew-pehr
...diesel.	...gazole / gasoil. gah-zohl / gah-zwahl

Parking

parking lot	parking par-keeng
parking garage	garage de stationnement gah-rahzh duh stah-see-ohn-mahn
parking space	place de parking plahs duh par-keeng
ticket-vending machine	horodateur or-oh-dah-tur
parking meter	parcomètre par-koh-meh-truh
available / full	libre / complet lee-bruh / kohn-play
Where can I park?	Où puis-je me garer? oo pweezh muh gah-ray
Is parking nearby?	Il y a un parking près d'ici? eel yah uhn par-keeng preh dee-see
Can I park here?	Je peux me garer ici? zhuh puh muh gah-ray ee-see
Is it safe?	C'est prudent? say prew-dahn
How long can I park here?	Je peux me garer ici pour combien de temps? zhuh puh muh gah-ray ee-see poor kohn-bee-an duh tahn
Is it free?	C'est gratuit? say grah-twee
Where do I pay?	Je paie où? zhuh pay oo
How much per hour / day?	Combien par heure / jour? kohn-bee-an par ur / zhoor

Get safe parking tips from your hotelier, and leave nothing of value in your car.

Many cities use remote meters for curbside parking. After you park, find the ticket-vending machine ***(horodateur)*** or parking meter ***(parcomètre).*** Insert coins to reach the desired amount of time, press the button to print out a ticket, and put it on your dashboard. Instructions on the machine or meter may list times you have to pay; for example, all days ***sauf*** (except) ***dimanches et jours feries*** (Sundays and holidays). Keep an eye on the ***durée maximale*** (maximum stay time).

Garages often have extremely narrow spaces and tight corners; drive carefully. After parking, take your ticket with you; when you come back, pay at the machine before returning to your car (pay with cash since most US credit and debit cards won't work in the machines). As you enter a big city, signs may direct you to various garages and indicate the number of available parking spaces (for example, ***129 places libres***).

Car Trouble and Parts

accident	accident ahk-see-dahn
fender-bender	accrochage ah-kroh-shahzh
breakdown	en panne ahn pahn
dealership / repair shop	concessionaire kohn-seh-see-oh-nair
strange noise	bruit curieux brwee kew-ree-uh
electrical problem	problème d'électricité proh-blehm day-lehk-tree-see-tay
warning light	feux de détresse fuh duh day-trehs
smoke	fumée few-may
My car won't start.	Ma voiture ne démarre pas. mah vwah-tewr nuh day-mar pah
My car is broken.	Ma voiture ne marche pas. mah vwah-tewr nuh marsh pah
This doesn't work.	Ça ne marche pas. sah nuh marsh pah

Please check this.	Merci de bien vouloir verifier ceci. mehr-see duh bee-an vool-wahr vehr-ee-fee-ay suh-see
oil	l'huile lweel
tire (flat)	pneu (crevé) pnuh (kruh-vay)
air in the tires	pression dans les pneus preh-see-ohn dahn lay pnuh
radiator	radiateur rahd-yah-tur
battery (dead)	batterie (à plat) bah-tuh-ree (ah plah)
sparkplugs	bougies boo-zhee
fuses	fusibles few-zee-bluh
headlights	phares far
taillights	feux arrières fuh ah-ree-ehr
turn signal	clignotant kleen-yoh-tahn
brakes	freins fran
window	fenêtre fuh-neh-truh
windshield	pare-brise par-breez
windshield wipers	essuie-glaces ehs-wee-glahs
engine	moteur moh-tur
fan belt	courroie du ventilateur koor-wah dew vahn-tee-lah-tur
starter	starter star-tehr
transmission	transmission trahns-mee-see-ohn
transmission (fluid)	(liquide de) transmission (lee-keed duh) trahns-mee-see-ohn
radio	radio rah-dee-oh
key	clé / clef klay / kleh
alarm	alarme ah-larm
It's overheating.	Le moteur surchauffe. luh moh-tur sewr-shohf
It's a lemon ("rattletrap").	C'est un tas de féraille. sayt uhn tah duh fay-rī
I need...	J'ai besoin... zhay buh-zwan

...a tow truck.	...d'un dépanneur. duhn day-pah-nur
...a mechanic.	...d'un mécanicien. duhn may-kah-nee-see-an
...a stiff drink.	...d'un bon coup à boire. duhn bohn koo ah bwahr

In France, people with car problems go to the dealership. If you're renting a troubled Renault, your rental agency may direct you to the nearest concessionaire Renault. For help with repair, see "Repairs" on page 284.

The Police

In any country, the flashing lights of a patrol car are a sure sign that someone's in trouble. If it's you, try this handy phrase: ***Pardon, je suis un touriste*** (Sorry, I'm a tourist). Or, for the adventurous: ***Si vous n'aimez pas ma conduite, vous n'avez que descendre du trottoir.*** (If you don't like how I drive, get off the sidewalk.) If you're in serious need of assistance, turn to the Help! chapter on page 271.

police officer	agent de police ah-zhahn duh poh-lees
driver's license	permis de conduire pehr-mee duh kohn-dweer
What seems to be the problem?	Quel est le problème? kehl ay luh proh-blehm
restricted zone	zone interdite / accès restreint zohn an-tehr-deet / ahk-seh rehs-tran
pedestrian-only	zone piétonne zohn pee-ay-tohn
speeding	dépasser la vitesse autorisée day-pah-say lah vee-tehs oh-toh-ree-zay
I didn't know the speed limit.	Je ne savais pas qu'elle était la limitation de vitesse. zhuh nuh sah-vay pah kehl ay-tay lah lee-mee-tah-see-ohn duh vee-tehs
parking ticket	ticket de parking tee-kay duh par-keeng

I didn't know where to park.	Je ne savais pas où me garer. zhuh nuh sah-vay pah oo muh gah-ray
I'm very sorry.	Je suis vraiment désolé. zhuh swee vray-mahn day-zoh-lay
Can I buy your hat?	Je peux acheter votre chapeau? zhuh puh ah-shuh-tay voh-truh shah-poh

FINDING YOUR WAY

Whether you're driving, walking, or biking, these phrases will help you get around.

Route-Finding Phrases

I'm going / We're going to _____.	Je vais / Nous allons à _____. zhuh vay / nooz ah-lohn ah _____
Do you have a...?	Avez-vous...? ah-vay-vooz
...city map	...un plan de la ville uhn plahn duh lah veel
...road map	...une carte routière ewn kart root-yehr
How many minutes...?	Combien de minutes...? kohn-bee-an duh mee-newt
...on foot	...à pied ah pee-yay
...by bicycle	...à bicyclette ah bee-see-kleht
...by car	...en voiture ahn vwah-tewr
How many kilometers to _____?	Combien de kilomètres à _____? kohn-bee-an duh kee-loh-meh-truh ah _____
What's the... route to Paris?	Quelle est la... route pour Paris? kehl ay lah... root poor pah-ree
...most scenic	...plus belle plew behl
...fastest	...plus directe plew dee-rehkt
...easiest	...plus facile plew fah-seel

...most interesting	...plus intéressante plewz an-tay-reh-sahnt
Point it out?	Montrez-moi? mohn-tray mwah
Where is this address?	Où se trouve cette adresse? oo suh troov seht ah-drehs

Directions

Following signs to ***centre-ville*** will land you in the heart of things.

downtown	centre-ville sahn-truh-veel
straight ahead	tout droit too drwah
to the left	à gauche ah gohsh
to the right	à droite ah drwaht
first	premier pruhm-yay
next	prochain proh-shan
intersection	carrefour kar-foor
corner	au coin oh kwan
block	paté de maisons pah-tay duh may-zohn
roundabout	rond-point rohn-pwan
stoplight	feu fuh
(main) square	place (principale) plahs (pran-see-pahl)
street	rue rew
avenue	avenue ah-vuh-new
boulevard	boulevard bool-var
curve	virage vee-rahzh
bridge	pont pohn
tunnel	tunnel tew-nehl
road	route root
ring road	périphérique pay-ree-fay-reek
expressway	autoroute oh-toh-root
north	nord nor

south	sud sewd
east	est ehst
west	ouest wehst
shortcut	raccourci rah-koor-see
traffic jam	bouchon boo-shohn

Lost Your Way

I'm lost.	Je suis perdu. zhuh swee pehr-dew
We're lost.	Nous sommes perdus. noo suhm pehr-dew
Can you help me?	Vous pouvez m'aider? voo poo-vay meh-day
Where am I?	Où suis-je? oo sweezh
Where is ____?	Où est ____? oo ay ____
How do I get to ____?	Comment est-ce que j'arrive à ____? koh-mahn ehs kuh zhah-reev ah ____
Can you show me the way?	Vous pouvez me montrer le chemin? voo poo-vay muh mohn-tray luh shuh-man

Reading Road Signs

Aire	Rest stop on expressway
Allumez vos feux	Turn on your lights
Attention	Caution
Attention travaux	Workers ahead
Autres directions (follow when leaving a town)	Other directions
Bouchon	Traffic jam ahead
Céder le passage	Yield
Centre-ville	Center of town
Centre commercial	Grouping of large, suburban stores (not city center)

Déviation	Detour
Doublage interdit	No passing
Entrée	Entrance
Feu	Traffic signal
Fluide	No traffic ahead
Horadateur	Parking meter
Interdit	Not allowed
Par temps de pluie	When raining (modified speed limit signs)
Parc de stationnement	Parking lot
Parking interdit	No parking
Péage	Toll
Priorité	Right-of-way
Priorité à droite	Right-of-way is for cars coming from the right
Prochaine sortie	Next exit
Ralentir	Slow down
Rappel	Remember to obey the sign
Réservé aux piétons	Pedestrians only
Route barrée	Road blocked
Rue piétonne	Pedestrian-only street
Sans issue	Dead end
Sauf riverains	Local access only
Sens unique	One-way street
Sortie	Exit
Sortie des camions	Work truck exit
Stationnement interdit	No parking
Stop	Stop
Télépéage	Automated toll booths
Toutes directions (follow when leaving a town)	All directions
Travaux	Construction
Virages	Curves
Voie piétonne	Pedestrian zone
Vous n'avez pas la priorité	You don't have the right of way (when merging)

For a list of other signs you might see, turn to page 21 in the French Basics chapter.

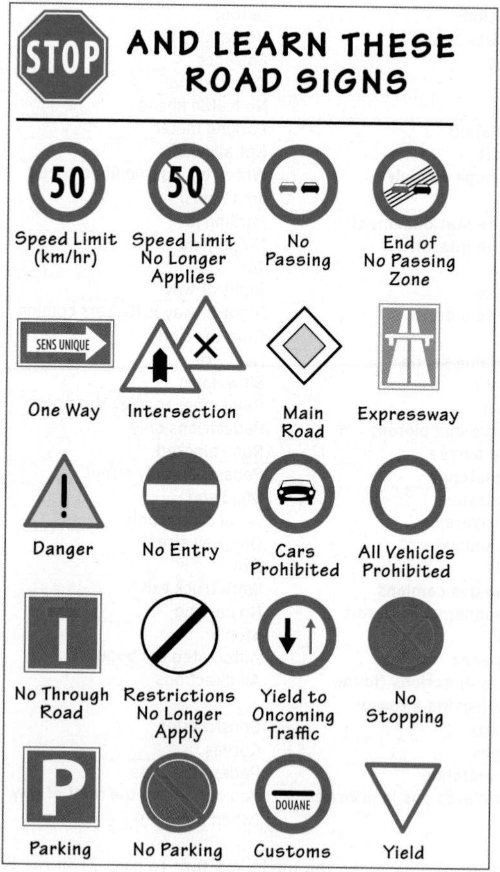
STOP
AND LEARN THESE ROAD SIGNS
50
Speed Limit (km/hr)
50
Speed Limit No Longer Applies
No Passing
End of No Passing Zone
SENS UNIQUE
One Way
Intersection
Main Road
Expressway
Danger
No Entry
Cars Prohibited
All Vehicles Prohibited
No Through Road
Restrictions No Longer Apply
Yield to Oncoming Traffic
No Stopping
P
Parking
No Parking
DOUANE
Customs
Yield

Going Places

On your travels through France, you're likely to see these place names. If French clerks at train stations and train conductors don't understand your pronunciation, write the town name on a piece of paper.

Alsace	ahl-sahs
Amboise	ahm-bwahz
Annecy	ahn-see
Antibes	ahn-teeb
Arles	arl
Arromanches	ah-roh-mahnsh
Avignon	ah-veen-yohn
Bayeux	bah-yuh
Beaune	bohn
Beynac	bay-nak
Bordeaux	bor-doh
Calais	kah-lay
Carcassonne	kar-kah-suhn
Chambord	shahn-bor
Chamonix	shah-moh-nee
Chartres	shar-truh
Chenonceau	shuh-nohn-soh
Cherbourg	shehr-boor
Chinon	shee-nohn
Collioure	kohl-yoor
Colmar	kohl-mar
Côte d'Azur	koht dah-zewr
Dijon	dee-zhohn
Dordogne	dor-dohn-yuh
Giverny	zhee-vehr-nee
Grenoble	gruh-noh-bluh
Honfleur	ohn-flur
Le Havre	luh hah-vruh
Loire	lwahr
Lyon	lee-ohn
Marseille	mar-say
Mont Blanc	mohn blahn
Mont St-Michel	mohn san-mee-shehl

Nantes	nahnt
Nice	nees
Normandy	nor-mahn-dee
Paris	pah-ree
Provence	proh-vahns
Reims	rans
Rouen	roo-ahn
Roussillon	roo-see-yohn
Sarlat	sar-lah
Strasbourg	strahs-boorg
Verdun	vehr-duhn
Versailles	vehr-sī
Villefranche	veel-frahnsh

SLEEPING

This chapter covers making reservations, hotel stays (including checking in, making requests, and dealing with difficulties), specific concerns (such as families and mobility issues), and hostels.

RESERVATIONS

Making a Reservation

reservation	réservation ray-zehr-vah-see-ohn
Do you have...?	Avez-vous...? ah-vay-voo
I'd like to reserve...	Je voudrais réserver... zhuh voo-dray ray-zehr-vay
...a room...	...une chambre... ewn shahn-bruh
...for one person / two people	...pour une personne / deux personnes poor ewn pehr-suhn / duh pehr-suhn
...for today / tomorrow	...pour aujourd'hui / demain poor oh-zhoor-dwee / duh-man
...for one night	...pour une nuit poor ewn nwee
two / three nights	deux / trois nuits duh / trwah nwee

Key Phrases: Sleeping

Do you have a room?	Avez-vous une chambre? ah-vay-voo ewn shahn-bruh
for one person / two people	pour une personne / deux personnes poor ewn pehr-suhn / duh pehr-suhn
today / tomorrow	aujourd'hui / demain oh-zhoor-dwee / duh-man
How much is it?	C'est combien? say kohn-bee-an
hotel	hôtel oh-tehl
inexpensive hotel	pension pahn-see-ohn
vacancy / no vacancy	chambre libre / complet shahn-bruh lee-bruh / kohn-play

June 21	le vingt et un juin luh vant ay uhn zhwan
How much is it?	C'est combien? say kohn-bee-an
Anything cheaper?	Rien de moins cher? ree-an duh mwan shehr
I'll take it.	Je la prends. zhuh lah prahn
My name is ____.	Je m'appelle ____. zhuh mah-pehl ____
Do you need a deposit?	Avez-vous besoin d'un acompte? ah-vay-voo buh-swan duhn ah-kohnt
Do you accept credit cards?	Vous prenez les cartes de crédit? voo pruh-nay lay kart duh kray-dee
Can I reserve with a credit card and pay in cash?	Je peux faire une réservation avec une carte de crédit et payer plus tard en liquide? zhuh puh fair ewn ray-zehr-vah-see-ohn ah-vehk ewn kart duh kray-dee ay pay-ay plew tar ahn lee-keed

French hotels are rated from one to five stars (check the blue-and-white plaque by the front door). For budget travelers, one or two stars is the best value. Prices vary widely under one roof. You'll save money if you get a room with a double bed ***(grand lit)*** instead of twin beds ***(deux petits lits),*** and a bathroom with a shower ***(salle d'eau)*** instead of a bathroom with a bathtub ***(salle de bains).*** You'll pay less for a room with just a toilet and sink (***cabinet de toilette,*** or **C. de T.**), and even less for a room with only a sink ***(lavabo seulement).***

Many people stay at a ***hôtel,*** but you have other choices:

Hôtel-château (oh-tehl-shah-toh): Castle hotel
Auberge (oh-behrzh): Small hotel with restaurant
Pension (pahn-see-ohn): Small hotel
Chambre d'hôte (shahn-bruh doht): B&B or room in a private home; a *table d'hôte* is a *chambre d'hôte* that offers an optional, reasonably priced home-cooked dinner.
Gîte (zheet): Country home rental
Auberge de jeunesse (oh-behrzh duh zhuh-nehs): Hostel

Getting Specific

I'd like a...	Je voudrais une... zhuh voo-dray ewn
...single room.	...chambre single. shahn-bruh san-guhl
...double room.	...chambre double. shahn-bruh doo-bluh
...triple room.	...chambre triple. shahn-bruh tree-pluh
...room for _____ people.	...chambre pour _____ personnes. shahn-bruh poor _____ pehr-suhn
with / without / and	avec / sans / et ah-vehk / sahn / ay
king-size bed	king size keeng "size"
queen-size bed	lit de cent-soixante lee duh sahn-swah-sahnt
double bed	grand lit grahn lee
twin beds...	deux petits lits / deux lits jumeaux... duh puh-tee lee / duh lee zhew-moh
...together / separate	....ensemble / séparés ahn-sahn-bluh / say-pah-ray
single bed	petit lit / lit jumeau puh-tee lee / lee zhew-moh
without footboard	sans pied de lit sahn pee-ay duh lee
private bathroom	salle de bain privée sahl duh ban pree-vay
toilet	WC vay say
shower	douche doosh
bathtub	baignoire behn-wahr
with only a sink	avec lavabo seulement ah-vehk lah-vah-boh suhl-mahn
shower outside the room	une douche sur le palier ewn doosh sewr luh pahl-yay
balcony	balcon bahl-kohn
view	vue vew
cheap	pas cher / bon marché pah shehr / bohn mar-shay

quiet	tranquille trahn-keel
romantic	romantique roh-mahn-teek
on the ground floor	au rez-de-chaussée oh ray-duh-shoh-say
Do you have...?	Avez-vous...? ah-vay-voo
...an elevator	...un ascenseur uhn ah-sahn-sur
...air-conditioning	...climatisation klee-mah-tee-zah-see-ohn
...Internet access	...accès à l'internet ahk-seh ah lan-tehr-neht
...Wi-Fi (in the room)	...Wi-Fi (dans la chambre) wee-fee (dahn lah shahn-bruh)
...parking	...un parking uhn par-keeng
...a garage	...un parking couvert uhn par-keeng koo-vehr
What is your...?	Quel est votre...? kehl ay voh-truh
...email address	...adresse email ah-drehs "email"
...cancellation policy	...conditions d'annulation kohn-dees-yohn dah-new-lah-see-ohn

In France, a room with one double bed is generally smaller than a room with two twin beds ***(deux petits lits).*** An American-size double bed (55 inches wide) is called ***un grand lit***. A queen-size bed is ***un lit de cent-soixante***—literally a 160-centimeter bed (63 inches wide). And ***le king size*** is usually two twin beds pushed together and sheeted as one big bed. You may find any of these in a French "double room." If you'll take either twins or a double, ask generically for ***une chambre pour deux*** (a room for two) to avoid being needlessly turned away. Taller guests may want to request a bed ***sans pied de lit*** (without footboard).

Nailing Down the Price

price	prix / tarif pree / tah-reef
Can I see the price list?	Je peux voir les tarifs? zhuh puh vwahr lay tah-reef

What Your Hotelier Wants to Know

If you'd like to reserve by email, your hotelier needs to know the following information: number and type of rooms (i.e., single or double); number of nights; date of arrival (written day/month/year); date of departure; and any special needs (bathroom in the room, cheapest room, twin beds vs. one big bed, crib, air-conditioning, quiet, view, ground floor, no stairs, and so on). Here's a sample email I'd send to make a reservation.

From: rick@ricksteves.com
Sent: Today
To: info@hotelcentral.com
Subject: Reservation request for 19-22 July

Dear Hotel Central,

I would like to reserve a double room for 2 people for 3 nights, arriving 19 July and departing 22 July. If possible, I would like a quiet room with a bathroom inside the room.

Please let me know if you have a room available and the price.

Thank you!
Rick Steves

The hotel will reply with its room availability and rates for your dates. This is not a confirmation—you must email back to say that you want the room at the given rate, and you'll likely be asked for your credit card number for a deposit.

How much is...?	Combien...? kohn-bee-an
...a room for ____ people	...une chambre pour ____ personnes ewn shahn-bruh poor ____ pehr-suhn
...your cheapest room	...la chambre la moins chère lah shahn-bruh lah mwan shehr
Is breakfast included?	Le petit déjeuner est compris? luh puh-tee day-zhuh-nay ay kohn-pree
Complete price?	Tout compris? too kohn-pree
Is it cheaper if...?	C'est moins cher si je...? say mwan shehr see zhuh
...I stay three nights	...vais rester trois nuits vay rehs-tay trwah nwee
...I pay in cash	...paie en liquide pay ahn lee-keed

Many hotels are willing to lower the price if you stay for longer periods and/or pay in cash. Rates can vary by season: High season ***(haute saison)*** is more expensive than low season ***(basse saison)***. In resort towns, some hotels offer half-pension ***(demi-pension),*** which includes two meals per day served at the hotel: breakfast and your choice of lunch or dinner. The price for half-pension is often listed per person rather than per room. Hotels that offer half-pension often require it in summer. The meals are usually good, but if you want more freedom, look for hotels that don't push half-pension.

Arrival and Departure

arrival	arrivée ah-ree-vay
arrival date	la date d'arrivée lah daht dah-ree-vay
departure date	la date de départ lah daht duh day-par
I'll arrive / We'll arrive...	J'arrive / Nous arrivons... zhah-reev / nooz ah-ree-vohn
I'll depart / We'll depart...	Je pars / Nous partons...... zhuh par / noo par-tohn
...June 16.	...le seize juin. luh sehz zhwan

...in the morning / afternoon / evening.	...dans la matinée / l'après-midi / la soirée. dahn lah mah-tee-nay / lah-preh-mee-dee / lah swah-ray
...Friday before 6 p.m.	...vendredi avant six heures du soir. vahn-druh-dee ah-vahn seez ur dew swahr
I'll stay...	Je reste... zhuh rehst
We'll stay...	Nous restons... noo rehs-tohn
...two nights.	...deux nuits. duh nwee
We arrive Monday, depart Wednesday.	Nous arrivons lundi, et partons mercredi. nooz ah-ree-vohn luhn-dee ay par-tohn mehr-kruh-dee

For help with saying dates in French, see "Time and Dates," starting on page 34.

Confirm, Change, or Cancel

It's smart to call a day or two in advance to confirm your reservation.

I have a reservation.	J'ai une réservation. zhay ewn ray-zehr-vah-see-ohn
My name is _____.	Je m'appelle _____. zhuh mah-pehl _____
I'd like to... my reservation.	Je voudrais... ma réservation. zhuh voo-dray... mah ray-zehr-vah-see-ohn
...confirm	...confirmer kohn-feer-may
...change	...modifier moh-dee-fee-ay
...cancel	...annuler ah-new-lay
The reservation is for...	La réservation est pour... lah ray-zehr-vah-see-ohn ay poor
...today / tomorrow.	...aujourd'hui / demain. oh-zhoor-dwee / duh-man
...August 13.	...le treize août. luh trehz oot

Did you find the reservation?	Avez-vous trouvé la réservation? ah-vay-voo troo-vay lah ray-zehr-vah-see-ohn
Is everything OK?	Ça va marcher? sah vah mar-shay
See you then.	À bientôt. ah bee-an-toh
I'm sorry, but I need to cancel.	Je suis désolé, mais j'ai besoin d'annuler. zhuh swee day-zoh-lay may zhay buh-zwan dah-new-lay
Are there cancellation fees?	Il y a des frais d'annulation? eel yah day fray dah-new-lah-see-ohn

Depending on how far ahead you cancel a reservation—and on the hotel's cancellation policy—you might pay a penalty. Most likely your credit card will be billed for one night.

AT THE HOTEL

Checking In

My name is ____.	Je m'appelle ____. zhuh mah-pehl
I have a reservation.	J'ai une réservation. zhay ewn ray-zehr-vah-see-ohn
one night	une nuit ewn nwee
two / three nights	deux / trois nuits duh / trwah nwee
Where is...?	Où est....? oo ay
...my room	...ma chambre mah shahn-bruh
...the elevator	...l'ascenseur lah-sahn-sur
...the breakfast room	...la salle du petit déjeuner lah sahl dew puh-tee day-zhuh-nay
Is breakfast included?	Le petit déjeuner est compris? luh puh-tee day-zhuh-nay ay kohn-pree
When does breakfast start and end?	Le petit déjeuner commence et termine à quelle heure? luh puh-tee day-zhuh-nay koh-mahns ay tehr-meen ah kehl ur

key	clé klay
Two keys, please.	Deux clés, s'il vous plaît. duh klay see voo play

Choosing a Room

Can I see...?	Je peux voir...? zhuh puh vwahr
...a room	...une chambre ewn shahn-bruh
...a different room	...une chambre différente ewn shahn-bruh dee-fay-rahnt
Do you have something...?	Avez-vous quelque chose de...? ah-vay-voo kehl-kuh shohz duh
...larger / smaller	...plus grand / moins grand plew grahn / mwan grahn
...better / cheaper	...meilleur / moins cher meh-yur / mwan shehr
...brighter	...plus clair plew klair
...quieter	...plus tranquille plew trahn-keel
...in the back	...derrière dehr-yehr
...with a view	...avec vue ah-vehk vew
...on a lower / higher floor	...sur un étage plus bas / plus haut sewr uhn ay-tahzh plew bah / plew oh
No, thank you.	Non, merci. nohn mehr-see
What a charming room!	Quelle chambre charmante! kehl shahn-bruh shar-mahnt
I'll take it.	Je la prends. zhuh lah prahn

Be aware that a room ***avec vue*** (with a view) can also come with more noise. If a ***tranquille*** room is important to you, say so.

Hotel Words

cancellation policy	conditions d'annulation kohn-dees-yohn dah-new-lah-see-ohn
check-in time	heure d'enrégistrement ur dahn-ray-zhee-struh-mahn
check-out time	heure limite d'occupation ur lee-meet doh-kew-pah-see-ohn
elevator	ascenseur ah-sahn-sur
emergency exit	issue / sortie de secours ee-sew / sor-tee duh suh-koor
fire escape	escalier d'incendie ehs-kahl-yay dan-sahn-dee
floor...	étage... ay-tahzh
...lower / higher	...plus bas / plus haut plew bah / plew oh
ground floor	rez-de-chaussée ray-duh-shoh-say
Internet access	accès a' l'internet ahk-seh ah lan-ter-neht
laundry	linge / lessive lanzh / luh-seev
parking	parking / garage par-keeng / gah-rahzh
price list	liste des tarifs leest day tah-reef
reservation	réservation ray-zehr-vah-see-ohn
a room...	une chambre... ewn shahn-bruh
...single	...single san-guhl
...double	...double doo-bluh
...triple	...triple tree-pluh
family room	une grande chambre / une suite ewn grahnd shahn-bruh / ewn sweet
stairs	escalier ehs-kahl-yay
suite	suite sweet
swimming pool	piscine pee-seen
view	vue vew
Wi-Fi	Wi-Fi wee-fee

In Your Room

air-conditioner	climatisation klee-mah-tee-zah-see-ohn
alarm clock	réveil ray-vay
baggage	bagages bah-gahzh
balcony	balcon bahl-kohn
bathroom	salle de bains sahl duh ban
bathtub	baignoire behn-wahr
bed	lit lee
bedspread	couvre-lit koo-vruh-lee
blanket	couverture koo-vehr-tewr
blinds	stores stor
city map	plan de la ville plahn duh lah veel
chair	chaise shehz
closet	placard plah-kar
corkscrew	tire-bouchon teer-boo-shohn
crib	berceau behr-soh
curtains	rideaux ree-doh
door	porte port
double bed	grand lit grahn lee
drain	descente d'eau day-sahnt doh
electrical adapter	adaptateur électrique ah-dahp-tah-tur ay-lehk-treek
electrical outlet	prise preez
faucet	robinet roh-bee-nay
hair dryer	sèche-cheveux sehsh-shuh-vuh
hanger	porte-manteau port-mahn-toh
key	clé klay
kitchenette	kitchenette keet-cheh-neht
lamp	lampe lahmp
lightbulb	ampoule ahn-pool
lock	serrure suh-rewr
mirror	miroir meer-wahr

pillow	oreiller oh-ray-yay
radio	radio rah-dee-oh
remote control...	télécommande... tay-lay-koh-mahnd
...for TV	...pour la télé poor lah tay-lay
...for air-conditioner	...pour la climatisation poor lah klee-mah-tee-zah-see-ohn
safe (n)	coffre-fort koh-fruh-for
scissors	ciseaux see-zoh
shampoo	shampooing shahn-pwan
sheets	draps drah
shower	douche doosh
shutters	volets voh-lay
single bed	petit lit / lit jumeau puh-tee lee / lee zhew-moh
sink	lavabo lah-vah-boh
sink stopper	bouchon pour le lavabo boo-shohn poor luh lah-vah-boh
soap	savon sah-vohn
telephone	téléphone tay-lay-fohn
television	télévision tay-lay-vee-zee-ohn
toilet	toilette twah-leht
toilet paper	papier toilette pahp-yay twah-leht
towel (hand)	petite serviette puh-teet sehr-vee-eht
towel (bath)	serviette de bain sehr-vee-eht duh ban
twin beds	deux petits lits / deux lits jumeaux duh puh-tee lee / duh lee zhew-moh
wake-up call	réveil téléphoné ray-vay tay-lay-foh-nay
washcloth	gant de toilette gahn duh twah-leht
water (hot / cold)	eau (chaude / froide) oh (shohd / frwahd)
window	fenêtre fuh-neh-truh
window screen	moustiquaire moos-tee-kair

If you don't see remote controls in the room (for the TV or air-conditioner), ask for them at the front desk. A comfortable setting for the air-conditioner is about 20 degrees Celsius. On French faucets, a **C** stands for ***chaud*** (hot)—the opposite of cold.

If you'd rather not struggle all night with a log-style French pillow, check in the closet to see if there's a fluffier American-style pillow, or ask for a ***coussin*** (koo-san).

Hotel Hassles

Combine these phrases with the words in the previous table to make simple and clear statements such as: ***La toilette ne marche pas***. (The toilet doesn't work.)

I have a problem in the room.	J'ai un problème dans la chambre. zhay uhn proh-blehm dahn lah shahn-bruh
Come with me.	Venez avec moi. vuh-nay ah-vehk mwah
The room is...	La chambre est... lah shahn-bruh ay
It's...	C'est... say
...dirty.	...sale. sahl
...moldy.	...moisie. mwah-zee
...smoky.	...enfumée. ahn-few-may
...stinky.	...puante. pew-ahnt
It's noisy.	C'est bruyante. say brew-yahnt
The room is too hot / too cold.	La chambre est trop chaude / trop froide. lah shahn-bruh ay troh shohd / troh frwahd
How can I make the room cooler / warmer?	Comment je peux rendre la chambre plus fraîche / chaude? koh-mahn zhuh puh rahn-druh lah shahn-bruh plew frehsh / shohd
There's no (hot) water.	Il n'y a pas d'eau (chaude). eel nee ah pah doh (shohd)

I can't open / shut / lock...	Je ne peux pas ouvrir / fermer / fermer à clé..... zhuh nuh puh pah oo-vreer / fehr-may / fehr-may ah klay
...the door / the window.	...la porte / la fenêtre. lah port / lah fuh-neh-truh
How does this work?	Comment ça marche? koh-mahn sah marsh
This doesn't work.	Ça ne marche pas. sah nuh marsh pah
When will it be fixed?	Quand est-ce qu'il sera réparé? kahn ehs keel suh-rah ray-pah-ray
The bed is too soft / hard.	Le lit est trop mou / dur. luh lee ay troh moo / dewr
I can't sleep.	Je ne peux pas dormir. zhuh nuh puh pah dor-meer
ants	fourmis foor-mee
bedbugs	punaises pew-nehz
cockroaches	cafards kah-far
mice	souris soo-ree
mosquitoes	moustiques moos-teek
I'm covered with bug bites.	Je suis couvert de piqures d'insectes. zhuh swee koo-vehr duh pee-kewr dan-sehkt
My... was stolen.	On m'a volé... ohn mah voh-lay
...money	...l'argent. lar-zhahn
...computer	...l'ordinateur. lor-dee-nah-tur
...camera	...l'appareil-photo. lah-pah-ray-foh-toh
I need to speak to the manager.	J'ai besoin de parler au gérant / directeur. zhay buh-swan duh par-lay oh zhay-rahn / dee-rehk-tur
I want to make a complaint.	Je veux faire une réclamation. zhuh vuh fair ewn ray-klah-mah-see-ohn
The visitors' book, please.	Le livre d'or, s'il vous plaît. luh lee-vruh dor see voo play

Keep your valuables with you, out of sight in your room, or in a room safe (if available). For help on dealing with theft or loss, including a list of items, see page 273.

Most reputable hotels have a visitors' book in which guests can write their comments, good or bad, about their stay and the service. Asking to see the ***livre d'or*** (literally "golden book") can inspire the hotelier to find a solution for your problem.

Hotel Help

Use the "In Your Room" words (on page 90) to fill in the blanks.

I'd like...	Je voudrais... zhuh voo-dray
Do you have...?	Avez-vous...? ah-vay-voo
a / another	un / un autre uhn / uhn oh-truh
extra	supplémentaire sew-play-mahn-tair
different	différent dee-fay-rahn
Please change...	Changez, s'il vous plaît... shahn-zhay see voo play
Please don't change...	Ne changez pas, s'il vous plaît... nuh shahn-zhay pah see voo play
...the towels / the sheets.	...les serviettes / les draps. lay sehr-vee-eht / lay drah
What is the charge to...?	Ça coûte combien pour...? sah koot kohn-bee-an poor
...use the telephone	...utiliser le téléphone ew-tee-lee-zay luh tay-lay-fohn
...use the Internet	...utiliser l'internet ew-tee-lee-zay lan-tehr-neht
Do you have Wi-Fi...?	Avez-vous le Wi-Fi...? ah-vay-voo luh wee-fee
...in the room / in the lobby	...dans les chambres / à la réception dahn lay shahn-bruh / ah lah ray-sehp-see-ohn

What is the network name / the password?	Quel est le nom du réseau / le mot de passe? kehl ay luh nohn dew ray-zoh / luh moh duh pahs
Where is a nearby...?	Où se trouve le... le plus proche? oo suh troov luh... luh plew prohsh
...full-service laundry	...blanchisserie service complet blahn-shee-suh-ree sehr-vees kohn-play
...self-service laundry	...laverie automatique lah-vuh-ree oh-toh-mah-teek
...pharmacy	...pharmacie far-mah-see
...Internet café	...café internet kah-fay an-tehr-neht
...grocery store	...supermarché / épicerie sew-pehr-mar-shay / ay-pee-suh-ree
...restaurant	...restaurant rehs-toh-rahn
Where do you go for lunch / dinner / coffee?	Vous allez où pour déjeuner / dîner / un café? vooz ah-lay oo poor day-zhuh-nay / dee-nay / uhn kah-fay
Will you call a taxi for me?	Pourriez-vous appeler un taxi pour moi? poor-yay-voo ah-puh-lay uhn tahk-see poor mwah
Where can I park?	Je peux me garer où? zhuh puh muh gah-ray oo
What time do you lock up?	Vous fermez à quelle heure? voo fehr-may ah kehl ur
Please wake me at 7:00.	Réveillez-moi à sept heures, s'il vous plaît. ray-vay-ay-mwah ah seht ur see voo play
I'd like to stay another night.	Je voudrais rester encore une nuit. zhuh voo-dray rehs-tay ahn-kor ewn nwee

Will you call my next hotel...?	Pourriez-vous appeler mon prochain hotel...? poor-yay-voo ah-puh-lay mohn proh-shan oh-tehl
...for tonight	...pour ce soir poor suh swahr
...to make / to confirm a reservation	...pour faire / confirmer une réservation poor fair / kohn-feer-may ewn ray-zehr-vah-see-ohn
Will you call another hotel for me? (if hotel is booked)	Vous pourriez contacter un autre hôtel pour moi? voo poor-yay kohn-tahk-tay uhn oh-truh oh-tehl poor mwah
I will pay for the call.	Je paierai l'appel. zhuh pay-uh-ray lah-pehl

Checking Out

When is check-out time?	A quelle heure on doit libérer la chambre? ah kehl ur ohn dwah lee-bay-ray lah shahn-bruh
Can I check out later?	Je peux libérer la chambre plus tard? zhuh puh lee-bay-ray lah shahn-bruh plew tar
I'll leave...	Je pars... zhuh par
We'll leave...	Nous partons... noo par-tohn
...today / tomorrow.	...aujourd'hui / demain. oh-zhoor-dwee / duh-man
...very early.	...très tôt. treh toh
Can I pay now?	Je peux régler la note maintenant? zhuh puh ray-glay lah noht man-tuh-nahn

The bill, please.	La note, s'il vous plaît. lah noht see voo play
I think this is too high.	Je pense que c'est trop. zhuh pahns kuh say troh
Can you explain / itemize the bill?	Vous pouvez expliquer / détailler cette note? voo poo-vay ehk-splee-kay / day-teh-yay seht noht
Do you accept credit cards?	Vous prenez les cartes de crédit? voo pruh-nay lay kart duh kray-dee
Is it cheaper if I pay in cash?	C'est moins cher si je paie en liquide? say mwan shehr see zhuh pay ahn lee-keed
Everything was great.	C'était super. say-tay sew-pehr
I slept like a baby.	J'ai dormi comme un enfant. zhay dor-mee kohm uhn ahn-fahn
Can I / Can we...?	Je peux / Nous pouvons...? zhuh puh / noo poo-vohn
...leave baggage here until ____ o'clock	...laisser les baggages ici jusqu'à ____ heure leh-say lay bah-gahzh ee-see zhews-kah ____ ur
A tip for you.	Un pourboire pour vous. uhn poor-bwahr poor voo

Your bill will include a small ***taxe du séjour,*** the daily hotel tax.

SPECIAL CONCERNS

Families

Do you have...?	Vous avez...? vooz ah-vay
...a family room	...une grande chambre / une suite ewn grahnd shahn-bruh / ewn sweet
...a family rate	...un tarif famille uhn tah-reef fah-mee

...a discount for children	...un tarif réduit pour enfants uhn tah-reef ray-dwee poor ahn-fahn
I have / We have...	J'ai / Nous avons... zhay / nooz ah-vohn
...one child.	...un enfant. uhn ahn-fahn
...two children.	...deux enfants. duhz ahn-fahn
_____ months old	de _____ mois duh _____ mwah
_____ years old	de _____ ans duh _____ ahn
Do you accept children?	Vous recevez des enfants? voo ruh-suh-vay dayz ahn-fahn
age limit	limite d'âge lee-meet dahzh
I'd like / We'd like...	Je voudrais / Nous voudrions... zhuh voo-dray / noo voo-dree-ohn
...a crib.	...un berceau. uhn behr-soh
...an extra bed.	...un lit supplémentaire. uhn lee sew-play-mahn-tair
...bunk beds.	...lits superposés. lee sew-pehr-poh-zay
babysitting service	service de babysitting sehr-vees duh "babysitting"
Is... nearby?	Il y a... près d'ici? eel yah... preh dee-see
...a park	...un parc uhn park
...a playground	...un parc avec des jeux uhn park ah-vehk day zhuh
...a swimming pool	...une piscine ewn pee-seen

Mobility Issues

For related phrases, see page 312 in the Personal Care and Health chapter.

Do you have...?	Vous avez...? vooz ah-vay
...an elevator	...un ascenseur uhn ah-sahn-sur

...a ground floor room	...une chambre au rez-de-chaussée ewn shahn-bruh oh ray-duh-shoh-say
...a wheelchair-accessible room	...une chambre accessible à un fauteuil roulant ewn shahn-bruh ahk-suh-see-bluh ah uhn foh-tuh-ee roo-lahn

AT THE HOSTEL

Europe's cheapest beds are in hostels, open to travelers of any age. Official hostels (affiliated with Hostelling International) are usually big and institutional. Independent hostels are more casual, with fewer rules.

hostel	auberge de jeunesse oh-behrzh duh zhuh-nehs
dorm bed	lit dortoir lee dor-twahr
How many beds per room?	Il y a combien de lits par chambre? eel yah kohn-bee-an duh lee par shahn-bruh
dorm for women only	dortoir uniquement pour les femmes dor-twahr ew-neek-mahn poor lay fahm
co-ed dorm	dortoir mixte dor-twahr meekst
double room	chambre double shahn-bruh doo-bluh
family room	salle de séjour sahl duh say-zhoor
Is breakfast included?	Le petit déjeuner est compris? luh puh-tee day-zhuh-nay ay kohn-pree
curfew	couvre-feu koov-ruh-fuh
lockout	portes fermées port fehr-may
membership card	carte de membre kart duh mahn-bruh

EATING

Dig into this chapter's phrases for dining at restaurants, special concerns (including dietary restrictions, children, and being in a hurry), types of food and drink, and shopping for your picnic. The next chapter is a Menu Decoder.

French restaurants normally serve from noon to 2 p.m. and from 7 p.m. until about 10 p.m. Cafés and brasseries are generally open throughout the day. The menu is posted right on the front door or window, and "window shopping" for your meal is a fun, important part of the experience. While the slick self-service restaurants are easy to use, you'll often eat better for the same money in a good little family bistro. The inside seating in all French restaurants is now non-smoking.

RESTAURANTS

Diners around the world recognize French food as a work of art. French cuisine is sightseeing for your taste buds.

Styles of cooking include ***haute cuisine*** (classic, elaborately prepared, multi-course meals), ***cuisine bourgeoise*** (the finest-quality home cooking), ***cuisine des provinces*** (traditional dishes of specific regions), and ***nouvelle cuisine*** (a focus on smaller portions and closer attention to the texture and color of the ingredients).

Types of Restaurants

Restaurant: Generally elegant, expensive eatery serving haute cuisine

Café / Brasserie: Informal eateries offering quick, simple food and drink; *brasseries* often serve meals throughout the day

Bistro: Small, usually casual neighborhood restaurant offering straightforward, traditional food

Auberge / Hostellerie / Relais: Country inn serving high-quality traditional food

Crêperie: Street stand or café specializing in crêpes (thin pancakes, usually served with sweet fillings)

Salon de thé: Tea and coffee house offering pastries, desserts, and sometimes light meals

Buffet-express / Snack bar: Cafeteria, usually near a train or bus station

...a table...	...une table...	ewn tah-bluh
...for one / two.	...pour un / deux.	poor uhn / duh
...inside / outside.	...à l'intérieur / dehors.	ah lan-tay-ree-ur / duh-or
...by the window.	...à côté de la fenêtre.	ah koh-tay duh lah fuh-neh-truh
...with a view.	...avec une vue.	ah-vehk ewn vew
quiet	tranquille	trahn-keel
Is this table free?	Cette table est libre?	seht tah-bluh ay lee-bruh
Can I sit here?	Je peux m'asseoir ici?	zhuh puh mah-swahr ee-see
Can we sit here?	Nous pouvons nous asseoir ici?	noo poo-vohn nooz ah-swahr ee-see
How long is the wait?	Combien de temps faut-il attendre?	kohn-bee-an duh tahn foh-teel ah-tahn-druh
How many minutes?	Combien de minutes?	kohn-bee-an duh mee-newt
Where are the toilets?	Où sont les toilettes?	oo sohn lay twah-leht

At a ***café*** or a ***brasserie***, if the table is not set, it's fine to seat yourself and just have a drink. However, if it's set with a placemat and cutlery, you should wait to be seated and plan to order a meal. If you're unsure, ask the server ***Je peux m'asseoir ici?*** (Can I sit here?) before taking a seat.

Reservations

reservation	réservation	ray-zehr-vah-see-ohn
Are reservations recommended?	Les réservations sont conseillées?	lay ray-zehr-vah-see-ohn sohn kohn-seh-yay

I'd like to make a reservation...	Je voudrais faire une réservation... zhuh voo-dray fair ewn ray-zehr-vah-see-ohn
...for one person / for myself.	...pour moi-même. poor mwah-mehm
...for two people.	...pour deux personnes. poor duh pehr-suhn
...for today / tomorrow.	...pour aujourd'hui / demain. poor oh-zhoor-dwee / duh-man
...for lunch / dinner.	...pour le déjeuner / le dîner. poor luh day-zhuh-nay / luh dee-nay
...at _____ o'clock.	...à _____ heures. ah _____ uhr
My name is _____.	Je m'appelle _____. zhuh mah-pehl _____
I have a reservation for _____ people.	J'ai une réservation pour _____ personnes. zhay ewn ray-zehr-vah-see-ohn poor _____ pehr-suhn

The Menu

Here are a few food categories and other restaurant lingo you might see on the menu.

menu	carte kart
The menu (in English), please.	La carte (en anglais), s'il vous plaît. lah kart (ahn ahn-glay) see voo play
fixed-price meal	menu / prix fixe muh-new / pree feeks
special of the day	plat du jour plah dew zhoor
specialty of the house	spécialité de la maison spay-see-ah-lee-tay duh lah may-zohn
fast service special	formule rapide for-mewl rah-peed
tourist menu (fixed-price meal)	menu touristique muh-new too-ree-steek

A Sample Menu of the Day

Choose a first course, second course, dessert, and beverage.

Restaurant La Mer
18, rue de la Gare, Marseille

MENU TOURISTIQUE €22

Entrée au choix (FIRST COURSE CHOICES)

- SOUPE DE POISSONS (FISH SOUP)
- 12 ESCARGOTS EN COQUILLE (SNAILS IN SHELL)
- SALADE NIÇOISE
- SUGGESTION DU CHEF

Plat au choix (SECOND COURSE CHOICES)

- PLATEAU FRUITS DU MER (PLATTER OF MIXED COLD SEAFOOD)
- POISSON DU MARCHE (FISH FROM THE MARKET)
- POULET BASQUAISE (CHICKEN BASQUE STYLE)
- STEAK-FRITES, SAUCE A L'ECHALOTE (STEAK W/FRIES + SHALLOT SAUCE)

Dessert au choix (DESSERT CHOICES)

- FROMAGE (CHEESE)
- PATISSERIE DU JOUR (PASTRY OF THE DAY)
- GLACE OU SORBET (ICE CREAM OR SHERBET)
- CREME BRULEE

~SERVICE COMPRIS~ (SERVICE INCLUDED)

Merci et Bon Appetit!

children's plate	assiette d'enfant ahs-yeht dahn-fahn
seniors' menu	une carte de seniors ewn kart duh seen-yor
breakfast	petit déjeuner puh-tee day-zhuh-nay
lunch	déjeuner day-zhuh-nay
dinner	dîner dee-nay
dishes (prepared dishes)	des plats day plah
warm / cold plates	plats chauds / froids plah shoh / frwah
appetizers	hors d'oeuvres or duh-vruh
sandwiches	sandwichs sahnd-weech
bread	pain pan
cheese	fromage froh-mahzh
soup	soupe soop
salad	salade sah-lahd
first course	entrée ahn-tray
main course	plat principal plah pran-see-pahl
fish	poisson pwah-sohn
poultry	volaille voh-lī
meat	viande vee-ahnd
seafood	fruits de mer frwee duh mehr
egg dishes	plats d'oeufs plah duhf
side dishes	plats d'accompagnement plah dah-kohn-pahn-yuh-mahn
vegetables	légumes lay-gewm
fruit	fruit frwee
dessert	dessert day-sehr
drink menu	carte des consommations kart day kohn-soh-mah-see-ohn
beverages	boissons bwah-sohn
beer	bière bee-ehr
wine	vin van

service included	service compris sehr-vees kohn̲-pree
service not included	service non compris sehr-vees nohn̲ kohn̲-pree
hot / cold	chaud / froid shoh / frwah
comes with	servi avec sehr-vee ah-vehk
choice of	le choix de luh shwah duh

In French restaurants, you can order off the menu, which is called a ***carte***, or you can order a multi-course, fixed-price meal, which, confusingly, is called a ***menu*** (so if you ask for a ***menu*** instead of the ***carte***, you'll get a fixed-price meal). Most restaurants also have a few special dishes of the day, called ***plat du jour***, or simply ***plat***.

Menus, which usually include three courses, are generally a good value and will help you pace your meal like the locals: You'll get your choice of soup, appetizer, or salad; your choice of three or four main courses with vegetables; plus a cheese course and/or a choice of desserts. Wine and other drinks are generally extra. Certain premium items add a few euros to the price, clearly noted on the menu (***supplément*** or ***sup.***). Many restaurants offer less expensive, abbreviated versions of their ***menu*** at lunchtime, allowing you to select two courses rather than three or four. These pared-down ***menus*** are sometimes called ***formules*** and feature an ***entrée et plat*** (first course and main dish) or ***plat et dessert*** (main dish and dessert).

If you order ***à la carte*** (from what we would call the "menu"), you'll have a wider selection of food. It's traditional to order an ***entrée*** (which—again, confusingly—is a starter rather than a main dish) and a ***plat principal*** (main course). The ***plats*** are generally more meat-based, while the ***entrées*** are where you can get your veggies. (The ***menu***, while time-consuming if you're in a rush, creates the appropriate balance of veggies to meat.) Elaborate meals may also have ***entremets***—tiny dishes served between courses.

Service compris (s.c.) means that the tip is included.

Ordering

To get a waiter's attention, simply ask ***S'il vous plaît?*** (Please?). If you have allergies or dietary restrictions, see page 117.

waiter	Monsieur muhs-yuh
waitress	Mademoiselle / Madame mahd-mwah-zehl / mah-dahm
I'm / We're ready to order.	Je suis / Nous sommes prêt à commander. zhuh swee / noo suhm preh ah koh-mahn-day
I need / We need more time.	J'ai besoin de / Nous avons besoin de plus de temps. zhay buh-zwan duh / nooz ah-vohn buh-zwan duh plew duh tahn
I'd like / We'd like...	Je voudrais / Nous voudrions... zhuh voo-dray / noo voo-dree-ohn
...just a drink.	...une consommation seulement. ewn kohn-soh-mah-see-ohn suhl-mahn
...to see the menu.	...voir la carte. vwahr lah kart
Do you have...?	Avez-vous...? ah-vay-voo
...an English menu	...une carte en anglais ewn kart ahn ahn-glay
...a lunch special	...un plat du jour uhn plah dew zhoor
...half portions	...des demi-portions day duh-mee-por-see-ohn
What do you recommend?	Qu'est-ce que vous recommandez? kehs kuh voo ruh-koh-mahn-day
What's your favorite dish?	Quel est votre plat favori? kehl eh voh-truh plah fah-voh-ree
What is better? (point to menu items)	Qu'est-ce qui vaut mieux? kehs kee voh mee-uh
What is...?	Qu'est-ce qui est...? kehs kee ay
Is it...?	C'est...? say
...good	...bon bohn

...affordable	...abordable ah-bor-dah-bluh
...expensive	...cher shehr
...local	...de la région / du pays duh lah ray-zhee-ohn / dew pay-ee
...fresh	...frais fray
...fast (already prepared)	...déjà préparé day-zhah pray-pah-ray
...spicy (hot)	...piquant pee-kahn
Is it filling?	C'est copieux? say koh-pee-uh
Make me happy.	Rendez-moi content. rahn-day mwah kohn-tahn
Around _____ euros.	Environ _____ euros. ahn-vee-rohn _____ uh-roh
What is that? (pointing)	C'est quoi ça? say kwah sah
How much is it?	C'est combien? say kohn-bee-an
Nothing with eyeballs.	Rien avec des yeux. ree-an ah-vehk dayz yuh
Can I substitute (something) for _____?	Je peux substituer (quelque chose) pour _____? zhuh puh sewb-stee-tew-ay (kehl-kuh shohz) poor _____
Can I / Can we get it "to go"?	Je peux / Nous pouvons prendre ça "à emporter"? zhuh puh / noo poo-vohn prahn-druh sah ah ahn-por-tay

Once you're seated, the table is yours for the entire lunch or dinner period. The waiter or waitress is there to serve you, but only when you're ready. When going to a good restaurant with an approachable staff, I like to say, "Make me happy," and set a price limit.

Some eateries will let you split a dish; others won't. If you are splitting a main dish, it's polite to get one or two ***entrées*** (starters) as well. In most cases, it's fine for a person to get only a ***plat*** (main dish). You can never split a multi-course ***menu***.

If you want just a simple meal—like soup, a salad, a sandwich, or an omelet—go to a ***café*** or ***brasserie*** instead of a ***restaurant***.

There's always one more question at the end of any sales encounter (whether finishing a meal or buying cheese at a ***fromagerie***): Will there be anything else? The French have a staggering number of ways to say this, including: ***Ça sera tout?*** (Will that be all?), ***Et avec ça?*** (And with this?), ***Vous-avez terminé?*** (Have you finished?), ***Désirez-vous autre chose?*** (Would you like anything else?), ***Ça vous a plû?*** (Have you enjoyed it?), and so on. Your response can be a simple ***Ça va, merci.*** (Everything is fine, thanks.)

Tableware and Condiments

I need / We need a...	J'ai besoin / Nous avons besoin... zhay buh-zwan / nooz ah-vohn buh-zwan
...napkin.	...d'une serviette. dewn sehrv-yeht
...knife.	...d'un couteau. duhn koo-toh
...fork.	...d'une fourchette. dewn foor-sheht
...spoon.	...d'une cuillère. dewn kwee-yehr
...cup.	...d'une tasse. dewn tahs
...glass.	...d'un verre. duhn vehr
...carafe.	...d'une carafe. dewn kah-rahf
Please...	S'il vous plaît... see voo play
...another table setting.	...d'un autre couvert. duhn oh-truh koo-vehr
...another plate.	...d'une autre assiette. dewn oh-truh ahs-yeht
silverware	des couverts day koo-vehr
water	d'eau doh
bread	de pain duh pan
butter	de beurre duh bur
margarine	de margarine duh mar-gah-reen
salt / pepper	de sel / de poivre duh sehl / duh pwah-vruh

sugar	de sucre duh sew-kruh
artificial sweetener	de faux-sucre duh foh-sew-kruh
honey	de miel duh mee-ehl
mustard	de moutarde duh moo-tard
ketchup	de ketchup duh "ketchup"
mayonnaise	de mayonnaise duh mah-yoh-nehz
toothpick	d'un cure-dents duhn kewr-dahn

The Food Arrives

Your meal might begin with an ***amuse-bouche***—literally, "palate amusement" (included with your meal). After bringing your food, your server might wish you a cheery ***"Bon appétit!"***

Looks delicious!	Ça a l'air délicieux! sah ah lair day-lee-see-uh
Is it included with the meal?	C'est inclus avec le repas? say an-klew ah-vehk luh ruh-pah
I did not order this.	Je n'ai pas commandé ça. zhuh nay pah koh-mahn-day sah
We did not order this.	Nous n'avons pas commandé ça. noo nah-vohn pah koh-mahn-day sah
Can you heat this up?	Vous pouvez réchauffer ça? voo poo-vay ray-shoh-fay sah
A little.	Un peu. uhn puh
More. / Another.	Plus. / Un autre. plew / uhn oh-truh
One more, please.	Encore un, s'il vous plaît. ahn-kor uhn see voo play
The same.	La même chose. lah mehm shohz
Enough.	Assez. ah-say
Finished.	Terminé. tehr-mee-nay
Thank you.	Merci. mehr-see

Complaints

This is...	C'est... say
...dirty.	...sale. sahl
...greasy.	...graisseux. gray-suh
...salty.	...salé. sah-lay
...undercooked.	...pas assez cuit. pah ah-say kwee
...overcooked.	...trop cuit. troh kwee
...inedible.	...immangeable. an-mahn-zhah-bluh
...cold.	...froid. frwah
...disgusting.	...dégoûtant. day-goo-tahn
Do any of your customers return?	Avez-vous des clients qui reviennent? ah-vay-voo day klee-ahn kee ruh-vee-ehn
Yuck!	Berk! behrk

Compliments to the Chef

Yummy!	Miam-miam! myahm-myahm
Delicious!	Délicieux! day-lee-see-uh
Magnificent!	Magnifique! mahn-yee-feek
Very tasty!	Très bon! treh bohn
I love French food.	J'aime la cuisine française. zhehm lah kwee-zeen frahn-sehz
My compliments to the chef!	Félicitations au chef! fay-lee-see-tah-see-ohn oh shehf

If you've really enjoyed the meal, learn and use this phrase liberally: ***Félicitations au chef!*** (My compliments to the chef!). French chefs take their work seriously and appreciate knowing you were satisfied.

Paying

bill	addition ah-dee-see-ohn
The bill, please.	L'addition, s'il vous plaît. lah-dee-see-ohn see voo play
Together.	Ensemble. ahn-sahn-bluh
Separate checks.	Notes séparées. noht say-pah-ray
Credit card OK?	Carte de crédit OK? kart duh kray-dee "OK"
This is not correct.	Ce n'est pas exact. suh nay pah ehg-zahkt
Can you explain this?	Vous pouvez expliquez ça? voo poo-vay ehk-splee-kay sah
Can you itemize the bill?	Vous pouvez détailler cette note? voo poo-vay day-tay-yay seht noht
What if I wash the dishes?	Et si je lave la vaisselle? ay see zhuh lahv lah vay-sehl
May I have a receipt, please?	Je peux avoir une facture, s'il vous plaît? zhuh puh ah-vwahr ewn fahk-tewr see voo play
Thank you very much.	Merci beaucoup. mehr-see boh-koo

In France, slow service is good service (fast service would rush the diners). Out of courtesy, your waiter will not bring your bill until you ask for it. Here's a good strategy: When you're done with your dessert, your waiter will ask if you'd like some coffee (which is typically taken after, rather than with, the dessert). This gives you the perfect opening to ask for the bill.

If you're paying with your credit card in cafés and restaurants, the waiter will come by your table with a little machine that the French jokingly call the "game boy." This device will print a receipt for you to sign. If splitting the bill, tell your server the amount you want to charge to each card. If you want to leave a tip, do it in cash (see next section).

It's extremely rare for the French to request separate checks; usually they just split the bill evenly or take turns treating each other.

Tipping

Because a service charge is already included in the bill, an additional tip is not required, but appreciated. My French friends, who understand that it bothers Americans to "undertip," suggest this: Imagine that the bill already includes a 15 percent tip, then add whatever you feel is appropriate—maybe 5 percent for good service, or up to 10 percent for exceptional service. It's often most convenient to simply round up the bill (for example, for an €18.80 check, round up to €20)—hand your payment to the waiter and say ***C'est bon*** (say bohn), meaning "It's good—keep the change." If you order your food at a counter, don't tip.

tip	pourboire poor-bwahr
service included	service compris sehr-vees kohn-pree
service not included	service non compris sehr-vees nohn kohn-pree
Is tipping expected?	Je dois laisser un pourboire? zhuh dwah lay-say uhn poor-bwahr
What percent?	Quel pourcentage? kehl poor-sahn-tahzh
Keep the change.	Gardez la monnaie. gar-day lah moh-nay
Change, please.	La monnaie, s'il vous plaît. lah moh-nay see voo play
This is for you.	C'est pour vous. say poor voo

SPECIAL CONCERNS

In a Hurry

Europeans take their time at meals, so don't expect speedy service. However, if you're in a rush, be proactive and let your server know in advance, or seek out a ***brasserie*** or restaurant that offers ***service rapide*** (fast food).

I'm / We're in a hurry.	Je suis / Nous sommes pressé. zhuh swee / noo suhm preh-say
I'm sorry.	Désolé. day-zoh-lay
I need / We need...	J'ai besoin / Nous avons besoin... zhay buh-swan / nooz ah-vohn buh-swan
...to be served quickly.	...d'être servi vite. deh-truh sehr-vee veet
I must / We must...	Je dois / Nous devons... zhuh dwah / noo duh-vohn
...leave in 30 minutes / one hour.	...partir dans trente minutes / une heure. par-teer dahn trahnt mee-newt / ewn ur
Will the food be ready soon?	Ce sera prêt bientôt? suh suh-rah preh bee-an-toh
The bill, please.	L'addition, s'il vous plaît. lah-dee-see-ohn see voo play

Allergies and Other Dietary Restrictions

Think of your meal (as the French do) as if it's a finely crafted creation by a trained artist. The chef knows what goes well together, and substitutions are considered an insult to his training. Picky eaters should just take it or leave it. However, French restaurants are willing to accommodate genuine dietary restrictions and other special concerns (or at least point you to an appropriate choice on the menu). These phrases might help. If the food you're unable to eat doesn't appear in this list, look for it in the Menu Decoder (next chapter). You'll find vegetarian phrases in the next section.

I'm allergic to...	Je suis allergique à... zhuh sweez ah-lehr-zheek ah
I cannot eat...	Je ne peux pas manger de... zhuh nuh puh pah mahn-zhay duh
He / She cannot eat...	Il / Elle ne peut pas manger de... eel / ehl nuh puh pah mahn-zhay duh

He / She has a life-threatening allergy to...	Il / Elle a une allergie très grave à... eel / ehl ah ewn ah-lehr-zhee treh grahv ah
No...	Non... nohn
...dairy products.	...aux produits laitiers. oh proh-dwee layt-yay
...any kind of nut.	...aux toutes sortes de noix. oh toot sort duh nwah
...peanuts.	...aux cacahuètes. oh kah-kah-weht
...walnuts.	...aux noix. oh nwah
...wheat / gluten.	...au blé / au gluten. oh blay / oh glew-tehn
...shellfish.	...crustacés. krew-stah-say
...salt / sugar.	...sel / sucre. sehl / sew-kruh
I'm a diabetic.	Je suis diabétique. zhuh swee dee-ah-bay-teek
He / She is lactose intolerant.	Il / Elle est intolérant au lactose. eel / ehl ay an-toh-lay-rahnt oh lahk-tohz
I'd like / We'd like a meal that's...	Je voudrais / Nous voudrions un repas qui est... zhuh voo-dray / noo voo-dree-ohn uhn ruh-pah kee ay
...kosher.	...casher. kah-shehr
...halal.	...halal. ah-lahl
...low-fat.	...allege en matières grasses. ah-lehzh ahn mah-tee-yehr grahs
Low cholesterol.	Allégé. ah-lay-zhay
No caffeine.	Décaféiné. day-kah-fay-nay
No alcohol.	Sans alcool. sahnz ahl-kohl
Organic.	Biologique. bee-oh-loh-zheek
I eat only insects.	Je ne mange que les insectes. zhuh nuh mahnzh kuh layz an-sehkt

Vegetarian Phrases

Many French people think "vegetarian" means "no red meat" or "not much meat." If you're a strict vegetarian, be very specific: Tell your server what you don't eat—and it can be helpful to clarify what you do eat. Write it out on a card and keep it handy.

I'm a...	Je suis... zhuh swee
...vegetarian. (male)	...végétarien. vay-zhay-tah-ree-an
...vegetarian. (female)	...végétarienne. vay-zhay-tah-ree-ehn
...strict vegetarian.	...strict végétarien. streekt vay-zhay-tah-ree-an
...vegan. (m / f)	...végétalien / végétalienne. vay-zhay-tah-lee-an / vay-zhay-tah-lee-ehn
Is any animal product used in this?	Il y a des produits d'origine animale dedans? eel yah day proh-dwee doh-ree-zheen ah-nee-mahl duh-dahn
What is vegetarian? (pointing to menu)	Qu'est-ce qu'il y a de végétarien? kehs keel yah duh vay-zhay-tah-ree-an
I don't eat...	Je ne mange pas... zhuh nuh mahnzh pah
I'd like this without...	Je voudrais cela sans... zhuh voo-dray suh-lah sahn
...meat.	...viande. vee-ahnd
...eggs.	...oeufs. uhf
...animal products.	...produits d'origine animale. proh-dwee doh-ree-zheen ah-nee-mahl
I eat...	Je mange... zhuh mahnzh
Do you have...?	Avez-vous...? ah-vay-voo
...anything with tofu	...quelque chose avec du tofu kehl-kuh shohz ah-vehk dew toh-few
...a veggie burger	...un hamburger végétarien uhn ahn-bur-gehr vay-zhay-tah-ree-an

Children

Do you have a...?	Vous avez...? vooz ah-vay
...children's menu	...une carte d'enfants ewn kart dahn-fahn
...children's portion	...une assiette enfant ewn ahs-yeht ahn-fahn
...half-portion	...une demi-portion ewn duh-mee-por-see-ohn
...high chair	...une chaise haute ewn shehz oht
...booster seat	...un réhausseur uhn ray-oh-sur
noodles / rice	pâtes / riz paht / ree
with butter	avec beurre ah-vehk bur
without sauce	pas de sauce pah duh sohs
sauce or dressing on the side	sauce à part sohs ah par
pizza	pizza "pizza"
...cheese only	...juste fromage zhewst froh-mahzh
...pepperoni	...chorizo shoh-ree-zoh
grilled ham and cheese sandwich	croque monsieur krohk muhs-yuh
hot dog and fries	saucisse-frites soh-sees-freet
hamburger	hamburger ahn-bur-gehr
cheeseburger	cheeseburger sheez-bur-gehr
French fries	frites freet
ketchup	ketchup "ketchup"
milk	lait lay
straw	paille pī-yuh
More napkins, please.	Des serviettes, s'il vous plaît. day sehrv-yeht see voo play

WHAT'S COOKING?

Breakfast

French hotel breakfasts are small, expensive, and often optional. The basic continental breakfast has three parts: ***boisson chaude***—a hot drink, such as ***café au lait*** (coffee with milk), ***thé*** (tea), or ***chocolat chaud*** (hot chocolate); ***viennoiserie***—your choice of sweet rolls, including ***croissants;*** and ***une tartine***—a fancy word for a ***baguette*** with ***beurre*** (butter) and ***confiture*** (jam). You may also get some ***jus de fruit*** (fruit juice, usually orange), but it likely costs extra. Many hotels now provide breakfast buffets with fruit, cereal, yogurt, and cheese (usually for a few extra euros and well worth it).

You can save money by breakfasting at a ***bar*** or ***café,*** where it's usually acceptable to bring in a ***croissant*** from the neighboring ***boulangerie*** (bakery). Or just order ***une tartine*** with your ***café au lait.*** French people almost never eat eggs for breakfast, but if you're desperate, you can get an ***omelette*** almost any time of day at a café.

I'd like / We'd like...	Je voudrais / Nous voudrions... zhuh voo-dray / noo voo-dree-oh<u>n</u>
breakfast	petit déjeuner puh-tee day-zhuh-nay
bread	pain pa<u>n</u>
roll	petit pain puh-tee pa<u>n</u>
little loaf of bread	baguette bah-geht
toast	toast "toast"
butter	beurre bur
jam	confiture koh<u>n</u>-fee-tewr
honey	miel mee-ehl
fruit cup	salade de fruits sah-lahd duh frwee
pastry	pâtisserie pah-tee-suh-ree
croissant	croissant krwah-sah<u>n</u>
cheese	fromage froh-mahzh
yogurt	yaourt yah-oort
cereal	céréale say-ray-ahl

Key Phrases: What's Cooking?

food	nourriture noo-ree-tewr
breakfast	petit déjeuner puh-tee day-zhuh-nay
lunch	déjeuner day-zhuh-nay
dinner	dîner dee-nay
bread	pain pan
cheese	fromage froh-mahzh
soup	soupe soop
salad	salade sah-lahd
fish	poisson pwah-sohn
chicken	poulet poo-lay
meat	viande vee-ahnd
vegetables	légumes lay-gewm
fruit	fruit frwee
dessert	dessert day-sehr

milk	lait lay
coffee / tea	café / thé kah-fay / tay
fruit juice	jus de fruit zhew duh frwee
orange juice (fresh)	jus d'orange (pressé) zhew doh-rahnzh (preh-say)
hot chocolate	chocolat chaud shoh-koh-lah shoh

Pastries

Baked goods are divided into two general categories: a ***boulangerie*** specializes in breads and yeasty sweet rolls (such as ***croissants*** or ***brioche,*** collectively called ***viennoiserie***). A ***pâtisserie*** deals with cakes and other treats. It's said that a baker cannot be both good at bread and good at pastry. That's not always the case, though at cooking school, they major in one or the other. In general, people eat ***viennoiserie*** earlier in the day and ***pâtisserie*** later in the day. Here are a few examples of ***viennoiserie,*** which break into general categories.

These ***viennoiserie*** are made with puff pastry ***(pâte feuilletée)***—buttery, crispy, and flaky:

croissant krwah-sahn
classic French crescent roll

pain au chocolat pan oh shoh-koh-lah
buttery, flaky pastry filled with chocolate (sometimes called "chocolate croissant")

palmier pahlm-yay
"palm"-shaped, light and delicate buttery pastry

chausson aux pommes shoh-sohn oh pohm
"slipper" filled with apples (like an apple turnover)

grillé pommes gree-yay pohm
apple-filled pastry with "grill" pattern

anglaise ahn-glehz
"English" apple pastry with large vents cut into the top

oranais oh-rahn-ay
apricot danish

jesuit zhehz-weet
pastry filled with almond crème, shaped like a Jesuit's triangular hat

mille-feuille meel-fuh-ee
light pastry with a "thousand sheets" of delicate dough and layers of cream; a.k.a. Napoleon

pithivier pee-teev-yay
spiral pie made of puff pastry, usually filled with almond paste

vol-au-vent vohl-oh-vahn
hollow, cylindrical pastry that's so light it's called "windblown"; generally cherry-filled, but sometimes savory

jambon-mornay zhahn-bohn-mor-nay
savory puff pastry with ham and cheese

Pastries *(cont.)*

These are puffier and more bread-like:

brioche bree-ohsh
big, puffy roll made with eggs

cramique krah-meek
brioche bread with raisins ("ceramic")

pain aux raisins / escargot raisins
pan oh ray-zan / ehs-kar-goh ray-zan
spiral, "snail"-shaped, glazed pastry with raisins

pain au lait pan oh lay
"milk bread"; small, flaky roll

tresse trehs
"braid"-shaped brioche

cannelé kah-nuh-lay
small, "fluted" pastry with caramelized crust and custard filling

These are heavier, using an eggy dough with lots of butter and no yeast (called ***pâte à choux***):

beignet behn-yay
deep-fried dough triangle sprinkled with powdered sugar

profiterole proh-fee-tuh-rohl
cream puff

chouquette shoo-keht
dense little baked doughnut speckled with sugar

éclair ay-klair oblong, iced sweet roll filled with custard

religieuse ruh-lee-zhee-uhz round éclair shaped like a nun

Other goodies are prepared in a variety of ways:

macaron mah-kah-rohn
cookie with a puffy but hard crust sandwiching a thin layer of cream

madeleine mah-duh-lehn
bite-size buttery sponge cake with a shell-like shape

mignardise meen-yar-deez
miniature petit four (see next)

petit four puh-tee foor
bite-sized, frosted cake served at parties

roulé aux noix roo-lay oh nwah
"walnut roll" with a layer of nutty paste

tarte tart
miniature pie, generally filled with fruit

For other types of desserts—as well as handy phrases for fillings in many of the above items—see page 156.

What's Probably Not for Breakfast

You likely won't see any of these items at a traditional French breakfast table, but you may see them at international hotels or cafés catering to foreigners.

omelet	omelette oh-muh-leht
eggs	des oeufs dayz uhf
fried eggs	oeufs au plat uhf oh plah
scrambled eggs	oeufs brouillés uhf broo-yay
boiled egg...	oeuf à la coque... uhf ah lah kohk
...soft / hard	...mollet / dur moh-lay / dewr
poached egg	oeuf poché uhf poh-shay
ham	jambon zhahn-bohn

Snacks and Quick Lunches

omelet	omelette oh-muh-leht
quiche...	quiche... keesh
...with cheese	...au fromage oh froh-mahzh
...with ham	...au jambon oh zhahn-bohn
...with onions	...aux oignons ohz ohn-yohn

...with leeks	...aux poirreaux	oh pwah-roh
...with mushrooms	...aux champignons	oh shah<u>n</u>-peen-yoh<u>n</u>
...with bacon, cheese, and onions	...lorraine	lor-rehn
...with tuna	...au thon	oh toh<u>n</u>
...with salmon	...au saumon	oh soh-moh<u>n</u>
paté	pâté	pah-tay
onion tart	tarte à l'oignon	tart ah lohn-yoh<u>n</u>
cheese tart	tarte au fromage	tart oh froh-mahzh

Light meals are quick and easy at ***cafés, brasseries,*** and ***bars*** throughout France. (These are about the same, except that ***brasseries*** serve food all day, whereas some ***cafés*** close their kitchens between lunch and dinner—around 4 p.m. to 6 p.m.—but stay open to serve snacks and drinks.) These places generally have more limited menus than restaurants, but they offer more budget options.

A ***salade, crêpe*** (see next), ***quiche,*** or ***omelette*** is a fairly cheap way to fill up, even in Paris. Each can be made with various extras like ham, cheese, mushrooms, and so on.

Crêpes

The quintessentially French thin pancake called a ***crêpe*** (rhymes with "step," not "grape") is a good budget standby: It's filling, usually inexpensive, and generally quick. A place that sells them is a ***crêperie*** (krehp-eh-ree).

Crêpes generally come in two types: ***sucrée*** (sweet) and ***salée*** (savory). Technically, a savory ***crêpe*** should be made with a heartier buckwheat batter, and is called a ***galette*** (gah-leht). However, many cheap and lazy ***crêperies*** use the same sweet batter ***(de froment)*** for both their sweet and savory ***crêpes***.

For savory ***crêpes,*** the standard toppings include ***fromage*** (cheese, usually Swiss-style Gruyère or Emmental), ***jambon*** (ham), ***oeuf*** (an egg that's cracked and scrambled right on the hot plate), and ***champignons*** (mushrooms).

For sweet ***crêpes,*** common toppings are ***chocolat*** (chocolate syrup), Nutella (the delicious milk chocolate-hazelnut spread), jam or jelly, and powdered sugar.

savory crêpe	crêpe salée	krehp sah-lay
buckwheat crêpe	galette	gah-leht
with...	au...	oh
...cheese	...fromage	froh-mahzh
...ham	...jambon	zhahn-bohn
...eggs	...oeufs	uhf
...mushrooms	...champignons	shahn-peen-yohn
sweet crêpe	crêpe sucrée	krehp sew-kray
with...	au...	oh
...sugar	...sucre	sew-kruh
...chocolate	...chocolat	shoh-koh-lah
...Nutella	...Nutella	new-teh-lah
...jam	...confiture	kohn-fee-tewr
...whipped cream	...chantilly	shahn-tee-yee
...apple jam	...compote de pommes	kohn-poht duh pohm
...chestnut cream	...crème de marrons	krehm duh mah-rohn
...orange liqueur	...Grand Marnier	grahn marn-yay
chickpea crêpe	socca	soh-kah

During slow times, the ***crêperie*** chef might make several ***crêpes*** to be stacked up, then reheated later. Don't be surprised if he doesn't make a fresh one for you.

Sandwiches

I'd like a sandwich.	Je voudrais un sandwich. zhuh voo-dray uhn sahnd-weech
toasted	grillé gree-yay
cheese	fromage froh-mahzh
tuna	thon tohn
fish	poisson pwah-sohn
chicken	poulet poo-lay
turkey	dinde dand
ham	jambon zhahn-bohn
salami	salami sah-lah-mee
boiled egg	oeuf dur uhf dewr
garnished with veggies	crudités krew-dee-tay
lettuce	salade sah-lahd
tomato	tomate toh-maht
onions	oignons ohn-yohn
mustard	moutarde moo-tard
mayonnaise	mayonnaise mah-yoh-nehz
without mayonnaise	sans mayonnaise sahn mah-yoh-nehz
peanut butter	beurre de cacahuètes bur duh kah-kah-weht
jam / jelly	confiture kohn-fee-tewr
pork sandwich	sandwich au porc sahnd-weech oh por
grilled / heated	grillé / réchauffé gree-yay / ray-shoh-fay
Does this come cold or warm?	C'est servi froid ou chaud? say sehr-vee frwah oo shoh

Sandwiches, as well as small quiches, often come ready-made at ***boulangeries*** (bakeries). When buying a sandwich, you might see signs for ***emporté*** (to go) or ***sur place*** (to eat here).

Types of Sandwiches

Here are a few basic sandwich options you're likely to see.

canapé kah-nah-pay
small, open-faced sandwich

croque madame krohk mah-dahm
grilled ham and cheese sandwich topped with a fried egg

croque monsieur krohk muhs-yuh
grilled ham and cheese sandwich

jambon beurre zhahn-bohn bur
ham and butter (boring for most)

jambon crudités zhahn-bohn krew-dee-tay
ham with tomatoes, lettuce, cucumbers, and mayonnaise

pain salé pan sah-lay
bread rolled up with salty bits of bacon, cheese, or olives

pan bagnat pahn bahn-yah
tuna salad (salade niçoise) stuffed into a hollowed-out soft roll

poulet crudités poo-lay krew-dee-tay
chicken with tomatoes, lettuce, maybe cucumbers, and mayonnaise

saucisson beurre soh-see-sohn bur
thinly sliced sausage and butter

tartine tar-teen
baguette slice with toppings (like an open-faced sandwich)

thon crudités tohn krew-dee-tay
tuna with tomatoes, lettuce, maybe cucumbers, and mayonnaise

à la provençale ah lah proh-vahn-sahl
with marinated peppers, tomatoes, and eggplant

à la italienne ah lah ee-tahl-yehn
grilled panini

A slice of baguette topped with just about anything is called a ***tartine.*** These all-purpose, open-faced sandwiches are so beloved that French youth use the word ***tartine*** as a slang term meaning "cool."

Crunchy, grilled ***croque*** sandwiches (literally "crunch")—such as the ***croque madame*** or the ***croque monsieur***—are a French café staple.

Other variations include ***croque provençal*** (with tomato), ***croque norvégien*** (with smoked salmon), ***croque tartiflette*** (with potatoes), ***croque sucré*** (a sweet variation with powdered sugar), and even ***croque hawaiian*** (with pineapple).

If You Knead Bread

A good baker ***(boulanger)*** is a highly valued commodity within his or her community; it's said that "good bread makes a happy village." Here are a few of the many types of bread you'll find in French ***boulangeries***.

pain pan
bread

baguette bah-geht
big ol' "stick" of white bread

baguette de tradition bah-geht duh trah-dee-see-yohn
traditional baguette, made according to government specifications

flûte flewt
"flute," slightly slimmer than a baguette

bâtard bah-tar
"bastard," larger version of a baguette

ficelle fee-sehl
"string," super-thin baguette

couronne koo-ruhn
"crown," ring-shaped baguette that can be broken into individual rolls

gros pain groh pan
"fat" baguette

miche meesh
large round loaf

boule bool
round loaf (like a squashed "ball")

pain de campagne pan duh kahn-pahn-yuh
"country bread" with various grains and a thicker crust (often a large circular loaf)

pain complet pan kohn-play
wholemeal bread

multicéréales mewl-tee-say-ray-ahl
multigrain

pain au froment pan oh froh-mahn
wheat bread

pain de seigle pan duh seh-gluh
rye bread

pain au levain pan oh luh-van
sourdough ("yeast") bread

pain bis pan bees
dark-grain bread

pain pavé pan pah-vay
"cobblestone"-shaped bread, often rye

pain de mie pan duh mee
American-style sandwich bread

pain viennois pan vee-ehn-wah
soft, shiny, slightly sweeter baguette

pain doré / pain perdu pan doh-ray / pan pehr-dew
French toast ("golden bread" / "lost bread")

pain d'épices pan day-pees
gingerbread ("spice bread")

petit pain puh-tee pan
roll

Poilâne pwah-lahn
big, round loaf of rustic bread with floured crust

tartine tar-teen
baguette slice slathered with toppings, often butter and / or jam

brioche bree-ohsh
sweet, soft bun (for more pastries, see page 122)

fougasse foo-gahs
spindly, lace-like bread sometimes flavored with nuts, herbs, olives, or ham

If You Knead Bread *(cont.)*

pain brié pan̲ bree-ay
dense, crusty, football-shaped bread with ridges

pissaladière pee-sah-lah-dee-yehr
bread dough topped with onions, olives, and anchovies

croûte au fromage kroot oh froh-mahzh
cheese pastry

gougères goo-zhehr
savory cream puffs made with cheese

Other terms you might see at a ***boulangerie*** include ***quotidien*** (everyday), ***ordinaire*** (ordinary), ***de ménage*** or ***fait maison*** (homemade), ***paysanne*** (peasant), ***à l'ancienne*** (old-fashioned), and ***de fantasie*** (fancy; sometimes means sold by the piece). ***Gana*** and ***Banette*** are specific brands of baguettes.

Say Cheese

Like fine wines, French cheeses come in a staggering variety—each one with its own subtle features. Cheeses range from very fresh (aged one day) to aged for weeks. The older the cheese, the more dried and shrunken. Cheeses come in many shapes (round, logs, pyramids) and various sizes (from single-bite mouthfuls to wheels that will feed you for several meals). Some are sprinkled with herbs or spices; others are speckled with edible mold; and still others are more adorned, such as those rolled in ash ***(à la cendre)*** or wrapped in leaves ***(banon).***

Broadly speaking, French cheeses are divided into a few categories:

cheese	fromage froh-mahzh
goat	chèvre sheh-vruh
cow	vache vahsh
sheep / ewe	brebis bruh-bee
blue	bleu bluh
gooey cheese with edible rind (like brie)	à pâte molle ah paht mohl

Specific Qualities of Cheese

Once you've settled on the type of cheese, you can hone in on the characteristics you'd like.

I like cheese that is...	J'aime le fromage qui est... zhehm luh froh-mahzh kee ay
young (smooth)	ferme fehrm
aged (mature, stronger flavor)	bien fait bee-an̲ fay
mild or soft	doux doo
sharp	fort for
hard / soft / semi-soft	dur / mou / plutôt mou dewr / moo / plew-toh moo
nutty	le goût de noisettes luh goo duh nwah-zeht
pungent	relevé ruh-luh-vay
with herbs	aux herbes ohz ehrb
with spices	aux épices ohz ay-pees
rolled in ashes	aux cendres oh san̲-druh
creamy	à la crème ah lah krehm
of the region	de la région duh lah ray-zhee-ohn̲
rind	croûte kroot
bloomy / washed / natural	fleurie / lavée / naturelle fluh-ree / lah-vay / nah-tew-rehl
interior part of cheese	pâte paht

When it comes to soft, like brie, there are two types of rinds: A "bloomy" rind ***(croûte fleurie)*** is mild and lighter-colored (white or off-white), while a washed rind ***(croûte lavée)*** is orange or reddish and more pungent. Harder cheeses usually have a natural rind ***(croûte naturelle)***—hard and inedible.

In the Cheese Shop

Visit a ***fromagerie*** or a ***crémerie*** (cheese shop) and experiment, using the terms in the previous table. Consider simply putting yourself in the ***fromagerie*** clerk's capable hands—ask her to choose for you. She might appreciate the chance to help you select a few that complement each other and show off her craft. Don't expect to be offered a taste.

Some cheeses come in hockey-puck-sized disks called ***crottin*** (kroh-tan̲). You can't just buy part of a ***crottin***—you must get the whole thing. Other cheeses come in larger wheels that can be sliced. When cutting you a ***tranche*** (trahn̲sh; slice), the ***fromagerie*** clerk will want to know how much you want: ***Comme ça?*** (Like this?) ***Plus?*** (More?) ***Moins?*** (Less?). And especially for the little ***crottins*** of soft cheeses, plan to eat them the same day—they don't keep.

cheese shop	fromagerie / crémerie froh-mah-zhuh-ree / kray-muh-ree
cheese platter	plâteau de fromages plah-toh duh froh-mahzh
I would like three types of cheese for a picnic.	Je voudrais trois sortes de fromage pour une pique-nique. zhuh voo-dray trwah sort duh froh-mahzh poor ewn peek-neek
I like a cheese that is ____ and ____. (use phrases in previous table)	J'aime un fromage qui est ____ et ____. zhehm uhn̲ froh-mahzh kee ay ____ ay ____
Choose for me, please.	Choisissez pour moi, s'il vous plaît. shwah-zee-say poor mwah see voo play
What type?	Quel sorte? kehl sort
Like this. (showing size)	Comme ça. kohm sah

Ossau-Iraty oh-soh-ee-rah-tee
smooth, firm, buttery ewe's cheese

Pavé d'Auge pah-vay dohzh
spicy, tangy, square-shaped cow cheese

Pélardon pay-lar-dohn
nutty, round goat cheese

Picodon pee-koh-dohn
spicy goat cheese

Pont l'Evêque pohn lay-vehk
flavorful, smooth, square-shaped cow cheese with an earthy flavor

Port Salut por sah-lew
semi-soft, sweet cow cheese served in a wedge

Pur Brebis pewr bruh-bee
"pure sheep" cheese from the Pyrenees

Reblochon ruh-bloh-shohn
soft, gooey, mild, creamy, Brie-like cow cheese

Roquefort rohk-for
powerful, blue-veined, tangy sheep cheese

Selles-sur-Cher sehl-sewr-shehr
mild goat cheese

Saint-Marcellin san-mar-suh-lan
soft cow cheese with white edible rind

Sainte-Maure sant-mor
soft, creamy goat cheese in a cylindrical shape (Loire)

Saint-Nectaire san-nehk-tair
semi-soft, nutty cow cheese sold in big rounds

Tomme (de Savoie) tohm (duh sah-vwah)
mild, semi-soft cow cheese

Valençay vah-lahn-say
firm, nutty, ash- and mold-covered goat cheese shaped like a flat-topped pyramid

Soups and Stews

soup (of the day)	soupe (du jour) soop (dew zhoor)
broth	bouillon boo-yohn
...chicken	...de poulet duh poo-lay
...beef	...de boeuf duh buhf
...with noodles	...aux nouilles oh noo-ee
...with rice	...au riz oh ree
thick vegetable soup	potage de légumes poh-tahzh duh lay-gewm
Provençal vegetable soup	soupe au pistou soop oh pee-stoo
onion soup	soupe à l'oignon soop ah lohn-yohn
cream of asparagus soup	crème d'asperges krehm dah-spehrzh
potato and leek soup	vichyssoise vee-shee-swah
garlic soup	soupe à l'ail / tourin soop ah lī / too-ran
shellfish chowder	bisque beesk
seafood stew	bouillabaisse boo-yah-behs
meat and vegetable stew	pot au feu poht oh fuh
meat stew	ragoût rah-goo

Salads

Salads are usually served with a vinaigrette dressing and often eaten after the main course (to aid digestion).

salad...	salade... sah-lahd
...green / mixed	...verte / mixte vehrt / meekst
...with goat cheese	...au chèvre chaud oh sheh-vruh shoh
...chef's	...composée kohn-poh-zay
seafood	...océane oh-say-ahn
tuna	...de thon duh tohn

...veggie	...crudités krew-dee-tay
...with ham / cheese / egg	...avec jambon / fromage / oeuf ah-vehk zhahn-bohn / froh-mahzh / uhf
lettuce	laitue / salade lay-tew / sah-lahd
tomatoes	tomates toh-maht
onions	oignons ohn-yohn
cucumber	concombre kohn-kohn-bruh
oil / vinegar	huile / vinaigre weel / vee-nay-gruh
dressing on the side	sauce à part sohs ah par
What is in this salad?	Qu'est-ce qu'il ya dans cette salade? kehs keel yah dahn seht sah-lahd

Salad Specialties

Here are a few salads you'll see on café menus. They're typically large—one is perfect for lunch or a light dinner.

salade niçoise sah-lahd nee-swahz
green salad topped with green beans, tomatoes, anchovies, olives, hard-boiled eggs, and tuna

salade au chèvre chaud sah-lahd oh sheh-vruh shoh
green salad topped with warm goat cheese on toasted bread croutons

salade composée sah-lahd kohn-poh-zay
"composed" of multiple ingredients, which can include bacon, Comté or Roquefort cheese, egg, walnuts, and ham

salade paysanne sah-lahd pī-sahn
usually comes with potatoes, walnuts, tomatoes, ham, and egg

salade aux gésiers sah-lahd oh gay-zee-ay
salad with chicken gizzards (and often slices of duck)

salade lyonnaise sah-lahd lee-oh-nehz
croutons, fried bits of ham, and a poached egg on a bed of lettuce

First Courses and Appetizers

These smaller dishes are typically served at the start of the meal. See also "Soups and Stews" and "Salads" on page 138.

artichauts à la vinaigrette ar-tee-shoh ah lah vee-nay-greht
artichokes in a vinaigrette dressing

bouchée à la reine boo-shay ah lah rehn
pastry shell filled with creamed veal brains and mushrooms

crudités krew-dee-tay
raw and lightly cooked fresh vegetables with vinaigrette

escargots ehs-kar-goh
snails baked in the shell with garlic butter

(pâté de) foie gras (pah-tay duh) fwah grah
rich, expensive goose- or duck-liver spread

huîtres wee-truh
oysters (usually served on the half shell)

oeuf mayo uhf mah-yoh
hard-boiled egg topped with mayonnaise

oeufs en meurette uhf ahn muh-reht
poached eggs in a red wine sauce, often served on a large crouton

pâté pah-tay
smooth, highly seasoned ground meat (usually pork, sometimes game, poultry liver, or rabbit) that's served in slices with mustard and cornichons (little pickles)

pommes de terre duchesse pohm duh tehr dew-shehs
"duchess potatoes"—mashed potatoes that are baked

quenelles keh-nehl
dumplings with meat or fish in white sauce

soufflé soo-flay
fluffy eggs baked with savory fillings (cheese, meat, and vegetables)

tapenade tah-puh-nahd
paste made from olives, anchovies, lemon, and olive oil

terrine tehr-een
chunkier form of pâté (see above) served in a deep pan

Seafood

seafood	fruits de mer frwee duh mehr
assorted seafood	assiette de fruits de mer ahs-yeht duh frwee duh mehr
fish	poisson pwah-sohn
shellfish	crustacés / coquillages krew-stah-say / koh-kee-ahzh
anchovies	anchois ahn-shwah
clams	palourdes pah-loord
cod	cabillaud kah-bee-yoh
crab	crabe krahb
halibut	flétan flay-tahn
herring	hareng ah-rahn
lobster	homard oh-mar
mussels	moules mool
oysters	huîtres wee-truh
prawns	scampi skahn-pee
salmon	saumon soh-mohn
salty cod	morue moh-rew
sardines	sardines sar-deen
scallops	coquilles Saint-Jacques koh-keel san-zhahk
shrimp	crevettes kruh-veht
squid	calamar kah-lah-mar
trout	truite trweet
tuna	thon tohn
How much for a portion?	C'est combien la portion? say kohn-bee-an lah por-see-ohn
What's fresh today?	Qu'est-ce que c'est frais aujourd'hui? kehs kuh say fray oh-joord-wee
How do you eat this?	Comment est-ce que ça se mange? koh-mahn ehs kuh sah suh mahnzh

Do you eat this part?	Ça se mange? sah suh mahnzh
Just the head, please.	Seulement la tête, s'il vous plaît. suhl-mahn lah teht see voo play

Poultry

poultry	volaille voh-lī
chicken	poulet poo-lay
duck	canard kah-nar
goose	oie wah
turkey	dinde dand
breast	le blanc / le filet luh blahn / luh fee-lay
thigh	la cuisse lah kwees
drumstick	le pilon luh pee-lohn
white meat	viande blanche vee-ahnd blahnsh
eggs	des oeufs dayz uhf
free-range	élevé en liberté / élevé en plein air ay-luh-vay ahn lee-behr-tay / ay-luh-vay ahn plehn air
How long has this been dead?	Il est mort depuis longtemps? eel ay mor duh-pwee lohn-tahn

Meat

meat	viande vee-ahnd
meat cured with salt / smoked meat	viandes salées / viandes fumées vee-ahnd sah-lay / vee-ahnd few-may
beef	boeuf buhf
boar	sanglier sahn-glee-ay
cold cuts	assiette de charcuterie ahs-yeht duh shar-kew-tuh-ree
cutlet	côtelette koh-tuh-leht

Avoiding Mis-Steaks

By American standards, the French undercook meats. In France, rare (***saignant***, literally "bloody") is nearly raw, medium ***(à point)*** is rare, and well done ***(bien cuit)*** is medium. These shorter cooking times help the meat from getting overcooked, since French steak is usually thinner and tougher than American steak. Also for this reason, French steak is always served with sauces (***au poivre*** is a pepper sauce; ***une sauce roquefort*** is a blue-cheese sauce).

alive	vivant vee-vahn
raw	cru krew
very rare	bleu bluh
rare	saignant sehn-yahn
medium	à point ah pwan
well-done	bien cuit bee-an kwee
very well-done	très bien cuit treh bee-an kwee
almost burnt	presque carbonisé prehs-kuh kar-boh-nee-zay
thick hunk of prime steak	pavé pah-vay
flank steak	bavette bah-veht
hanger steak	onglet ohn-glay
sirloin	faux-filet foh-fee-lay
rib-eye steak	entrecôte ahn-truh-koht
tenderloin	médaillon may-dī-yohn
T-bone	côte de boeuf koht duh buhf
fillet	filet fee-lay
tenderloin of T-bone	tournedos toor-nuh-doh

frog legs	cuisses de grenouilles kwees duh greh-noo-ee
ham	jambon zhahn-bohn
lamb	agneau ahn-yoh
mixed grill	grillades gree-yahd
mutton	mouton moo-tohn
organs	organes or-gahn
oxtail	queue de boeuf kuh duh buhf
pork	porc por
rabbit	lapin lah-pan
roast beef	rosbif rohs-beef
sausage	saucisse soh-sees
blood sausage	boudin noir boo-dan nwahr
snails	escargots ehs-kar-goh
steak	bifteck beef-tehk
veal	veau voh
venison	viande de chevreuil vee-ahnd duh shuh-vruh-ee
Is this cooked?	C'est cuit? say kwee

Meat, but...

These are the cheapest items on a menu for good reason.

brains	cervelle sehr-vehl
calf pancreas	ris de veau ree duh voh
calf liver	foie de veau fwah duh voh
calf kidneys	rognons de veau rohn-yohn duh voh
calf head	tête de veau teht duh voh
horse meat	viande de cheval vee-ahnd duh shuh-vahl
sausage made of intestines	andouillette ahn-doo-yeht

liver	foie fwah
tongue	langue lahng
tripe	tripes / tablier de sapeur treep / tah-blee-ay duh sah-pur
dish of sheep's feet and tripe	pieds et paquets pee-ay ay pah-kay

Main Course Specialties

The "French Regional Specialties" sidebar (on pages 148-149) lists some unique dishes you'll find in certain areas of France, but the following (some of which started as regional dishes) have become standard menu items nationwide.

boeuf bourguignon buhf boor-geen-yohn
beef stew slowly cooked in red wine and served with onions, bacon, potatoes, and mushrooms (Burgundy)

boudin blanc boo-dan blahn
bratwurst-like sausage

confit de canard kohn-fee duh kah-nar
duck that has been preserved in its own fat, then cooked in its fat, and often served with potatoes cooked in the same fat (Dordogne)

coq au vin kohk oh van
chicken braised ever so slowly in red wine, cooked until it melts in your mouth (Burgundy)

daube dohb
long and slowly simmered dish (usually with beef, sometimes with lamb), typically paired with noodles or other pasta

escalope normande ehs-kah-lohp nor-mahnd
turkey or veal in a cream sauce (Normandy)

gigot d'agneau zhee-goh dahn-yoh
leg of lamb often grilled and served with white beans; the best lamb, *pré salé*, has been raised in salt-marsh lands (Provence)

Main Course Specialties *(cont.)*

magret de canard mah-gray duh kah-nar
sliced duck breast

poulet rôti poo-lay roh-tee
roasted chicken on the bone—French comfort food

ratatouille rah-tah-too-ee
mix of vegetables (often eggplant, zucchini, onions, and peppers) in a thick, herb-flavored tomato sauce (Provence)

saumon soh-mohn
salmon usually from the North Sea and served with sauce, most commonly a sorrel *(oseille)* sauce; *saumon tartare* is raw salmon

steak haché (à cheval) stehk ah-shay (ah shuh-vahl)
lean, gourmet hamburger patty served sans bun (with an egg on top)

steak tartare stehk tar-tar
very lean, raw hamburger served with savory seasonings (usually Tabasco, capers, raw onions, salt, and pepper on the side) and topped with a raw egg yolk

How Food Is Prepared

aged	vieilli vee-ay-ee
assorted	assiette / variés ahs-yeht / vah-ree-ay
baked	cuit au four kweet oh foor
boiled	bouilli boo-yee
braised	braisé breh-zay
breaded	pané pah-nay
broiled	grillé gree-yay
browned	doré doh-ray
cold	froid frwah
cooked	cuit kwee
chopped	haché ah-shay
crispy	croustillant kroo-stee-ahn

cured (salted / smoked)	salé / fumé sah-lay / few-may
deep-fried	frit free
fillet	filet fee-lay
fresh	frais fray
fried	frit free
garnish	garniture gar-nee-tewr
glazed	glacé glah-say
grated	râpé rah-pay
grilled	grillé gree-yay
homemade	fait maison fay may-zohn
hot	chaud shoh
in cream sauce	en crème ahn krehm
juicy	juteux zhew-tuh
marinated	mariné mah-ree-nay
medium	à point ah pwan
melted	fondu fohn-dew
microwave	four à micro-ondes foor ah mee-kroh-ohnd
mild	doux doo
minced	haché ah-shay
mixed	mixte meekst
pan-fried	poêlé poh-eh-lay
pickled	au vinaigre oh vee-nay-gruh
poached	poché poh-shay
rare	saignant sehn-yahn
raw	cru krew
roasted	rôti roh-tee
sautéed	sauté soh-tay
smoked	fumé few-may
steamed	à la vapeur ah lah vah-pur
stuffed	farci far-see
well-done	bien cuit bee-an kwee

French Regional Specialties

Alps (Chamonix): Try ***raclette*** (melted cheese over potatoes and meats), ***fondue savoyarde*** (cheese fondue), ***gratin savoyard*** (potatoes with cheese), ***tartiflette*** (scalloped potatoes with melted cheese), and ***croziflette*** (like ***tartiflette*** with buckwheat pasta).

Alsace (Colmar): Flavored by German heritage, Alsace is known for ***choucroute garnie*** (sauerkraut and sausage), ***Rösti*** (like hash browns), ***Spätzle*** (soft egg noodles), ***tarte à l'oignon*** (onion tart), ***tarte flambée*** (like a thin-crust pizza with cream, onion, and bacon bits), ***Baeckeoffe*** (stew of onions, meat, and potatoes), and ***poulet/coq au Riesling*** (chicken/rooster slow-cooked in white wine).

Basque Country (St-Jean-de-Luz): This region is known for its spicy red peppers called ***piments d'Espelette.*** Anything ***basquaise*** ("Basque-style") is cooked with tomato, eggplant, red pepper, and garlic. Dishes include ***ttoro*** (seafood stew) and ***marmitako*** (hearty tuna stew). The local dry-cured ham, ***jambon de Bayonne,*** is famous throughout France. ***Gâteau basque*** is a buttery cherry-and-almond cake.

Brittany (Dinan): Look for ***galettes*** (savory buckwheat crêpes), ***huîtres*** (oysters), and the frothy, fermented milk drink called ***lait ribot***. Many dishes are prepared ***marinière***, with a white-wine and shallot sauce.

Burgundy (Beaune): This wine region excels in ***coq au vin*** (chicken with wine sauce), ***boeuf bourgignon*** (beef stew cooked with wine, bacon, onions, potatoes, and mushrooms), ***oeufs en meurette*** (eggs poached in red wine), ***escargots*** (snails in garlic), ***jambon persillé*** (ham with garlic and parsley preserved in gelatin), ***gougères*** (eggy cheese puffs), and ***moutarde de Dijon*** (hot Dijon mustard).

Champagne (Reims): Dishes include ***salade de pissenlit*** (warm dandelion salad with bacon), ***potée champenoise*** (rabbit blood pudding), ***jambon de Reims*** (ham cooked in champagne and wrapped in a pastry shell), and ***truite*** (trout).

Dordogne/Périgord (Sarlat): The speciality here is ***foie gras*** (goose-liver pâté). Also try the ***confit de canard*** (duck cooked in its own fat), ***salade périgourdine*** (mixed green salad with ***foie gras,*** gizzards, and various duck parts), ***pommes de terre sarladaise*** (potatoes fried in duck fat), and anything with ***noix*** (walnuts).

Languedoc (Carcassonne): Try the hearty ***cassoulet*** (white bean, duck, and sausage stew), ***canard*** (duck), ***cargolade*** (snail, lamb, and sausage stew), and ***aligot*** (mashed potatoes with cheese).

Loire Valley (Amboise): Savor the fresh ***truite*** (trout), ***veau*** (veal), ***rillettes*** (cold, minced, shredded pork paté), ***fromage du chèvre*** (goat cheese), ***aspèrges*** (asparagus), and ***champignons*** (mushrooms).

Lyon: The culinary capital of France specializes in ***salade lyonnaise*** (croutons, fried ham, and a poached egg on a bed of lettuce), green lentils ***(lentilles)*** served on a salad or with sausages, ***quenelles de brochet*** (fish dumplings in a creamy sauce), and ***filet de sandre*** (whitefish).

Normandy (Bayeux): Munch some ***moules*** (mussels) and ***escalope Normande*** (veal in cream sauce). Swallow some ***cidre*** (hard apple cider) or ***calvados*** (apple brandy). ***Trou Normand*** is apple sorbet swimming in ***calvados.***

Provence (Avignon): Sample the ***soupe au pistou*** (vegetable soup with garlic, cheese, and basil), ***ratatouille*** (eggplant, zucchini, tomatoes, onions, and green peppers), ***brandade de morue*** (salted cod in garlic cream), ***tapenade*** (a spread of pureed olives, garlic, and anchovies), ***tians*** (gratin-like vegetable dishes), ***artichauts à la barigoule*** (artichokes stuffed with garlic, ham, and herbs), and ***riz de Camargue*** (a reddish, chewy, nutty-tasting rice). ***Tourte de blettes*** is a confused "pie," made with Swiss chard, that's both savory and sweet.

Riviera (Nice): Dive into various fish stews: ***bouillabaisse*** (the classic, spicy fish stew), ***soupe de poisson*** (cheaper, simpler alternative to ***bouillabaisse***), ***bourride*** (creamy fish soup), and ***baudroie*** (fishy soup cooked with vegetables and garlic). Other classics include ***salade niçoise*** (potatoes, tomatoes, olives, tuna, green beans, hard-boiled egg and anchovies) and ***pan bagnat*** (a ***salade niçoise*** on a bun).

French Cooking Styles

à l'anglaise ah lahn-glehz
boiled ("English")

au jus oh zhew
in its natural juices

basquaise bahs-kehz
with tomato, eggplant, red pepper, and garlic ("Basque-style")

bourguignon boor-geen-yohn
cooked in red wine ("Burgundy-style")

confit kohn-fee
any meat cooked in its own fat

fines herbes feen ehrb
with chopped fresh herbs

forestière foh-rehs-tee-yehr
with mushrooms

gratinée grah-tee-nay
topped with cheese, then broiled

jardinière zhar-deen-yehr
with vegetables

meunière muhn-yehr
coated with flour and fried in butter ("miller's wife")

nouvelle cuisine noo-vehl kwee-zeen
small portions of dishes from fresh ingredients; popular, relatively low-fat, and expensive

provençale proh-vahn-sahl
with tomatoes, garlic, olive oil, and herbs ("Provence-style")

roulade roo-lahd
anything "rolled" around a filling

savoyard sah-voy-ar
hearty alpine food, typically with melted cheese and / or potatoes

French Sauces

Sauces are a huge part of French cooking. In the early 20th century, the legendary French chef Auguste Escoffier identified five French "mother sauces" from which all others are derived: ***béchamel*** (milk-based white sauce), ***espagnole*** (veal-based brown sauce), ***velouté*** (stock-based white sauce), ***hollandaise*** (egg yolk-based white sauce), and ***tomate*** (tomato-based red sauce).

aïoli ah-ee-oh-lee
garlic mayonnaise

béchamel bay-shah-mehl
creamy, milk-based sauce

béarnaise bayr-nehz
sauce of egg yolks, butter, tarragon, white wine, and shallots

beurre blanc bur blahn
sauce of butter, white wine, and shallots

beurre noisette bur nwah-zeht
browned butter

crème fraîche krehm frehsh
"fresh cream" (similar to, but thinner than, sour cream)

crème normande krehm nor-mahnd
sauce of cream, cider, and spices

demi-glace duh-mee-glahs
"half-glazed" brown sauce

espagnole ehs-pahn-yohl
flavorful veal-based sauce

hollandaise oh-lahn-dayz
sauce of butter and egg yolks

marinière mah-reen-yehr
sauce of white wine, parsley, and shallots

mornay mor-nay
white sauce with grated Gruyère cheese

rouille roo-ee
thickened reddish mayonnaise heady with garlic and spicy peppers

soubise soo-beez
béchamel sauce (see above) with onion

tomate toh-maht
red sauce with tomato base

velouté vuh-loo-tay
light sauce, usually chicken or fish stock, thickened with flour

Flavors and Spices

spicy (hot)	piquant pee-kahn
spicy (flavorful)	épicée ay-pee-say
(too) salty	(trop) salé (troh) sah-lay
sour	aigre ay-gruh
sweet	doux doo
bitter	amer ah-mehr
cayenne	poivre de Cayenne pwah-vruh duh kah-yehn
cilantro	coriandre koh-ree-ahn-druh
cinnamon	cannelle kah-nehl
citrus fruits	agrumes ah-grewm
garlic	ail ī
herbs	herbes ehrb
horseradish	raifort ray-for
mint	menthe mahnt
paprika	paprika pah-pree-kah
parsley	persil pehr-seel
pepper	poivre pwah-vruh
saffron	safran sah-frahn
salt	sel sehl
sugar	sucre sew-kruh

You can look up more herbs and spices in the Menu Decoder (next chapter).

Veggies and Sides

vegetables	légumes lay-gewm
mixed vegetables	légumes variés lay-gewm vah-ree-ay
with vegetables	garni gar-nee
artichoke	artichaut ar-tee-shoh
arugula (rocket)	roquette roh-keht
asparagus	asperges ah-spehrzh
avocado	avocat ah-voh-kah
beans	haricots ah-ree-koh
beets	betterave beh-tuh-rahv
broccoli	brocoli broh-koh-lee
cabbage	chou shoo
carrots	carottes kah-roht
cauliflower	chou-fleur shoo-flur
corn	maïs mah-ees
cucumber	concombre kohn-kohn-bruh
eggplant	aubergine oh-behr-zheen
endive	endive ahn-deev
fennel	fenouil fuh-noo-ee
garlic	ail ī
green beans	haricots verts ah-ree-koh vehr
leeks	poireaux pwah-roh
lentils	lentilles lahn-teel
mushrooms	champignons shahn-peen-yohn
olives	olives oh-leev
onions	oignons ohn-yohn
peas	petits pois puh-tee pwah
pepper...	poivron... pwah-vrohn
...green / red / yellow	...vert / rouge / jaune vehr / roozh / zhohn
pickles	cornichons kor-nee-shohn
potato	pomme de terre pohm duh tehr

radish	radis rah-dee
rice	riz ree
spaghetti	spaghetti "spaghetti"
spinach	épinards ay-pee-nar
tomatoes	tomates toh-maht
truffles	truffes trewf
turnip	navet nah-vay
zucchini	courgette koor-zheht

In Provence, where olives are a specialty, you'll find several varieties. For example, ***tanche*** are plump, full-flavored, and black, while ***picholine*** are green and buttery.

There are also multiple types of mushrooms. The basic version is ***champignon*** (or ***champignon de Paris***). Others include ***chanterelle ou girolle*** (big, yellow, wild chanterelle), ***cèpe*** (classic porcini-like boletus mushroom), ***morille*** (honeycomb-shaped morel mushroom), ***mousseron*** (meadow mushroom), and ***pleurote*** (oyster mushroom).

Fruits

fruit	fruit frwee
fruit cup	salade de fruits sah-lahd duh frwee
fruit smoothie	smoothie aux fruits smoo-zee oh frwee
apple	pomme pohm
apricot	abricot ah-bree-koh
banana	banane bah-nahn
berries	fruits rouges frwee roozh
blueberry	myrtille meer-tee
cantaloupe	melon muh-lohn
cherry	cerise suh-reez
cranberry	canneberge kah-nuh-behrzh
date	datte daht
fig	figue feeg

grapefruit	pamplemousse pahn-pluh-moos
grapes	raisins ray-zan
lemon	citron see-trohn
melon	melon muh-lohn
orange	orange oh-rahnzh
peach	pêche pehsh
pear	poire pwahr
pineapple	ananas ah-nah-nahs
plum	prune prewn
pomegranate	grenade gruh-nahd
prune	pruneau prew-noh
raisin	raisin sec ray-zan sehk
raspberry	framboise frahn-bwahz
strawberry	fraise frehz
tangerine	mandarine mahn-dah-reen
watermelon	pastèque pah-stehk

While ***fraise*** is a basic word for "strawberry," the French have more than 600 variations: ***fraises des bois*** are tiny, sweet, and less visually appealing strawberries found in nearby forests; other variations include ***gariguettes*** and ***maras des bois***. Buy ***une barquette*** (small basket) to put them in, and suddenly your two-star hotel room is a three-star.

Likewise, the French have various names for watermelon: a ***pastèque*** is a particularly sweet one; a ***citre*** (also called a ***gigérine, barbarine,*** or ***méréville***) is used only for making jams or pies.

Nuts to You

nuts	noix nwah
almond	amande ah-mahnd
chestnut	marron / châtaigne mah-rohn / shah-tehn-yuh
coconut	noix de coco nwah duh koh-koh

hazelnut	noisette nwah-zeht
peanut	cacahuète kah-kah-weht
pine nut	pignon de pin peen-yohn duh pan
pistachio	pistache pee-stahsh
seeds	graines grehn
sunflower	tournesol toor-nuh-sohl
walnut	noix nwah

Just Desserts

I'd like...	Je voudrais... zhuh voo-dray
We'd like...	Nous voudrions... noo voo-dree-ohn
dessert	dessert day-sehr
cookies	biscuits / petits gâteaux bees-kwee / puh-tee gah-toh
cake	gâteau gah-toh
ice cream...	glace... glahs
...scoop	...boule bool
...cone	...cornet kor-nay
...cup	...bol bohl
...vanilla	...vanille vah-nee
...chocolate	...chocolat shoh-koh-lah
...strawberry	...fraise frehz
sorbet	sorbet sor-bay
fruit cup	salade de fruits sah-lahd duh frwee
tart	tartelette tar-tuh-leht
pie	tarte tart
whipped cream	crème chantilly krehm shahn-tee-yee
pastry	pâtisserie pah-tee-suh-ree
crêpes	crêpes krehp
sweet crêpes	crêpes sucrées krehp sew-kray
candy	bonbon bohn-bohn

chocolates	chocolats shoh-koh-lah
low calorie	bas en calories bah ahn kah-loh-ree
homemade	fait maison fay may-zohn
We'll split one.	Nous le partageons. noo luh par-tah-zhohn
Two forks / spoons, please.	Deux fourchettes / cuillères, s'il vous plaît. duh foor-sheht / kwee-yehr see voo play
I shouldn't, but...	Je ne devrais pas, mais... zhuh nuh duh-vray pah may
Magnificent!	Magnifique! mahn-yee-feek
It's heavenly!	C'est divin! say dee-van
Death by pleasure.	C'est à mourrir de plaisir. say ah moo-reer duh play-zeer
Orgasmic.	Orgasmique. or-gahz-meek
A moment on the lips, forever on the hips.	Un moment sur les lèvres et pour toujours sur les hanches. uhn moh-mahn sewr lay lehv-ruh ay poor too-zhoor sewr lay ahnsh

Crème de la Crème

These are some of the desserts you'll likely see at restaurants.

baba au rhum bah-bah oh room
brioche-like cake drenched in rum and served with whipped cream

bavarois / crème bavaroise bah-var-wah / krehm bah-var-wahz
gelatin-thickened "Bavarian cream" pudding

café gourmand kah-fay goor-mahn
coffee served with an assortment of small desserts—a great way to sample several desserts and learn your favorite

clafoutis klah-foo-tee
baked fruit-custard pie

crème brûlée krehm brew-lay
rich caramelized custard

Crème de la Crème *(cont.)*

crème caramel krehm kah-rah-mehl
flan (solid custard) in caramel sauce

crêpes suzette krehp sew-zeht
crêpes flambéed with an orange brandy sauce

financier fee-nahns-yay
rectangular brown-butter sponge cake

fondant au chocolat / moelleux au chocolat
fohn-dahn oh shoh-koh-lah / mweh-luh oh shoh-koh-lah
molten chocolate cake with a runny (not totally cooked) center

fromage blanc froh-mahzh blahn
fresh white cheese eaten with sugar

gâteau gah-toh
cake, usually layered with pastry cream

île flottante eel floh-tahnt
meringues floating in cream sauce

mousse au chocolat moos oh shoh-koh-lah
ultra-light chocolate mousse

nougat de Montélimar noo-gah duh mohn-tay-lee-mar
rich, chewy confection made with nuts, honey, and sometimes lavender

poires au vin rouge pwahr oh van roozh
pears poached in red wine and spices

profiterole proh-fee-tuh-rohl
cream puff, often filled with ice cream

riz au lait reez oh lay
rice pudding

soufflé au chocolat soo-flay oh shoh-koh-lah
chocolate soufflé

tarte tatin tart tah-tan
upside-down caramelized apple pie

tartes tart
narrow strips of fresh fruit, baked in a crust and served in thin slices

tourteau fromager toor-toh froh-mah-zhay
goat-cheese cake

You may also see ***glaces*** (ice creams) and ***sorbets*** (sorbets). For a wide range of pastries, see page 122.

If you order espresso, it will always come after dessert. To have coffee with dessert, ask for ***café avec le dessert*** (kah-fay ah-vehk luh day-sehr).

DRINKING

Every ***café*** or ***bar*** has a complete price list posted (and refills aren't free). In bigger cities, prices go up when you sit down. It's cheapest to stand at the ***comptoir*** (counter); drinks cost a bit more ***en salle*** (at a table indoors) or on the ***terasse*** (at a table outside). The outdoor seating is worth the extra cost in pleasant weather, with tidy sidewalk tables all set up facing the street, as if ready to watch a show.

Water

mineral water...	eau minérale... oh mee-nay-rahl
...carbonated	...gazeuse gah-zuhz
...not carbonated	...non gazeuse nohn gah-zuhz
tap water (in a restaurant)	une carafe d'eau ewn kah-rahf doh
(not) drinkable	(non) potable (nohn) poh-tah-bluh
Is the water safe to drink?	L'eau est potable? loh ay poh-tah-bluh

The French typically order ***eau minérale*** (and wine) with their meals. But if you want free tap water, ask for ***une carafe d'eau, s'il vous plaît***. (The technical term for "tap water," ***l'eau du robinet***, sounds crass to waiters.)

Milk

whole milk	lait entier lay ahnt-yay
skim milk	lait écrémé lay ay-kray-may
fresh milk	lait frais lay fray

Key Phrases: Drinking

drink	verre vehr
(mineral) water	eau (minérale) oh (mee-nay-rahl)
tap water (in a restaurant)	une carafe d'eau ewn kah-rahf doh
milk	lait lay
juice	jus zhew
coffee	café kah-fay
tea	thé tay
wine	vin van
beer	bière bee-ehr
Cheers!	Santé! sahn-tay

cold / warm	froid / chaud frwah / shoh
straw	paille pī-yuh

Juice and Other Drinks

fruit juice	jus de fruit zhew duh frwee
100% juice	cent pour cent jus sahn poor sahn zhew
orange juice	jus d'orange zhew doh-rahnzh
freshly squeezed	pressé preh-say
apple juice	jus de pomme zhew duh pohm
cranberry juice	jus de canneberge zhew duh kah-nuh-behrzh
grape juice	jus de raisin zhew duh ray-zan
grapefruit juice	jus de pamplemousse zhew duh pahn-pluh-moos
pineapple juice	jus d'ananas zhew dah-nah-nahs
fruit smoothie	smoothie aux fruits smoo-zee oh frwee

lemonade	citron pressé see-trohn preh-say
iced tea	thé glacé tay glah-say
(diet) soda	soda ("light") soh-dah ("light")
energy drink	boisson énergétique bwah-sohn ay-nehr-zhay-teek
with / without...	avec / sans... ah-vehk / sahn
...sugar	...sucre sew-kruh
...ice	...glaçons glah-sohn
25... (small)	Vingt-cinque... vant-sank
33... (medium)	Trente-trois... trahnt-trwah
50... (large)	Cinquante... san-kahnt
...centiliters.	...centilitres. sahn-tee-lee-truh

When you order a drink, state the size in centiliters (don't say "small," "medium," or "large," because the waiter might bring a bigger drink than you want). For something small, ask for 25 ***centilitres*** (about 8 ounces); for a medium drink, order 33 ***centilitres*** (about 12 ounces—a normal can of soda); a large is 50 ***centilitres*** (about 16 ounces); and a super-size is one ***litre*** (lee-truh; about a quart—which is more than I would ever order in France).

Coffee Talk

The French define various types of espresso drinks by how much milk is added. Here are the most common coffee drinks:

coffee (espresso)	café kah-fay
a shot of espresso with no milk	un café / un express uhn kah-fay / uhn ehk-sprehs
espresso shot with a "hazelnut"-size dollop of milk	une noisette ewn nwah-zeht
coffee with milk (similar to American latte)	un café crème uhn kah-fay krehm

coffee with lots of milk (in bowl-like cup)	un café au lait uhn kah-fay oh lay
coffee with whipped cream	un café avec chantilly uhn kah-fay ah-vehk shahn-tee-yee
a double espresso with milk	un grand crème uhn grahn krehm
espresso with a touch of apple brandy (calvados)	café-calva kah-fay-kahl-vah
espresso with water (like an Americano)	un café allongé / café longue uhn kah-fay ah-lohn-zhay / kah-fay lohng
instant coffee	Nescafé "Nescafé"
decaffeinated / decaf	décaféiné / déca day-kah-fay-nay / day-kah
sugar	sucre sew-kruh

To the French, milk is a delicate form of nutrition: You need it in the morning, but as the day goes on, too much can upset your digestion. Therefore, the amount of milk that's added to coffee decreases as the day goes on. A ***café au lait***—espresso with milk in a bowl-like cup—is exclusively for breakfast time. You can get a ***café crème*** around midday, but getting one later might be frowned upon. If you want an after-dinner coffee, try a ***café noisette*** (literally "hazelnut")—a shot of espresso cut with just a hazelnut-sized dollop of cream. You're welcome to order a milkier coffee drink late in the day, but don't be surprised if you get a funny look.

Other Hot Drinks

hot water	l'eau chaude loh shohd
hot chocolate	chocolat chaud shoh-koh-lah shoh
tea	thé tay
lemon	citron see-trohn
tea bag	sachet de thé sah-shay duh tay
plain tea	thé nature tay nah-tewr

herbal tea	tisane tee-zahn
lemon tea	thé au citron tay oh see-trohn
orange tea	thé à l'orange tay ah loh-rahnzh
peppermint tea	thé à la menthe tay ah lah mahnt
fruit tea	thé de fruit tay duh frwee
green tea	thé vert tay vehr
chai tea	thé chai tay "chai"

You may see the word ***infusion,*** which means anything that's suspended in water to provide flavor (such as tea and herbal teas).

French Wine Lingo

These terms will help you navigate French wine—whether you're choosing from a wine list at a restaurant or sampling vintages at a winery. Winemakers and sommeliers are happy to work with you...*if* they can figure out what you want (which they expect you to already know). It helps to know what you like—study and use the terms below.

wine	vin van
house wine	vin de la maison van duh lah may-zohn
cheapest wine	vin ordinaire van or-dee-nair
I'd like / We'd like a wine that is _____ and _____.	Je voudrais / Nous voudrions un vin _____ et _____. zhuh voo-dray / noo voo-dree-ohn uhn van _____ ay _____
local	du pays dew pay-ee
of the region	de la région duh lah ray-zhee-ohn
red	rouge roozh
white	blanc blahn
rosé	rosé roh-zay
sparkling	pétillant / mousseux / bouché (for cider) pay-tee-yahn / moo-suh / boo-shay
light	léger lay-zhay

full-bodied (heavy)	robuste / costaud roh-bewst / koh-stoh
sweet	doux doo
semi-dry	demi-sec duh-mee-sehk
dry	sec sehk
very dry	brut brewt
tannic	tannique tah-neek
oaky	goût du fût de chêne goo duh foo duh sheh-nuh
fruity (jammy)	confituré kohn-fee-tew-ray
fine	fin / avec finesse fan / ah-vehk fee-nehs
ready to drink (mature)	prêt à boire preh ah bwahr
not ready to drink	fermé fehr-may
from old vines	de vieille vignes duh vee-yay-ee veen-yuh
chilled	bien frais / rafraîchi bee-an fray / rah-fray-shee
at room temperature	chambré shahn-bray
cork	bouchon boo-shohn
corkscrew	tire-bouchon teer-boo-shohn
corked (spoiled from a bad cork)	bouchonné boo-shoh-nay
vineyard	vignoble veen-yoh-bluh
harvest	vendange vahn-dahnzh

The French believe that the specific qualities of wine are a unique product of its place of origin (microclimate, soil, geology, culture, and so on). This uniquely French concept is known as ***terroir*** (tehr-wahr, literally "soil") and also applies to cheese and other foods.

Ordering Wine

I would like...	Je voudrais... zhuh voo-dray
We would like...	Nous voudrions... noo voo-dree-ohn
...the wine list.	...la carte des vins. lah kart day van
...a glass...	...un verre... uhn vehr
...a small pitcher...	...un pichet... uhn pee-shay
...a carafe...	...une carafe... ewn kah-rahf
...a half bottle...	...une demi-bouteille... ewn duh-mee-boo-tay
...a bottle...	...une bouteille... ewn boo-tay
...a barrel...	...un tonneau... uhn toh-noh
...of red wine.	...de vin rouge. duh van roozh
...of white wine.	...de vin blanc. duh van blahn
of the region	de la région duh lah ray-zhee-ohn
house wine	vin de la maison van duh lah may-zohn
What is a good vintage?	Quelles est un bon millésime? kehl ay uhn bohn mee-lay-zeem
What do you recommend?	Qu'est-ce que vous recommandez? kehs kuh voo ruh-koh-mahn-day
Choose for me, please.	Choisissez pour moi, s'il vous plaît. shwah-zee-say poor mwah see voo play
Around ____ euros.	Au tour de ____ euro. oh toor duh ____ uh-roh
Another, please.	Un autre, s'il vous plaît. uhn oh-truh see voo play

You can put yourself in the capable hands of your server to match a wine to your meal. Say ***Choisissez pour moi, s'il vous plaît*** (Choose for me, please). To avoid paying more than you'd like, add ***Au tour de ____ euro*** (Around ____ euros).

If all you want is a basic table wine, you can order ***vin de la maison*** (house wine). It might not be available by the glass, but a ***pichet*** (small pitcher) of a quarter-liter isn't much bigger than a generously poured

Regional Wines

In France, wine is a work of art. Each wine-growing region and each vintage has its own distinct personality. I prefer drinking wine from the region I'm in. Ask for ***vin de la région,*** available at reasonable prices.

While Americans think of wine in terms of the type of grape (Merlot, Cabernet Sauvignon, Riesling), the French usually think in terms of the place of origin—whether a region ***(Côtes du Rhône),*** a specific town or village ***(Gigondas),*** or even a particular winery ***(Domaine du Grand Montmirail).***

Here's a rundown of what each region specializes in:

Alsace: The wines here (mostly whites) are German-influenced. This is one region where wines are named for their grapes: Try the Riesling, Sylvaner, Pinot Gris (formerly "Tokay"), Muscat, or Gewürztraminer.

Bordeaux: This region offers some of the world's most elegant, expensive red wines—such as Château Lafite Rothschild—along with Sauternes (a sweet dessert wine) and Graves (a fine white).

Burgundy: From Chablis to Beaujolais, you'll find great fruity reds, dry whites, and crisp rosés. For inexpensive but good reds, look for Bourgogne and Passetoutgrain. For whites, consider those from Mâcon and Chalon; St-Véran whites are also a good value. For rosé, try Marsannay.

Champagne: This hilly region pops the cork on the finest sparkling wine in the world.

glass. If you don't want a whole bottle of wine for the table, look on the menu for a section of ***vins au verre*** (wines sold by the glass).

Wine Labels

The information on a French wine label can give you a lot of details about the wine. Here are several terms to help you identify and choose a specific wine.

Dordogne (Périgord): Wines to sample are Bergerac (red, white, and rosé), Pecharmant (red, must be at least four years old), Cahors (a full-bodied red), and Monbazillac (sweet dessert wine).

Languedoc: Good-value reds include Corbières, Minervois, and Côtes du Roussillon.

Loire Valley: For whites, choose between the excellent, expensive Sancerres and the cheaper but still tasty Touraine Sauvignons, the light Muscadets, and the sweeter Vouvrays. The better reds come from Chinon and Bourgeuil.

Lyon: Gamay Beaujolais grapes produce a light, fruity, easy-to-drink red wine; most big reds here are Syrahs. Look for Saint-Joseph, Crozes-Hermitage, and the rich, perfumy whites from Condrieu.

Normandy and Brittany: Rather than wines, Normandy and Brittany specialize in apple-based beverages—such as the powerful Calvados apple brandy and alcoholic apple cidre.

Provence: The three main growing areas are Côtes du Rhône, Côtes de Provence, and Côteaux d'Aix-en-Provence; all three produce rich, fruity reds and dry, fresh rosés. Some of the main options to look for include Châteauneuf-du-Pape (velvety), Gigondas (spicy), Beaumes de Venise (sweet Muscat), Rasteau (robust), and Tavel (dry, crisp rosé).

AOC (appellation d'origine contrôlée): Meets nationwide laws for production of the highest-quality French wines
Appellation: Area in which a wine's grapes are grown
Cave: Cellar
Cépage: Grape variety (Syrah, Chardonnay, etc.)
Côte / Côteau: Hillside or slope
Cru: Superior growth
Domaine: Wine estate

Étiquette: Label
Fût: Wine barrel
Grand vin: Excellent wine
Millésime: Vintage (specific year)
Mis en bouteille au château / à la domaine: Estate-bottled (where it was made)
Mis en bouteille dans nos caves: Bottled in our cellars
Tonneau: Wine barrel
VDQS (vin délimité de qualité supérieure): Quality standards for specific regional wines
Vin de table: Table wine (can be a blend of several wines)
Vin du pays: Wine from a given area (a step up from *vin de table*)

Beer

I'd like / We'd like...	Je voudrais / Nous voudrions... zhuh voo-dray / noo voo-dree-ohn
beer	une bière ewn bee-ehr
from the tap	pression preh-see-ohn
bottle	bouteille boo-tay
light / dark	blonde / brune blohnd / brewn
local / imported	régionale / importée ray-zhee-oh-nahl / an-por-tay
a small beer	un demi uhn duh-mee
a large beer	une chope ewn shohp
lager	blonde blohnd
pilsner	pils / pilsner peel / peels-nehr
ale	bière anglaise légère / ale bee-ehr ahn-glehz lay-zhehr / ehl
wheat	bière blanche bee-ehr blahnsh
porter	bière brune bee-ehr brewn
stout	bière de malte forte bee-ehr duh mahlt fort
microbrew	bière artisanale bee-ehr ar-tee-zah-nahl
low-calorie ("lite")	biere "light" bee-ehr "light"

shandy	panaché pah-nah-shay
a non-alcoholic beer	une bière non-alcoolisée ewn bee-ehr nohn-ahl-koh-lee-zay
hard apple cider	cidre see-druh

American soft drinks can be far more expensive than wine or beer. If you want something refreshing, but don't want a whole glass of beer, consider a ***panaché***—half lemon-lime soda, half beer.

Bar Talk

Would you like to go out for a drink?	Voulez-vous prendre un verre? voo-lay-voo prahn-druh uhn vehr
I'll buy you a drink.	Je vous offre un verre. zhuh voo oh-fruh uhn vehr
It's on me.	C'est moi qui paie. say mwah kee pay
The next one's on me.	Le suivant est sur moi. luh swee-vahn ay sewr mwah
What would you like?	Qu'est-ce que vous prenez? kehs kuh voo pruh-nay
I'll have a ____.	Je prends un ____. zhuh prahn uhn ____
I don't drink alcohol.	Je ne bois pas d'alcool. zhuh nuh bwah pah dahl-kohl
What is the local specialty?	Quelle est la spécialité régionale? kehl ay lah spay-see-ah-lee-tay ray-zhee-oh-nahl
Straight.	Sec. sehk
With / Without...	Avec / Sans... ah-vehk / sahn
...ice.	...glaçons. glah-sohn
One more.	Encore une. ahn-kor ewn
I'm a little drunk.	Je me sens un peu ivre. zhuh muh sahn uhn puh ee-vruh
Cheers!	Santé! sahn-tay

To your health!	À votre santé! ah voh-truh sahn-tay
Long live France!	Vive la France! veev lah frahns
I'm hung over.	J'ai la gueule de bois. zhay lah guhl duh bwah

Spirits Specialties

An ***apéritif*** is served before dinner, and a ***digestif*** is served after dinner. Ask what's local.

Typical ***apéritifs*** are ***Champagne, bière*** (beer), and these:

kir keer
a thumb's level of crème de cassis (black currant liqueur) topped with white wine

kir royal keer roh-yahl
Champagne with cassis

pastis pahs-tees
sweet anise (licorice) drink that comes on the rocks with a glass of water—cut it to taste

pineau pee-noh
cognac and grape juice

port por
fortified wine

Here are some common ***digestifs*** (for after the meal):

armagnac ar-mahn-yahk
cognac's cheaper twin brother (from a different region)

B&B bay ay bay
brandy and Bénédictine

calvados kahl-vah-dohs
apple brandy from Normandy

Chambord shahn-bor
raspberry liqueur

Chartreuse / Bénédictine shar-truhz / bay-nay-deek-teen
two distinct, herb-based liqueurs, made by monks with secret formulas

cognac kohn-yahk
wine-distilled brandy from the Charentes region; well-known brands are Rémy Martin, Hennessy, and Martel

Cointreau kwan-troh
orange liqueur

crème de cassis krehm duh kah-sees
black currant liqueur

crème de menthe krehm duh mahnt
mint liqueur

eaux de vie oh duh vee
fruit brandy, literally "waters of life"; *framboise* (strawberry), *poire williams* (pear), and *kirsch* (cherry) are best-known

Grand Marnier grahn marn-yay
orange brandy

marc mark
regional brandy, e.g., marc de Bourgogne

For a non-alcoholic alternative, try one of the many flavored syrups mixed with bottled water (***sirops à l'eau***; see-roh ah loh). ***Un diabolo menthe*** is 7-Up with mint syrup, and ***un diabolo grenadine*** is with cherry syrup. ***Orangina*** is a carbonated orange juice with pulp, and ***limonade*** (lee-moh-nahd) is Sprite or 7-Up.

PICNICKING

Gather supplies early for a picnic lunch; you'll probably visit several small stores to assemble a complete meal, and many close at noon for their lunch break. For convenience, you can assemble your picnic at a ***supermarché*** or ***hypermarché*** (supermarket)—but smaller shops or a ***marché*** (open-air market) are more fun and offer the best selection. Look for a ***boulangerie*** (bakery), a ***crémerie*** or ***fromagerie*** (cheeses), a ***charcuterie*** or ***traiteur*** (deli items, prepared salads, meats, and pâtés), an ***épicerie*** or ***magasin d'alimentation*** (small grocery with fruit, veggies, and so on), and a ***pâtisserie*** (delicious pastries). Late-night grocery stores are called ***dépanneurs*** (day-pah-nur).

Tasty Picnic Words

picnic	pique-nique peek-neek
sandwich	sandwich sahnd-weech
bread	pain pan
roll	petit pain puh-tee pan
ham	jambon zhahn-bohn
sausage	saucisse soh-sees
cheese	fromage froh-mahzh
mustard...	moutarde... moo-tard
mayonnaise...	mayonnaise... mah-yoh-nehz
...in a tube	...en tube ahn tewb
olives...	olives... oh-leev
pickles...	cornichons... kor-nee-shohn
...in a jar	...dans un pot dahnz uhn poh
yogurt	yaourt yah-oort
fruit	fruit frwee
juice	jus zhew
cold drinks	boissons fraîches bwah-sohn frehsh
container	barquette bar-keht
spoon / fork...	cuillère / fourchette... kwee-yehr / foor-sheht
...made of plastic	...en plastique ahn plah-steek
cup / plate...	gobelet / assiette... goh-blay / ahs-yeht
...made of paper	...en papier ahn pahp-yay

To weigh and price your produce at more modern stores, put it on the scale, push the photo or number (keyed to the bin it came from), and then stick your sticker on the food. When buying produce in a market or from a produce stand, resist the temptation to touch, and wait your turn to be served.

Picnic-Shopping Phrases

Meat and cheese are sold by the gram. One hundred grams is about a quarter pound, enough for two sandwiches.

Is it self-service?	C'est libre service? say lee-bruh sehr-vees
Fifty grams.	Cinquante grammes. san-kahnt grahm
One hundred grams.	Cent grammes. sahn grahm
More. / Less.	Plus. / Moins. plew / mwan
A piece.	Un morceau. uhn mor-soh
A slice.	Une tranche. ewn trahnsh
Four slices.	Quatre tranches. kah-truh trahnsh
Sliced.	Tranché. trahn-shay
Half.	La moitié. lah mwaht-yay
A few.	Quelques. kehl-kuh
A handful.	Une poignée. ewn pwahn-yay
A small bag.	Un petit sachet. uhn puh-tee sah-shay
A bag, please.	Un sachet, s'il vous plaît. uhn sah-shay see voo play
Ripe for today?	Pour manger aujourd'hui? poor mahn-zhay oh-joord-wee
Can I taste it?	Je peux goûter? zhuh puh goo-tay
Can you make me...?	Vous pouvez me faire...? voo poo-vay muh fair
Can you make us...?	Vous pouvez nous faire...? voo poo-vay noo fair
...a sandwich	...un sandwich uhn sahnd-weech
...two sandwiches	...deux sandwichs duh sahnd-weech
to take out	à emporter ah ahn-por-tay
Can you please slice it?	Pourriez-vous le couper en tranches, s'il vous plaît? poor-yay-voo luh koo-pay ahn trahnsh see voo play

Does it need to be cooked?	Il faut le faire cuire? eel foh luh fair kweer
Can I use the microwave?	Je peux utiliser le micro-onde? zhuh puh ew-tee-lee-zay luh mee-kroh-ohnd
Ready to eat?	Prêt à manger? preh ah mahn-zhay
May I borrow a...?	Je peux emprunter...? zhuh puh ahn-pruhn-tay
Do you have a...?	Vous avez...? vooz ah-vay
Where can I buy / find a...?	Où puis-je acheter / trouver un...? oo pwee-zhuh ah-shuh-tay / troo-vay uhn
...corkscrew	...tire-bouchon teer-boo-shohn
...can opener	...ouvre boîte oo-vruh bwaht
...bottle opener	...décapsuleur day-kahp-sew-lur
Is there a park nearby?	Il y a un parc près d'ici? eel yah uhn park preh dee-see
Where is a good place to picnic?	Il y a un coin sympa pour pique-niquer? eel yah uhn kwan san-pah poor peek-nee-kay
Is picnicking allowed here?	On peut pique-niquer ici? ohn puh peek-nee-kay ee-see

Don't forget the wine for your ***pique-nique***. While public consumption is forbidden back home, the French see no problem with sipping a glass of wine ***en plein air***—in parks, on benches or along the riverbank. In fact, on a balmy summer evening when Parisians line up along the Seine for picnics, the soundtrack is the popping of corks.

Deli Items

To get some prepared food for your picnic, drop by a ***charcuterie***, a ***traiteur***, or a ***rôtisserie***. Note that a ***traiteur*** is literally a "caterer"—a place where someone might come to buy items they plan to serve at a party in their home. Much of the food can be eaten as-is, but other items might need to be heated or cooked. If you're not sure, ask ***Il faut le faire cuire?*** (Does this need to be cooked?) or ***Prêt à manger?*** (Ready to eat?).

Meat Dishes

The French slow-cook various meats to create meatloaf-like blocks that can be sliced or spread on a sandwich. Lined up in a case, they all look about the same: a block of meat and spices. But there's a lot of variety:

pâté pah-tay
a soft, spreadable meat dish; the most famous pâté is *foie gras* (made with duck or goose liver)

confit kohn-fee
meat that is slow-cooked, then preserved in its own fat

rillettes ree-yeht
meat that is stewed, shredded, then mixed with fat and packed into a brick

mousse moos
meat that has been whipped to become smooth and airy

jambon persillé zhahn-bohn pehr-see-yay
cold ham layered in a garlic-parsley gelatin

Don't confuse ***pâté*** (processed block of meat) with ***pâtes*** (pasta). And don't mistake ***confit*** (slow-cooked meat preserved in its own fat) for ***confiture*** (fruit jam).

Foie gras—the famous French ***pâté*** of goose or duck liver—comes in several forms. The more expensive ***entier*** is a piece cut right from the product, whereas ***bloc*** has been blended to make it easier to spread; ***mousse*** has been whipped for an even creamier consistency.

Salads

You can order a ***barquette*** (bar-keht; small plastic container) of any ***salade*** to spiff up your picnic. Just see what looks good in the display case, and keep an eye out for these favorites.

carrottes râpées kah-roht rah-pay
grated carrots in vinaigrette

céleri remoulade say-luh-ree ruh-moo-lahd
celery root in a cream sauce, usually with mayonnaise and mustard

cervelas vinaigrette sehr-vuh-lah vee-nay-greht
pork sausage with vinaigrette sauce

salade piémontaise sah-lahd pee-ay-mohn-tehz
French potato salad, usually with sausage, pickles, and mayonnaise

museau de porc / boeuf mew-zoh duh por / buhf
the nose (and other assorted bits) of a pig / cow chopped up and mixed in with parsley and vinaigrette (not for beginners)

betteraves rouges beh-tuh-rahv roozh
red beets

salade camarguaise sah-lahd kah-mar-gehz
salad with rice and veggies

taboulé tah-boo-lay
couscous salad

Produce Markets

It's considered rude for customers to touch produce; instead, tell the clerk what you want. Pointing and gesturing go a long way. Pay careful attention, as the unit of measure can differ. It could be ***par*** (per) ***kg*** (for ***kilogram,*** which is the same as a kilo)***, par kilo, par ½ kg, par ¼ kg, par 500 g, par 100 g,*** and so on. ***Un livre*** is 500 grams (about a pound in the US). You'll also see items priced by ***la piéce*** (piece), ***la botte*** (bunch), ***la barquette*** (container), or ***le pot*** (for plants).

kilo (1,000 grams)	kilo kee-loh
½ kilo (500 grams)	demi-kilo / livre duh-mee-kee-loh / lee-vruh
¼ kilo (250 grams)	quart-kilo kar-kee-loh
100 grams	cent grammes sahn grahm
that	ça sah

this much	comme ça kohm sah
more / less	plus / moins plew / mwan
a little more / less	un peu plus / moins uhn puh plew / mwan
too much	trop troh
enough	suffisament sew-fee-zah-mahn
piece	la piéce lah pee-ehs
bunch	la botte lah boht
one / two	un / deux uhn / duh
container	la barquette lah bar-keht
pot (for plants)	le pot luh poh

MENU DECODER

This handy French-English decoder won't list every word on the menu, but it'll help you get ***riz et veau*** (rice and veal) instead of ***ris de veau*** (calf pancreas).

Note that decoding a menu can be particularly challenging in France, where ingredients are lovingly described in painstaking detail. For simplicity, I've listed the most prevalent terms and commonly seen variations, but this decoder is far from exhaustive when it comes to listing every melon or mushroom under the French sun.

Menu Categories

When you pick up a menu, you'll likely see these categories of offerings, and they'll generally appear in this order.

Petit déjeuner	Breakfast
Déjeuner	Lunch
Dîner	Dinner
Entrées	First course; appetizers
Chaud	Hot
Froid	Cold
Sandwiches	Sandwiches
Salades	Salads
Potages, Soupes	Soups
Menu	Fixed-price meal(s)
Spécialités	Specialties
Plats	Dishes
Plats principals	Main dishes
Viande	Meat
Porc	Pork
Volaille	Poultry
Poisson	Fish
Fruits de mer	Seafood
Garnitures	Side dishes
Légumes	Vegetables
Carte des consommations	Drink menu
Carte des vins	Wine list
Fromages	Cheeses
Desserts	Desserts

Enfants	Children
Suggestion du jour / Plat du jour	Daily special

And for the fine print:

Couvert	Cover charge
Service (non) compris	Service (not) included
Prix net	Tax included

Small Words

à la / à l'	in the style of
au / aux / avec	with
de / d' / des / du	of
et	and
ou	or
sans	without
sur	over

If you see ***à la*** or ***à l'*** on a menu, the next word might not appear in this decoder. That's because these phrases mean "in the style of," and often are followed by flowery, artsy, obscure descriptions. Even if you knew the exact meaning, it might not make things much clearer.

FRENCH / ENGLISH

A

abricot apricot
accompagné de accompanied by
acide sour; acidic
affiné aged
agneau lamb
agneau de pré salé lamb raised on salt-marsh lands
agrume citrus
ail / aillet garlic; garlic shoot
aile wing (poultry or fowl)
aïoli garlic mayonnaise
airelle wild cranberry
Aisy cendré soft cow cheese coated in ash
alcool alcohol
aligot mashed potatoes with cheese
aloyau sirloin
amande almond
amer bitter
amuse-bouche appetizer
ananas pineapple
anchoïade garlic and anchovy paste
anchois anchovies
(à l') ancienne in the old style
andouille pungent tripe sausage
anémone de mer anemone
aneth dill
anglaise "English" apple pastry
(à l') anglaise boiled
anis anise
AOC certified origin, designation for top-quality wine as well as cheese and butter
apéritif before-dinner drink
appellation area in which a wine's grapes are grown
araignée de mer spider crab
armagnac brandy produced in southwest France
artichaut artichoke
artichaut à la barigoule artichoke stuffed with garlic, ham, and herbs
artisanal from a small producer
asperge asparagus
assiette plate
assiette de charcuterie cold cuts
assiette d'enfant children's plate
au gratin topped with cheese and browned
au jus meat served in its natural juices
au vinaigre pickled
aubergine eggplant
Auvergne cow cheese sold in big wheels
avocat avocado
baba au rhum rum-soaked brioche
Baeckeoffe meat-and-potato stew
bagna cauda anchovy and butter sauce
baguette long loaf of bread
bain-marie water bath
ballon roll

banane banana
Banon soft goat cheese, wrapped in chestnut leaves
bar sea bass
barbarine watermelon used in pies and preserves
(à la) barigoule brown sauce with artichokes and mushrooms
barquette basket
basilic basil
basquaise Basque-style: cooked with tomato, eggplant, red pepper, and garlic
bâtard half-length baguette
baudroie monkfish
bavarois rich "Bavarian cream" custard
bavette flank steak; skirt steak
Béarnaise sauce of egg and wine
Beaufort hard, sharp, aged cow cheese
béchamel creamy, milk-based sauce
beignet deep-fried doughnut
Bénédictine herb-based liqueur
betterave beet
beurre (doux / demi-sel / salé) butter (unsalted / salted / very salted)
beurre blanc sauce of butter, white wine, and shallots
beurre de cacahuètes peanut butter
beurre manié butter-and-flour thickening agent
beurre noisette browned butter
biche deer
bien cuit well-done (meat)
bien fait aged, mature (cheese)
bière beer
bière brune dark beer
bifteck steak (can be tough)
biologique organic
bis, pain / bisse, pain dark-grain bread
biscuit cookie
biscuit de Savoie sponge cake
bisque shellfish chowder
blanc white
blanc (de volaille) breast (chicken)
blanc d'oeuf egg white
blanquette slow-cooked stew with rich white sauce
blette chard
bleu blue (cheese); very rare (meat)
bleu d'Auvergne pungent blue cow cheese from Auvergne
boeuf beef
(de) bois "of the woods" (wild)
boisson beverage
bonbon candy
bonite bonito (skipjack tuna)
bouché sparkling (cider)
bouchée bite-size ("mouthful"), usually describes a small puff pastry
bouchée à la reine pastry shell with creamed sweetbreads and mushroom
boudin blanc bratwurst-like sausage
boudin noir blood sausage

bouillabaisse seafood stew
bouilli boiled
bouillon broth
boulangerie / boulanger bakery
boule scoop (ice cream)
boulette de viande meatball
bouquet garni "bouquet" of herbs used to flavor soups, then removed
bourguignon cooked in red wine
bourride creamy fish soup
Boursin soft, creamy, herbed cow cheese
bouteille bottle
braisé braised
brandade de morue salted cod in garlic cream
brebis, fromage de sheep-milk cheese
brick fritter
Brie (de Meaux) mild, soft (almost runny) cow cheese
brié, pain dense, crusty bread
Brillat-Savarin buttery, slightly sour variant of Brie cheese
brioche buttery roll made with eggs
Brocciu sweet, fresh goat or ewe cheese
brochet pike
brochette skewer
brocoli broccoli
brouillé scrambled
Brousse du Rove fresh, creamy goat cheese
brune dark (beer)
brunoise finely chopped vegetables
brut very dry (wine or cider)
Cabécou pungent, nutty goat cheese
cabillaud cod
cacahuète peanut
café coffee
café allongé / café longue "long" coffee (espresso with water, like an Americano)
café au lait coffee with lots of milk
café avec chantilly coffee with whipped cream
café calva espresso with a touch of brandy
café crème coffee with milk
café décaféiné / café déca decaffeinated; decaf coffee
café gourmand coffee served with 2 or 3 small pastries
café noisette coffee with a dollop of milk
caille quail
caladon honey and almond cookie
calamar squid
calisson (d'Aix) marzipan cookie
calvados apple brandy
camarguaise, salade salad with rice and veggies
Camembert pungent, semi-creamy cow cheese
(de) campagne / campagnarde country-style; rustic
canapé appetizer; finger food

canard duck
cannelé "fluted" custard and caramel pastry
cannelle cinnamon
Cantal aged, semi-hard cow cheese
câpre caper
cardamome cardamom
cargolade snail, lamb, and sausage stew
carotte carrot
carpaccio thinly sliced raw meat or fish
carré (d'agneau / de porc) loin (lamb / pork)
carrelet plaice (flatfish)
carte menu
(à la) carte individual items on the menu
cassis black currant
cassonade brown sugar
cassoulet bean and meat stew
cavaillon, melon de small cantaloupe
cave wine cellar
céleri rave celery root
cendré with ashes
Cendré de Champagne Brie-like cheese covered in ash
(aux) cendres rolled in cinders (cheese)
cépage grape variety (wine)
cèpe boletus mushroom (similar to porcini)
cerf deer
cerise cherry
cervelas garlic pork sausage
cervelle brains
Chambord raspberry liqueur
chambré room temperature
champignon mushroom
chantilly / crème chantilly whipped cream
chapelure browned breadcrumbs
charbon de bois charcoal
charcuterie prepared meats such as sausages and pâtés
charentais, melon de yellow cantaloupe
Charolais high-quality beef; also a goat cheese from the Charolais region
Chartreuse herb-based liqueur
châtaigne chestnut
château wine bottled where it was made
chaud hot
chaud-froid cooked but served cold
chausson fruit-filled pastry
chausson aux pommes apple turnover
chêne, goût du fût de oaky (wine)
cheval horse
chèvre goat
chèvre chaud, salade au salad with warm goat cheese on toasted croutons
chevreuil, viande de venison
chiffonnade sliced into thin strips
chinois Chinese
chocolat chocolate

C

(le) choix de choice of
chope large beer
chorizo spicy sausage
chou cabbage
chou frisé kale
choucroute sauerkraut
choucroute garnie sauerkraut and sausage
chou-fleur cauliflower
chouquette eggy little baked doughnut
ciboulette chives
cidre hard apple cider
citre watermelon used in pies and preserves
citron lemon
clafoutis fruit tart made with egg batter
clou de girofle clove
cochon pig
cocotte casserole
cognac wine-distilled brandy
coing quince
Cointreau orange liqueur
colin hake (fish)
complet whole (whole grain); full
composée, salade "composed" salad with various ingredients
compote stewed fruit
compote de pommes applesauce
compris included
comptoir counter
Comté "Swiss cheese" from cow's milk
concassé coarsely chopped
concombre cucumber
confit a preserve, often fowl or pork cooked in its own fat
confiture preserves; jam
confituré jammy (wine)
consommé clear broth
copieux filling
coq rooster
coq au vin chicken braised in red wine
coque cockle
coquelet cockerel (young rooster)
coquille Saint-Jacques scallop
corbeille basket
coriandre cilantro; coriander
cornichon pickle
costaud full-bodied (wine)
côte rib or chop (meat)
côte de boeuf T-bone steak
côtelette cutlet
côtes chops (for meat); hillsides (for wine)
cou neck
coulis thick sauce, usually a purée of a single ingredient
Coulommiers soft, rich, creamy, Brie-like cow cheese
courge summer squash
courgette zucchini
couronne "crown," ring-shaped baguette
court-bouillon herbed liquid used to cook fish
couteau knife
couvert cover charge
crabe crab

cramique brioche bread with raisins
crème cream; custard
crème à l'anglaise custard sauce
crème bavaroise Bavarian cream pudding
crème brûlée caramelized custard
crème caramel custard with caramel sauce
crème chantilly whipped cream
crème de cassis black currant liqueur
crème de menthe mint liqueur
crème fraîche heavy, slightly soured cream
crème (velouté) d'asperges cream of asparagus soup
créole (ice cream) rum and tropical fruit (like rum raisin)
crêpe crêpe (thin pancake)
crêpe de froment sweet crêpe (made of wheat batter)
crêpe sucrées sweet crêpe
crêpe suzette crêpe flambéed with orange brandy sauce
cresson watercress
crevette shrimp
croissant classic French crescent roll
croque madame grilled ham, cheese, and egg sandwich
croque monsieur grilled ham and cheese sandwich
croquette deep-fried ball of potato and other ingredients
Crottin de Chavignol goat cheese from the Loire Valley
croustade pastry-wrapped dish (e.g., fruit filled)
croustillant crispy
croûte crust (bread); rind (cheese)
croûte au fromage cheese pastry
croziflette buckwheat pasta with melted cheese
cru raw; superior growth (wine)
crudité raw vegetable
cuillère spoon
cuisse thigh
cuisse de grenouille frog leg
cuit cooked
cuit au four baked
culotte rump (steak)
dariole small cylindrical mold
datte date
daube stew, usually meat
dauphine, pommes (de terre) fried puffs of mashed potatoes
décortiqué peeled; shelled
déglacé deglazed
dégustation tasting; sampling
déjeuner lunch
demi half; small beer
demi-bouteille half bottle
demi-glace brown sauce
demi-sec medium-dry (wine)
désossé boned; boneless
diabolo grenadine lemon-lime soda with cherry syrup
diabolo menthe lemon-lime soda with mint syrup

D

digestif after-dinner drink
dinde turkey
dîner dinner
domaine wine estate
doré browned
doux mild, sweet (wine); mild, soft (cheese)
douze / douzaine dozen
droit de bouchon corkage fee
duchesse, pommes (de terre) baked puffs of mashed potatoes
duxelles chopped mushrooms, shallots, and cream
eau water
eau de vie fruit brandy ("water of life")
échalote shallot
Echourgnac cow cheese with brown rind
éclair oblong, iced custard-filled roll
écrivisse crayfish
édulcorant artificial sweetener
élevé en liberté / en plein air free-range
émincé chopped
Emmentaler "Swiss cheese"
(à) emporter to go
endive endive
entier whole
entrecôte rib-eye steak
entrée first course; appetizers
entremet small dish served between courses (sometimes dessert)
épaule shoulder (of beef, pork, lamb)
éperlan smelt
épice spice
épicée spicy (flavorful, well-seasoned)
épice, pain d' gingerbread
épinard spinach
Époisses (de Bourgogne) gooey, pungent, rich cow cheese
érable maple
escalope thin slice of meat
escalope normande turkey or veal in cream sauce
escargot snail
escargot raisins "snail"-shaped raisin pastry
espagnole flavorful veal-based sauce
estragon tarragon
étiquette label (wine)
express espresso
façon in the style or fashion of
fait, bien aged, mature (cheese)
fait maison homemade
(de) fantaisie fancy (can mean bread sold by the piece)
far breton baked flan, often with prunes
farce stuffing
farci stuffed
faux-filet sirloin
faux-sucre artificial sweetener
fenouil fennel
ferme farm; firm, young (cheese)
fermé not ready to drink (wine)
fermier / fermière farm-raised
feuille de vigne grape leaf
feuilleté flaky or puff pastry

fève fava bean
ficelle "string," super-thin baguette
figue fig
filet fillet
fin fine (wine)
fines herbes chopped fresh green herbs (chives, parsley, tarragon, etc.)
flambée flaming
flétan halibut
fleur de courgette stuffed and batter-fried zucchini flower
fleurie, croûte "bloomy" (soft, edible) rind (cheese)
flûte "flute," a slim baguette
foie liver
foie gras d'oie (de canard) liver from a fattened goose (duck)
fondant au chocolat molten chocolate cake
fondue small pieces of food dipped in hot liquid for cooking
fondue bourguignonne beef fondue (cooked in oil)
fondue savoyarde cheese fondue
forestière with mushrooms
fort sharp, strong (cheese)
fougasse bread with tasty tidbits baked in, often herbs
fougasse monégasque almond and anise pastry
four, cuit au baked
Fourme d'Ambert pungent cow's-milk blue cheese
frais fresh
fraise / fraise des bois strawberry / wild strawberry
framboise raspberry
friand (au fromage) cheese puff
fricadelle meatball
fricassée fricassee
frit fried; deep-fried
froid cold
fromage cheese
fromage à la crème cream cheese
fromage aux herbes cheese with herbs
fromage blanc fresh white cheese
fromage bleu blue cheese
fromage de la région cheese of the region
froment wheat
froment, pain au wheat bread
fruit fruit
fruit de la passion passion fruit
fruité fruity (wine)
fruits de mer seafood
fruits rouges berries
fumé smoked
fût wine barrel
galette a round pastry, pancake, or cake; also a buckwheat crêpe
galette de pommes de terre hash browns
gambas big prawn
Gana brand name of baguette
gariguette small strawberry
garni garnished; with vegetables
garniture side dish
gâteau cake

gâteau basque cherry and almond cake
gaufre waffle
gazeuse carbonated
gelée jelly; aspic
gésier gizzard
gibier game
gibier à plume game bird
gigérine watermelon used in pies and preserves
gigot (d'agneau) leg (of lamb)
gingembre ginger
girolle chanterelle mushroom
glace ice cream
glacé frozen; very cold (iced tea); glazed
glaçon ice cube
gougère savory cream puff with cheese
gourmandise sweet treat
goût du fût de chêne oaky (wine)
goûté snack
grain seed
grand large
Grand Marnier orange liqueur
gras fat
gratinée topped with cheese and browned
grenade pomegranate
grenouille frog
grillade grilled meat; mixed grill
grillé grilled
grillé pommes apple-filled pastry with "grill" pattern
griotte sour cherry (morello)
gros pain "large" baguette
groseille red currant
Gruyère "Swiss cheese"
haché minced
hachis hash
hachis Parmentier shepherd's pie
hareng herring
haricot (vert) bean (green)
herbes herbs
Hollandaise sauce of egg and butter
homard lobster
hors d'oeuvre appetizer
huile oil
huître oyster
île flottante meringue floating in cream sauce
importée imported
(à la) italienne Italian-style; grilled panini (for sandwiches)
izarra herbal brandy (Basque)
jambon de Bayonne dry-cured ham
jambon de Reims ham cooked in Champagne and wrapped in a pastry shell
jambon-mornay savory puff pastry with ham and cheese
jambon persillé ham and parsley preserved in gelatin
jardinière with vegetables
jarret shank; hock; knuckle
jaune (d'oeuf) egg yolk
jésuite triangular pastry filled with almond crème
joue cheek

julienne in matchstick-sized slices
jus juice (fruit juice, but also meat juices)
jus lié gravy
juteux juicy
kaki persimmon
kasher kosher
ker-y-pom shortbread and apple biscuit
kir white wine with black currant liqueur
kir royal champagne with black currant liqueur
kouign amann buttery, caramelized cake
Kuglehopf glacé raisin-and-almond cake with cherry liqueur
lait milk
lait demi-écrémé low-fat milk
lait écrémé nonfat milk
lait entier whole milk
lait ribot fermented milk drink; buttermilk
laitue lettuce
langoustine small, lobster-like shellfish
Langres soft cow cheese
langue tongue
lapin rabbit
lard / lardon bacon / slab bacon
laurier bay leaf
lavée, croûte washed rind (cheese)
léger light (not heavy)
légume vegetable
lentille lentil
levain, pain au sourdough ("yeast") bread
levure yeast
liaison thickening agent
light light (low-calorie)
limande dab (flatfish)
lit (sur un lit de) bed (on a bed of)
Livarot pungent, creamy cow cheese
lotte monkfish
loup sea bass
(à la) lyonnaise with onions
lyonnaise, salade salad with croutons, fried ham, and poached egg
macaron delicate sandwich cookie
macédoine mix of diced vegetables or fruit
mâche lamb's lettuce
madeleine buttery sponge cake
magret (de canard) breast (of duck)
maïs corn
maison house (specialty)
manchon wing (duck, chicken)
mandarine tangerine
mangue mango
mara des bois strawberry variety
marc regional brandy
(du) marché of the market (of the day)
mariné marinated
marinière white-wine and shallot sauce

marjolaine marjoram
marmitako Basque tuna stew
marmite stew pot
marron chestnut
médaillon tenderloin
mélangé mixed
melon cantaloupe
melon charentais yellow cantaloupe
(de) ménage homemade
mendiant chocolate with nuts and dried fruit ("beggar")
menthe mint
menu fixed-price meal
menu de dégustation tasting menu
menu du jour menu of the day
méréville watermelon used in pies and preserves
merlan whiting (cod-like fish)
mesclun mixed greens
meunière fried in butter
meurette red wine sauce
miche large round loaf of bread
mie, pain de sandwich bread
miel honey
mignardise miniature petit four
mille-feuille puff pastry with many layers; Napoleon
millésime vintage (wine)
mirepoix diced mix of celery, onions, and carrots
mixte mixed
moelleux moist, creamy, sometimes not fully cooked; sweet (wine)
moelleux au chocolat molten chocolate cake
moisi / moisi noble mold / "noble mold" that makes cheese and wine delicious
molle, à pâte gooey cheese with edible rind
Montrachet soft, tangy goat cheese, often covered in ash
Morbier semi-soft cow cheese with a charcoal streak
morceau piece
morille morel mushroom
mornay white sauce with Gruyère cheese
Morteau smoked pork sausage
morue salty cod
moule mussel
mousse mousse
mousseron meadow mushroom
mousseux sparkling
moutarde mustard
mouton mutton
multicéréales multigrain
Munster stinky, soft, aged cow cheese
mûre blackberry
muscade nutmeg
museau snout
myrtille blueberry
naturelle, croûte hard rind (cheese)
navarin lamb stew
navet turnip
Nescafé instant coffee

niçoise, salade with tomatoes, green beans, anchovies, olives, hard-boiled eggs, and tuna
noir black
noisette hazelnut; espresso with a dollop of milk
noix walnut; nuts
noix de beurre a pat of butter
noix de coco coconut
noix de Saint-Jacques scallop
Normande cream sauce
nougat de Montélimar honey and nut nougat
nouille noodle
nouvelle new
oeuf egg
oeuf à la coque (mollet / dur) boiled egg (soft / hard)
oeuf au plat fried egg
oeuf brouillé scrambled egg
oeuf mayonnaise hard-boiled egg topped with mayo
oeufs de poisson fish roe
oie goose
oignon onion
olive olive
omelette montoise puffy omelet (Mont Saint-Michel)
onglet hanger steak
oranais apricot danish
Orangina carbonated orange juice with pulp
ordinaire ordinary
origan oregano
os à moelle marrowbone
oseille sorrel
Ossau-Iraty smooth, firm, buttery ewe's cheese
pain bread
pain au chocolat flaky pastry filled with chocolate
pain au froment wheat bread
pain au lait "milk bread"; smaller, less sweet brioche
pain au levain sourdough bread
pain aux raisins spiral, glazed raisin pastry
pain bis / pain bisse dark-grain bread
pain brié dense, crusty bread
pain complet whole-wheat bread
pain de campagne rustic country loaf
pain de seigle rye bread
pain d'épices gingerbread ("spice bread")
pain doré French toast
pain de mie sandwich bread
pain pavé "cobblestone"-shaped rye bread
pain perdu French toast
pain salé bacon, olive, and cheese roll
pain viennois soft, shiny, slightly sweeter baguette
paleron chuck (beef)
palmier "palm"-shaped buttery pastry
palourde clam
pamplemousse grapefruit
pan bagnat tuna salad sandwich (Riviera)

P

panaché half beer, half lemon-lime soda
pané breaded
panier basket
papaye papaya
(en) papillote cooked in parchment
paprika paprika
paquets, pieds et sheep's feet and tripe
parfumé flavored
pastèque watermelon
pastis sweet anise (licorice) drink, cut with water
pâte pastry; dough
pâte à choux eggy butter-and-flour pastry
pâte à tartiner spread (like Nutella or peanut butter)
pâte molle gooey cheese with edible rind
pâté seasoned ground meat shaped into a loaf, can also be made of fish
pâtes pasta
paupiette meat beaten thin, then rolled
pavé thick hunk of meat
Pavé d'Auge spicy, tangy, square-shaped cow cheese
pavé, pain "cobblestone"-shaped rye bread
paysanne country style
paysanne, salade salad with potatoes, walnuts, tomatoes, ham, and egg
PDT (pomme de terre) potato
pêche peach
Pélardon nutty goat cheese
pépin seed
perdrix partridge
périgourdine, salade mixed green salad with foie gras and gizzards
persil parsley
pétillant sparkling (wine, water)
petit small
petit déjeuner breakfast
petit four miniature cake
petit gâteau cookie
petit pain bread roll
petit pois small green pea
petit salé salt pork
pichet pitcher
picholine green, buttery olive
Picodon spicy goat cheese
pied (de cheval / de mouton) foot (horse / sheep)
pieds et paquets sheep's feet and tripe
piémontaise, salade potato salad with tomato and egg
pigeon squab (pigeon)
pignon pine nut
piment d'Espelette spicy red pepper
pineau cognac and grape juice
pintade guinea hen
piperade omelet with tomatoes and peppers
piquant spicy (hot)
pissaladière onion, olive, and anchovy bread
pissenlit dandelion leaf

pistache pistachio
pithivier spiral-shaped puff pastry pie
planche wooden board for cutting or serving
plat dish
plat du jour special of the day
plat principal main course
plateau platter
plateau de charcuterie platter of cured meats
plateau de fromages cheese platter
plateau mixte platter of both cheese and cured meats
pleurote oyster mushroom
poché poached
poêlée pan-fried
Poilâne big, round loaf of rustic bread
(à) point medium (meat)
poire pear
poire au vin rouge pear poached in red wine and spices
poireau leek
petit pois pea
poisson fish
poitrine de boeuf brisket (beef)
poitrine de porc pork belly
poivre / au poivre pepper / pepper sauce
poivre de Cayenne cayenne pepper
poivron bell pepper
pomme apple
pomme de terre potato
pommes (de terre) dauphine fried puffs of mashed potatoes
pommes (de terre) duchesse baked puffs of mashed potatoes
pommes (de terre) sarladaise potatoes fried in duck fat
pommes frites French fries
Pont l'Evêque flavorful, smooth, earthy cow cheese
porc pork
Port Salut soft, sweet cow cheese
porto fortified wine
potage soup, usually thick
potage de légumes thick vegetable soup
potée prepared in earthenware pot
potée champenoise meat, potato, and vegetable stew
potiron winter squash
poulet chicken
poulet rôti roast chicken
poulpe octopus
pour emporter to go
poussin young chicken
pré salé raised on salt-marsh lands
pression draft (beer)
prêt à boire ready to drink; mature (wine)
prix fixe fixed price
profiterole cream puff (sometimes with ice cream)
provençale with garlic and tomatoes
prune plum

P

pruneau prune
pur pure
purée mashed
purée de pomme de terre mashed potatoes
quatre-quarts pound cake
quenelle meat or fish dumpling
quenelle de brochet fish dumpling in a creamy sauce
queue de boeuf oxtail
quiche quiche
quiche lorraine quiche with bacon, cheese, and onions
quotidien everyday
racine root
raclette melted cheese over potatoes and meats
radis radish
ragoût stew
raie sting ray
raifort horseradish
raisin grape
raisin sec raisin
râpée grated
ratatouille tomato stew with vegetables (often eggplant, zucchini, etc.)
ravioli de Royans ravioli with goat cheese filling
Reblochon soft, gooey, mild, creamy, Brie-like cow cheese
réchauffée reheated
régionale local
réglisse licorice
religieuse round éclair (shaped like a nun)
rémoulade mayonnaise sauce (often mustard-flavored)
rillette cold, shredded pork
rillon belly (pork)
ris (d'agneau / de veau) sweetbreads (lamb / veal)
riz rice
riz au lait rice pudding
riz basmati basmati rice
riz complet brown rice
riz de Camargue nutty, chewy rice
riz jasmin jasmine rice
robuste full-bodied (wine)
rognon kidney
rognon blanc testicle
romarin rosemary
Roquefort powerful, blue-veined, tangy sheep cheese
roquette arugula (rocket)
rosbif roast beef
rosé rosé (wine)
rösti hash browns
rôti roasted
rouge red
rouget red mullet
rouille mayo with garlic and spicy peppers
roulade "rolled" around a filling
roulé aux noix sweet walnut roll with nutty filling
roux butter and flour thickening agent
sablé shortcrust pastry
safran saffron
saignant rare (meat)

Saint-Jacques, coquille / noix de scallop
Saint-Marcellin soft cow cheese
Saint-Nectaire semi-soft, nutty cow cheese
Saint-Pierre John Dory (fish)
Sainte-Maure soft, creamy goat cheese
saison, de seasonal
salade salad
salade au chèvre chaud salad with warm goat cheese on toasted croutons
salade camarguaise rice and veggie salad
salade composée "composed" salad with various ingredients
salade de pissenlit warm dandelion greens with bacon
salade lyonnaise salad with croutons, fried ham, and poached egg
salade niçoise salad with tuna, green beans, tomatoes, anchovies, olives, and hard-boiled eggs
salade paysanne potato, walnut, tomato, ham, and egg salad
salade périgourdine salad with foie gras and gizzards
salade piémontaise potato, tomato, and ham salad
salé savory, salty
salé cake savory loaf, often with ham and cheese or olives
sandre freshwater fish, like pike or perch
sanglier wild boar
sapeur, tablier de tripe dish
sarladaise, pommes (de terre) potatoes fried in duck fat
sauce verte tarragon-flavored mayo (sometimes with parsley)
saucisse sausage
saucisse-frites hot dog and fries
saucisson dried sausage; salami
sauge sage
saumon salmon
sauté sautéed
sauvage wild
savoyarde with melted cheese and/or potatoes
scampi prawns
scarole escarole
sec dry
seigle, pain de rye bread
sel salt
Selles-sur-Cher mild goat cheese
selon arrivage market price
semoule semolina (grain)
service compris service included
service non compris service not included
sole sole (fish)
sorbet sorbet
soubise onion-cream sauce
soufflé soufflé
soufflé au chocolat chocolate soufflé
soupe soup
soupe à l'oignon onion soup

soupe à l'ognion gratinée French onion soup
soupe au pistou Provençal vegetable soup with pesto
sous-vide vacuum-sealed and very slow-cooked in heated water (therefore very tender)
Spätzle soft egg noodles
spécialité specialty
spéculoos molasses cookie
steak haché gourmet hamburger patty
steak tartare raw minced beef
sucre sugar
tablier de sapeur tripe dish
taboulé couscous salad
tanche plump black olive
tannique tannic (wine)
tapenade olive spread
tarte pie; tart
tarte à l'oignon onion tart
tarte alsacienne fruit tart from Alsace
tarte au fromage cheese tart
tarte flambée thin-crust pizza with onion and bacon
tarte salée savory tart; quiche
tarte tatin upside-down apple pie
tartelette small tart
tartiflette scalloped potatoes with melted cheese
tartine baguette (sometimes toasted) with sweet or savory toppings
tasse cup
taureau bull meat
terrine pressed, chilled loaf of chopped meat or vegetables
tête head
thé tea
thon tuna
thym thyme
tian gratin-like vegetable dish
tiède lukewarm
tilapia tilapia
tire-bouchon corkscrew
tisane herbal tea
tomate tomato
Tomme (de Savoie) mild, semi-soft cow cheese
tonneau wine barrel
torchon cheese cloth
tourin garlic soup
tournedos steak tenderloin
tournée cut into a football shape, often potatoes or carrots
tournesol sunflower
tourte de blettes sweet and savory Swiss chard pie
tourteau crab (similar to Dungeness crab)
tourteau fromager sweet goat-cheese cake
tranche / tranché slice / sliced
tresse "braid"-shaped brioche
trévise radicchio
tripes tripe
trou Normand apple sorbet in apple brandy
truffe truffle
truite trout
ttoro Basque seafood stew
turbot turbot (flatfish)

unilatéral, (grillé) à l' (grilled) on one side
vache cow
Valençay firm, nutty, goat cheese
vanille vanilla
(à la) vapeur steamed
varié assorted
VDQS quality standards for regional wines
veau veal
végétarien vegetarian
velouté smooth sauce or soup
venaison venison
vendange harvest (wine)
verre glass
verrine small glass serving dish
vert green
viande meat
viande de chevreuil venison
viandes fumées smoked meats
viandes salées salt-cured meats
vichyssoise potato and leek soup
(de) vieille vignes from old vines (wine)
viennoise coated with egg and breadcrumbs
(de) vigne from the vine
vignoble vineyard
vin wine
vin de la maison house wine
vin du pays wine from a given area
vin ordinaire cheapest house wine
vinaigre vinegar
vinaigrette vinaigrette
volaille poultry
vol-au-vent cylindrical, filled pastry
yaourt yogurt

ENGLISH / FRENCH

A

aged affiné; bien fait (cheese)
alcohol alcool
almond amande
anchovy anchois
anemone anémone de mer
anise anis
appetizer hors d'oeuvre
apple pomme
apple cider, hard cidre
apple pie, upside-down tarte tatin
applesauce compote de pommes
apricot abricot
artichoke artichaut
artificial sweetener faux-sucre
arugula (rocket) roquette
asparagus asperge
assorted varié
avocado avocat
bacon / slab bacon lard / lardon
baked cuit au four
banana banane
basil basilic
bay leaf laurier
bean / green bean haricot / haricot vert
beef boeuf
beef steak bifteck
beer (small / large) bière (demi / chope)
beer, draft bière pression
beet betterave
bell pepper poivron
belly (pork) poitrine (de porc)
berries fruits rouges
beverage boisson
bitter amer
black noir
black currant cassis
blackberry mûre
blood sausage boudin noir
blue cheese fromage bleu
blueberry myrtille
boar sanglier
boiled à l'anglaise; bouilli
boiled egg (soft / hard) oeuf à la coque (mollet / dur)
boletus mushroom cèpe
boneless / deboned désossé
bottle bouteille
brains cervelle
braised braisé
brandy cognac
bread pain...
  dark-grain ...bisse
  rye ...de seigle
  sandwich ...de mie
  sourdough ...au levain
  wheat ...au froment
  whole wheat ...complet
breaded pané
breakfast petit déjeuner
breast (chicken) blanc (de volaille)
brioche brioche
brisket (beef) poitrine (de boeuf)
broccoli brocoli
broth bouillon; consommé
browned doré

butter (unsalted / salted / very salted) beurre (doux / demi-sel / salé)
cabbage chou
cake gâteau
candied confit
candy bonbon
cantaloupe melon
caper câpre
carafe carafe
carbonated gazeuse
cardamom cardamome
carrot carotte
casserole cocotte
cauliflower chou-fleur
cayenne pepper poivre de Cayenne
celery root céleri rave
chanterelle mushroom chanterelle; girolle
chard blette
cheek joue
cheese fromage
cheese, blue fromage bleu
cheese, cream fromage à la crème; fromage à tartiner
cheese of the region fromage de la région
cheese pastry croûte au fromage
cheese platter plateau de fromages
cheese puff gougère
cheese tart tarte au fromage
cheese with herbs fromage aux herbes
cheese-topped gratinée; au gratin
cherry / sour cherry cerise / griotte
chestnut châtaigne; marron
chicken / roast chicken poulet / poulet rôti
children's plate assiette d'enfant
chilled rafraîchi
Chinese chinois
chive ciboulette
chocolate chocolat
chocolate soufflé soufflé au chocolat
choice of le choix de
chop (meat) côte
chuck (beef) paleron
cilantro coriandre
cinnamon cannelle
citrus agrume
clam palourde
clove clou de girofle
cockle coque
coconut noix de coco
cod / rock cod / salt cod cabillaud / morue de roche / morue
coffee (espresso) café...
  with water (like an Americano) ...allongé; ...longue
  with lots of milk ...au lait
  with some milk ...crème
  with a dollop of milk ...noisette
coffee, decaf café déca
coffee, instant Nescafé
cold froid
cold cuts assiette de charcuterie

cooked cuit
cooked in its own fat confit
cooked in red wine Bourguignon
cookie petit gâteau; biscuit
coriander coriandre
corkage fee droit de bouchon
corked (wine) bouchonné
corkscrew tire-bouchon
corn maïs
course, first entrée
course, main plat principal
couscous couscous
cover charge couvert
cow vache
crab crabe; tourteau
crab, spider araignée de mer
cranberry (wild) airelle
crayfish écrivisse
cream crème
cream cheese fromage à la crème
cream puff (with ice cream) chou à la crème; profiterole
cream sauce Normande
crêpe crêpe
crêpe, savory buckwheat galette
crêpes flambéed with orange brandy sauce crêpes suzette
crêpes, sweet crêpes sucrées
crescent roll croissant
crisp / crispy croustillant
cucumber concombre
cumin cumin
cup tasse
custard crème
custard sauce crème à l'anglaise
custard with caramel sauce crème caramel
custard with caramelized top crème brulée
cutlet côtelette
dab (flatfish) limande
dark (beer) brune
dark-grain bread pain bisse; pain de seigle
date datte
deep-fried frit
deer biche; cerf; chevreuil
delicatessen charcuterie
diet (drinks) light
dill aneth
dinner dîner
doughnut beignet; merveille
dozen douzaine
draft beer pression
drink menu carte des consommations
dry / very dry (wine) sec / brut
duck / duck breast canard / magret de canard
dumpling (meat or fish) quenelle
egg(s) œuf(s)...
boiled (soft / hard) ...à la coque (mollet / dur)
fried ...au plat
scrambled ...brouillé
egg white blanc d'oeuf
egg yolk jaune d'oeuf
eggplant aubergine
endive endive
escarole scarole
espresso express

espresso with brandy café-calva
fat gras
fava bean fève
fennel fenouil
fig figue
fillet filet
first course entrée
fish poisson
fixed-price meal prix fixe; menu
flaming flambée
flank steak bavette
flavored parfumé
fork fourchette
free-range élevé en liberté; en plein air
French fries pommes frites; frites
French toast pain perdu; pain doré
fresh frais
fricassee fricassée
fried frit
fried eggs oeufs au plat
fried in butter meunière
fritter beignet
frog / frog leg grenouille / cuisse de grenouille
fruit fruit
fruit-filled pastry chausson
fruity (wine) fruité
full-bodied (wine) robuste; costaud
game gibier
game bird gibier à plume
garlic / garlic shoot ail / aillet
garlic mayonnaise aïoli
garnish garniture
ginger gingembre
gingerbread pain d'épices
gizzard gésier
glass verre
goat chèvre
goat cheese fromage de chèvre
goose oie
grape raisin
grape leaf feuille de vigne
grapefruit pamplemousse
grated râpée
gravy sauce
green vert
green bean haricot vert
grill, mixed grillade
grilled grillé
guinea hen pintade
half demi
half bottle demi-bouteille
halibut flétan
ham (de Bayonne) jambon (dry-cured)
ham and cheese sandwich (grilled) croque monsieur
ham, cheese, and egg sandwich (grilled) croque madame
hamburger hamburger; steak haché
harvest (wine) vendange
hash hachis
hash browns rösti; galette de pommes de terre
hazelnut noisette
herbal tea tisane
herring hareng
hock jarret

homemade fait maison; de ménage
honey miel
horse cheval
hot chaud
hot dog and fries saucisse-frites
house maison
house wine vin de la maison
ice cream glace
ice cube glaçon
imported importée
intestines tripes
jam confiture
juice / juicy jus / juteux
kidney rognon
knife couteau
kosher kasher
lamb agneau
lamb, leg of gigot d'agneau
lamb stew navarin
large grand
leek poireau
lemon citron
lentil lentille
lettuce laitue; mâche; mesclun: salade
licorice réglisse
light (beer) blonde
light (not heavy) léger
liver foie
lobster homard
lobster (small) langoustine
local régionale; du pays
loin (lamb / pork) carré (d'agneau / de porc)
lukewarm tiède
lunch déjeuner
mango mangue
maple érable
marinated mariné
marjoram marjolaine
market price selon arrivage
marrow / marrowbone moelle / os à moelle
mayonnaise / garlic mayonnaise mayonnaise / aïoli
meat viande
meat stew ragoût
meatball boulette (de viande); fricadelle
medium (meat) à point
medium (wine) demi-sec
menu carte
menu of the day menu du jour
mild, soft (cheese) doux
mild, sweet (wine) doux
milk lait
minced haché; hachis
mint menthe
mixed mixte
mixed grill grillades
monkfish lotte; baudroie
morel mushroom morille
multigrain multicéréales
mushroom champignon
(with) mushrooms forestière
mussel moule
mustard moutarde
mutton mouton
new nouvelle
noodle (pasta) nouille; pâtes
nutmeg muscade
octopus poulpe
oil huile

olive olive; picholine; tanche
onion oignon
onion tart tarte à l'oignon
orange orange
organic biologique
oyster huître
oyster mushroom pleurote
oxtail queue de boeuf
pan fried poêlée
papaya papaye
paprika paprika
parsley persil
partridge perdrix
passion fruit fruit de la passion
pasta pâtes
pâté pâté; terrine
peach pêche
peanut cacahuète
peanut butter beurre de cacahuètes
pea petit pois
pear poire
peeled décortiqué
pepper (bell) poivron
pepper (spice) poivre
pepperoni pepperoni
persimmon kaki
pickle cornichon
pickled au vinaigre
pie tarte
piece morceau
pike brochet
pine nut pignon
pineapple ananas
pistachio pistache
plate assiette
platter plateau
plum prune
poached poché
pomegranate grenade
pork porc
pork sausage (with garlic) cervelas
potato pomme de terre
potatoes, mashed purée de pommes de terre
poultry volaille
pound cake quatre-quarts
prawn scampi; gambas
preserves confiture
prune pruneau
puff pastry feuilleté
pure pur
quail caille
quiche quiche; tarte salée
quince coing
rabbit lapin
radicchio trévise
radish radis
raisin raisin sec
rare / very rare (meat) saignant / bleu
raspberry framboise
raw cru
raw hamburger steak tartare
raw vegetables crudités
red rouge
red currant groseille
rib-eye steak entrecôte
rice riz...
  basmati ...basmati
  brown ...complet
  pudding ...au lait
roast beef rosbif

roasted rôti
roe (fish eggs) oeufs de poisson
room temperature chambré
rooster coq
root racine
rosé (wine) rosé
rosemary romarin
rump (steak) culotte
saffron safran
sage sauge
salad salade
salmon saumon
salt sel
salt pork petit salé
sauce sauce...
  butter, white wine, and shallots ...beurre blanc
  cream ...normande
  egg and butter ...hollandaise
  egg and wine ...béarnaise
  white ...béchamel
  white, with Gruyère cheese ...mornay
sauerkraut choucroute
sausage saucisse
sausage, blood boudin noir
sautéed sauté
scallop coquille Saint-Jacques; noix de Saint-Jacques
scoop (ice cream) boule
scrambled / scrambled eggs brouillé / oeufs brouillés
sea bass loup
seafood fruits de mer
seafood stew bouillabaisse
seasonal de saison
seed grain; pépin
semi-dry (wine) demi-sec
semolina (grain) semoule
shallot échalote
shank (leg meat) jarret
sharp (cheese) fort
shepherd's pie hachis Parmentier
shelled décortiqué
shellfish chowder bisque; soupe de poisson
shoulder (of beef, pork, lamb) épaule
shrimp crevette
side dishes garnitures
sirloin aloyau; faux-filet
skewer brochette
slice / sliced tranche / tranché
small petit
smelt éperlan
smoked fumé
snack amuse-bouche; goûté
snails escargots
sole (fish) sole
sorbet sorbet
sorrel oseille
soufflé soufflé
soufflé, chocolate soufflé au chocolat
soup soupe; potage
  cream of asparagus crème (velouté) d'asperges
  onion (French-onion) soupe à l'oignon (gratinée)
  potato and leek vichyssoise
  Provençal vegetable soupe au pistou
  vegetable potage de légumes

sour acide
sour cream crème aigre; crème fraîche
sparkling mousseux
special of the day plat du jour
specialty spécialité
spice épice
spicy (flavorful) épicée
spicy (hot) piquant
spinach épinards
sponge cake biscuit de Savoie
spoon cuillère
squab pigeon
squash, summer courge
squash, winter potiron
squid calamar
steak steak; bifteck; entrecôte; côte de boeuf
steamed à la vapeur
stew daube; ragout; blanquette
stew, bean and meat cassoulet
stew, seafood bouillabaisse
strawberry / wild strawberry fraise / fraise des bois
stuffed / stuffing farci / farce
sugar sucre
sugar, brown cassonade
sunflower tournesol
sweet doux
sweetbreads (lamb / veal) ris (d'agneau / de veau)
sweetener, artificial faux-sucre
Swiss cheese Gruyère; Emmentaler
tangerine mandarine
tarragon estragon
tart / small tart tarte / tartelette
tea thé
tenderloin médaillon; tournedos
testicle rognon blanc
thigh (poultry) cuisse
thyme thym
tilapia tilapia
"to go" pour emporter; à emporter
tomato tomate
tongue langue
toothpick cure-dent
tripe tripes
trout truite
truffles truffes
tuna thon
turbot (fish) turbot
turkey dinde
turnip navet
vanilla vanille
veal veau
vegetable légume
vegetables, raw crudités
(with) vegetables jardinière; garni
vegetarian végétarien
venison viande de chevreuil
vinaigrette vinaigrette
vinegar vinaigre
vineyard vignoble
vintage date (wine) millésime
waffle gaufre
walnut noix
water eau
  carbonated gazeuse
  not carbonated non gazeuse

water bath bain-marie
watercress cresson
watermelon pastèque
well done / very well done (meat) bien cuit / très bien cuit
wheat froment; blé
whipped cream crème chantilly
white blanc
whiting (fish) merlan
whole (entire) entier
whole (full) complet
whole-grain bread pain complet
wild game gibier
wine vin...
  red ...rouge
  rosé ...rosé
  sparkling ...pétillant
  white ...blanc
wine, house vin de la maison
wine of the region vin de la région
yeast levure
yogurt yaourt
yolk (egg) jaune (d'oeuf)
zucchini courgette

SIGHTSEEING

Whether you're touring a museum, going on a city walking tour, visiting a church, or conquering a castle, these phrases will help you make the most of your sightseeing time.

WHERE?

Where is / are the...?	Où est / sont...? oo ay / sohn
tourist information office	l'office de tourisme loh-fees duh too-reez-muh
toilets	les toilettes lay twah-leht
main square	la place principale lah plahs pran-see-pahl
old town center	la vieille ville lah vee-yay veel
entrance	l'entrée lahn-tray
exit	la sortie lah sor-tee
museum	le musée luh mew-zay
cathedral	la cathédrale lah kah-tay-drahl
church	l'église lay-gleez
castle	le château luh shah-toh
palace	le palais luh pah-lay
ruins	les ruines lay rween
amusement park	le parc d'amusement luh park dah-mewz-mahn
aquarium	l'aquarium lah-kwah-ree-uhm
zoo	le zoo (le jardin zoologique) luh zoh (luh zhar-dan zwoh-loh-zheek)
best view	la meilleure vue lah meh-yur vew
viewpoint	le point de vue luh pwan duh vew
Is there a fair nearby?	Il y a une fête foraine dans les environs? eel yah ewn feht foh-rehn dahn layz ahn-vee-rohn
Is there a festival nearby?	Il y a une festival dans les environs? eel yah ewn fehs-tee-vahl dahn layz ahn-vee-rohn

Key Phrases: Sightseeing

ticket	billet bee-yay
How much is it?	C'est combien? say kohn-bee-an
price	prix pree
Is there a guided tour (in English)?	Il y a une visite guidée (en anglais)? eel yah ewn vee-zeet gee-day (ahn ahn-glay)
When?	Quand? kahn
What time does this open / close?	À quelle heuere c'est ouvert / fermé? ah kehl ur say oo-vehr / fehr-may

AT SIGHTS

Tickets and Discounts

ticket office	guichet / billetterie gee-shay / bee-yeh-teh-ree
ticket	billet bee-yay
combo-ticket	billet combiné bee-yay kohn-bee-nay
price	prix pree
discount	réduction ray-dewk-see-ohn
Is there a discount for...?	Il y a une réduction pour...? eel yah ewn ray-dewk-see-ohn poor
...children	...les enfants layz ahn-fahn
...youths	...les jeunes lay juhn
...students	...les étudiants layz ay-tew-dee-ahn
...families	...les familles lay fah-mee
...seniors	...les gens âgés lay zhahn ah-zhay
...groups	...les groupes lay groop
I am...	J'ai... zhay
He / She is...	Il / Elle a... eel / ehl ah
... _____ years old.	... _____ ans. _____ ahn

I am extremely old.	Je suis très âgé. zhuh swee trehz ah-zhay
Is the ticket good all day?	Le billet est valable toute la journée? luh bee-yay ay vah-lah-bluh toot lah zhoor-nay
Can I get back in?	Je peux rentrer? zhuh puh rahn-tray

Information and Tours

information	les renseignements lay rahn-sehn-yuh-mahn
tour	une visite ewn vee-zeet
in English	en anglais ahn ahn-glay
Is there a...?	Il y a...? eel yah
...city walking tour	...une promenade guidée de la ville ewn proh-muh-nahd gee-day duh lah veel
...guided tour	....une visite guidée ewn vee-zeet gee-day
...audioguide	...un audioguide uhn oh-dee-oh-geed
...local guide (who is available)	...un guide local (qui est disponible) uhn geed loh-kahl (kee ay dee-spoh-nee-bluh)
...city guidebook (for Paris)	...un guide touristique (de Paris) uhn geed too-rees-teek (duh pah-ree)
...museum guidebook	...un guide de musée uhn geed duh mew-zay
Is it free?	C'est gratuit? say grah-twee
How much is it?	C'est combien? say kohn-bee-an
How long does it last?	Ça dure combien de temps? sah dewr kohn-bee-an duh tahn
When is the next tour in English?	La prochaine visite en anglais est à quelle heure? lah proh-shehn vee-zeet ahn ahn-glay ay ah kehl ur

Some sights are tourable only by groups with a guide ***(un guide)***. Individuals usually end up with the next French tour. To get an English tour, call in advance to see if one's scheduled; individuals can often tag along with a large tour group.

Visiting Sights

opening times	horaires d'ouverture oh-rair doo-vehr-tewr
last entry	la dernière entrée lah dehrn-yehr ahn-tray
At what time does this open / close?	À quelle heuere c'est ouvert / fermé? ah kehl ur say oo-vehr / fehr-may
What time is the last entry?	La dernière entrée est à quelle heure? lah dehrn-yehr ahn-tray ay ah kehl ur
Do I have to check this bag?	Est-ce que je dois déposer ce sac à la consigne? ehs kuh zhuh dwah day-poh-zay suh sahk ah lah kohn-seen-yuh
bag check	consigne kohn-seen-yuh
floor plan	plan plahn
floor	étage ay-tahzh
collection	collection koh-lehk-see-ohn
exhibition...	exposition... ehks-poh-zee-see-ohn
...temporary / special	...temporaire / spéciale tahn-poh-rair / spay-see-ahl
...permanent	...permamente pehr-mah-nahnt
café	café kah-fay
elevator	ascenseur ah-sahn-sur
toilet	toilette twah-leht
Where is ____?	Où est ____? oo ay ____
I'd like to see ____.	Je voudrais voir ____. zhuh voo-dray vwahr ____
Photo / Video OK?	Photo / Vidéo OK? foh-toh / vee-day-oh "OK"

(No) flash.	(Pas de) flash.	(pah duh) flahsh
(No) tripod.	(Pas de) trépied.	(pah duh) tray-pee-yay
Will you take my / our photo?	Vous pouvez prendre ma / notre photo?	voo poo-vay prahn-druh mah / noh-truh foh-toh
Please let me in. (if room or sight is closing)	S'il vous plaît, laissez-moi entrer.	see voo play leh-say-mwah ahn-tray
I promise I'll be fast.	Je promets d'aller vite.	zhuh proh-may dah-lay veet
It was my mother's dying wish that I see this.	C'était le dernier souhait de ma mère que je voies ça.	say-tay luh dehrn-yay soo-way duh mah mehr kuh zhuh vwah sah

Once at the sight, get your bearings by viewing ***le plan*** (floor plan). ***Vous êtes ici*** means "You are here." Many museums have an official, one-way route that all visitors take—just follow signs for ***Sens de la visite.***

Signs at Sights

First figure out which line is for buying tickets (***billets d'entrée*** or ***caisse individuelle***), and which is for the entrance ***(entrée).*** Some larger museums have separate entrances for individuals ***(entrée individuels),*** for groups ***(entrée groupe),*** and for people who already have tickets reserved ***(entrée billets coupe-file).***

Entrée	Entrance
Resérvations	Reservations
Guichet / Billetterie	Ticket office
Billets	Tickets
Adultes	Adults
Enfants	Children
Jeunes	Youths
Étuidants	Students
Gens âgés	Seniors
Billet combiné	Combo-ticket

Réduction	Discount
Visite guidée	Guided tour
Exposition	Exhibition
Plan (d'orientation)	Map (orientation)
Vous êtes ici	You are here (on map)
Vestiaire	Cloakroom
Consigne	Bag check
Obligatoire	Required
Consigne automatique	Lockers
Audioguide	Audioguide
Ascenseurs	Elevators
Vers l'exposition	To the exhibition
Sens de la visite	Direction of visit ("this way")
Photos interdites	No photography
Flash / trépied interdit	No flash / tripod
Défense de toucher	Do not touch
Nourriture / boissons interdite	No eating / drinking
Non autorisé	Not allowed
Interdit	Forbidden
Travaux (de restauration) en cours	Work in restoration
En dépôt	Work on loan
Salle d'étude	Classroom
Accès réservé au personel autorisé	Staff only
Sortie interdite	Exit not allowed
Sortie	Exit
Sortie de secours	Emergency exit

Toilets can be marked ***toilettes*** or ***WC.***

MUSEUMS

Types of Museums

Many of France's national museums close on Tuesdays. For efficient sightseeing in Paris, buy a Museum Pass. It'll save you money and time (because you can bypass ticket-buying lines).

museum	musée mew-zay
gallery	galerie gah-luh-ree
art gallery	galerie d'art gah-luh-ree dar
painting gallery	galerie de peinture gah-luh-ree duh pan-tewr
modern art	art moderne ar moh-dehrn
contemporary art	art contemporain ar kohn-tahn-poh-ran
folk	art populaire ar poh-pew-lair
history	histoire ees-twahr
town / city	village / ville vee-lahzh / veel
children's	pour les enfants poor layz ahn-fahn
Jewish	juif zhweef
memorial	mémorial may-moh-ree-ahl

Art Appreciation

I like it.	Ça me plaît. sah muh play
It's so...	C'est si... say see
...beautiful.	...beau. boh
...ugly.	...laid. lay
...strange.	...bizarre. bee-zar
...boring.	...ennuyeux. ahn-nuh-yuh
...interesting.	...intéressant. an-tay-reh-sahn
...thought-provoking.	...provocateur. proh-voh-kah-tur
It's B.S.	C'est con. say kohn
I don't get it.	Je n'y comprends rien. zhuh nee kohn-prahn ree-an
Is it upside down?	C'est à l'envers? say ah lahn-vehr
Who did this?	Qui a fait ça? kee ah fay sah
How old is this?	C'est vieux? say vee-uh
Wow!	Sensass! sahn-sahs
My feet hurt!	J'ai mal aux pieds! zhay mahl oh pee-yay

Art and Architecture Terms

art	art ar
artist	artiste ar-teest
painting	peinture pan-tewr
portrait	portrait por-tray
sculptor	sculpteur skewlp-tur
sculpture	sculpture skewlp-tewr
architect	architecte ar-shee-tehkt
architecture	architecture ar-shee-tehk-tewr
original	original oh-ree-zhee-nahl
restored	restauré rehs-toh-ray
B.C. / A.D.	avant J.-C. / après J.-C. ah-vahn zhay-say / ah-preh zhay-say
century	siècle see-eh-kluh
style	style steel
prehistoric	préhistorique pray-ees-toh-reek
ancient	ancien ahn-see-an
classical	classique klah-seek
Roman	romain roh-man
Byzantine	byzantin bee-zahn-tan
Islamic	islamique ees-lah-meek
medieval	médiéval may-day-vahl
Romanesque	romanesque roh-mah-nehsk
Gothic	gothique goh-teek
Renaissance	Renaissance ruh-nay-sahns
Baroque	baroque bah-rohk
Neoclassical	néoclassique nay-oh-klah-seek
Romantic	romantique roh-mahn-teek
Impressionist	impressionniste an-preh-see-oh-neest
Art Nouveau	art nouveau ar noo-voh
Modern	moderne moh-dehrn

abstract	abstrait ahb-stray
contemporary	contemporaire kohn-tahn-poh-rair

Historical Terms

Roman	Romain roh-man
Gauls / Franks	Gaulois / Francs goh-lwah / frahn
Middle Ages	le Moyen Âge luh moy-ahn ahzh
Hundred Years' War	la Guerre de Cent Ans lah gehr duh sahnt ahn
Joan of Arc	Jeanne d'Arc zhahn dark
Renaissance	la Renaissance lah ruh-nay-sahns
Louis XIV (Sun King)	Louis Quatorze (le Roi-Soleil) loo-ee kah-torz (luh rwah-soh-lay)
Enlightenment	les Lumières lay lew-mee-ehr
Pre-Revolutionary France	l'Ancien Régime lahn-see-an ray-zheem
French Revolution	la Révolution française lah ray-voh-lew-see-ohn frahn-sehz
Reign of Terror	la Terreur lah tehr-ur
First Empire (Napoleon I)	le Premier Empire luh pruhm-yay ahn-peer
Second Empire (Napoleon III)	le Second Empire luh suh-gohnd ahn-peer
Gilded Age (1871-1914)	la Belle Époque lah behl ay-pohk
turn of 20th century	fin de siècle fan duh see-eh-kluh
World War I	la Première Guerre mondiale lah pruhm-yehr gehr mohnd-yahl
World War II	la Seconde Guerre mondiale lah suh-gohnd gehr mohnd-yahl
Nazi-Collaborationist France	Vichy France vee-shee frahns

resistance	la Résistance lah ray-zees-tahns
D-Day	Jour J zhoor zhee
postwar	l'après-guerre lah-preh-gehr
Fifth Republic (current French government)	la Cinquième République lah sank-yehm ray-pew-bleek
European Union (EU)	l'Union Européenne (UE) lewn-yohn ur-oh-pay-ehn (ew uh)

CHURCHES

cathedral	cathédrale kah-tay-drahl
church	église ay-gleez
chapel	chapelle shah-pehl
altar	autel oh-tehl
bells	cloches klohsh
carillon	carillon kah-ree-yohn
chapter house (meeting room)	chapitre shah-pee-truh
choir	choeur kur
cloister	cloître klwah-truh
cross	croix krwah
crypt	crypte kreept
dome	dôme dohm
organ	orgue org
pulpit	chaire shair
relic	relique ruh-leek
sacristy	sacristie sah-kree-stee
stained glass	vitraux vee-troh
steeple / bell tower	clocher kloh-shay
treasury	trésorerie tray-zoh-ree
pope	Le Pape luh pahp

Mass	messe mehs
When is the Mass?	La messe est quand? lah mehs ay kahn
Are there church concerts?	Il y a des concerts à l'église? eel yah day kohn-sehr ah lay-gleez
Can I climb the tower?	Puis-je monter le tour? pweezh mohn-tay luh toor

CASTLES AND PALACES

castle	château shah-toh
palace	palais pah-lay
royal residence	résidence royale ray-zee-dahns roh-yahl
fortified castle	château-fort shah-toh-for
kitchen	cuisine kwee-zeen
dungeon	cachot kah-shoh
moat	fossé foh-say
fortified walls	remparts rahn-par
tower	tour toor
fountain	fontaine fohn-tehn
garden	jardin zhar-dan
king	roi rwah
queen	reine rehn
knight	chevalier shuh-vahl-yay
fair maiden	épouse fidèle ay-pooz fee-dehl
dragon	dragon drah-gohn

ANCIENT SITES

ancient sites	sites anciens seet ahn-see-an
Gauls	Gaulois goh-lwah
Roman	Romain roh-man

walls	murailles	mew-rī
forum (main square)	forum	foh-ruhm
temple	temple	tahn-pluh
column	colonne	koh-lohn
mosaic	mosaïque	moh-zī-eek
theater	théâtre	tay-ah-truh
arena	arène	ah-rehn
aqueduct	aqueduc	ahk-dew

RECREATION AND ENTERTAINMENT

This chapter offers phrases for your recreational pleasure, whether you're going to the park or beach, swimming, biking, hiking, or enjoying other sports. It also covers your options for nightlife and entertainment.

RECREATION

Outdoor Fun

Where is the best place for...?	Où est le meilleur endroit pour...? oo ay luh meh-yur ahn-drwah poor
...biking	...faire du vélo fair dew vay-loh
...walking	...marcher mar-shay
...hiking	...faire de la randonnée fair duh lah rahn-doh-nay
...running	...courrir / faire du jogging koo-reer / fair dew zhoh-geeng
...picnicking	...pique-niquer peek-nee-kay
...sunbathing	...se bronzer suh brohn-zay
Where is a...?	Où est...? oo ay
...park	...un parc uhn park
...playground	...une aire de jeux ewn air duh juh
...snack shop	...un snack uhn "snack"
...toilet	...une toilette ewn twah-leht
Where can I rent...?	Où puis-je louer...? oo pweezh loo-ay
...a bike	...un vélo uhn vay-loh
...that	...ça sah
What's fun to do...?	Qu'est-ce qu'il y a d'amusant à faire...? kehs keel yah dah-mew-zahnt ah fair
...for a boy / a girl...	...pour un garçon / une fille... poor uhn gar-sohn / ewn fee
... _____ years old	...de _____ ans duh _____ ahn

At most any park, people (usually men) play ***boules*** (pronounced "bool," also called ***pétanque***). Each player takes turns tossing an iron ball, with the goal of getting it as close as possible to the small, wooden target ball ***(cochonnet)***.

At bigger parks, you can sometimes rent toy sailboats ***(voiliers de bassin)*** or see puppet shows ***(guignols)***—fun to watch in any language.

Swimming and Water Sports

swimming	natation nah-tah-see-ohn
to swim	nager nah-zhay
Where's a...?	Où est...? oo ay
...swimming pool	...une piscine ewn pee-seen
...water park	...un parc aquatique uhn park ah-kwah-teek
...(good) beach	...une (belle) plage ewn (behl) plahzh
...nude beach	...une plage naturiste ewn plahzh nah-tewr-eest
Is it safe for swimming?	On peut nager en sécurité? ohn puh nah-zhay ahn say-kew-ree-tay
Where can I buy / rent...?	Où puis-je acheter / louer...? oo pweezh ah-shuh-tay / loo-ay
swimsuit	un maillot de bain uhn mī-yoh duh ban
towel	une serviette ewn sehrv-yeht
sunscreen	une crème solaire ewn krehm soh-lair
sunglasses	des lunettes de soleil day lew-neht duh soh-lay
flip-flops	des tongues day tohn-guh
water shoes	des chaussons étanches day shoh-sohn ay-tahnsh
umbrella (for sun)	un parasol uhn pah-rah-sohl
umbrella (for rain)	un parapluie uhn pah-rah-plwee
lounge chair	une chaise longue ewn shehz lohng

Renting

Whether you're renting a bike or a boat, here's what to ask.

Where can I rent a...?	Où puis-je louer...? oo pweezh loo-ay
Can I rent a...?	Je peux louer...? zhuh puh loo-ay
...bike	...un vélo uhn vay-loh
...boat	...une bâteau ewn bah-toh
How much per...?	C'est combien par...? say kohn-bee-an par
...hour	...heure ur
...half-day	...demie-journée duh-mee-zhoor-nay
...day	...jour zhoor
Is a deposit required?	Une caution est obligatoire? ewn koh-see-ohn ay oh-blee-gah-twahr

inner tube	une chambre à air ewn shahn-bruh ah air
goggles	des lunettes de natation day lew-neht duh nah-tah-see-ohn
snorkel and mask	un tuba et une masque uhn tew-bah ay ewn mahsk
surfing	surf sewrf
surfboard	une planche de surf ewn plahnsh duh sewrf
windsurfing	planche à voile plahnsh ah vwahl
waterskiing	ski nautique skee noh-teek
jet ski	un jet ski uhn "jet ski"
paddleboard	un paddleboard uhn "paddleboard"
boat	un bâteau uhn bah-toh
rowboat	une barque ewn bark
paddleboat	un pédalo uhn pay-dah-loh

canoe / kayak	un canoë / un kayak uhn kah-noh-ay / uhn "kayak"
sailboat	un voilier uhn vwahl-yay

In France, nearly any beach is topless. For a nude beach, look for a ***plage naturiste.*** At some French beaches (especially along the Atlantic), be wary of ***grandes marées***—high tides.

Bicycling

bicycle / bike	bicyclette / vélo bee-see-kleht / vay-loh
mountain bike	VTT (vélo tout-terrain) vay tay tay (vay-loh too-tuh-ran)
I'd like to rent a bike.	Je voudrais louer un vélo. zhuh voo-dray loo-ay uhn vay-loh
two bikes	deux vélos duh vay-loh
kid's bike	vélo d'enfant vay-loh dahn-fahn
helmet	casque kahsk
map	carte kart
lock	antivol ahn-tee-vohl
chain	chaîne shehn
pedal	pédale pay-dahl
wheel	roue roo
tire	pneu pnuh
air / no air	air / pas d'air air / pah dair
pump	pompe pohmp
brakes	les freins lay fran
How does this work?	Ça marche comment? sah marsh koh-mahn
How many gears?	Combien de vitesses? kohn-bee-an duh vee-tehs
Is there a bike path?	Il y a une piste cyclable? eel yah ewn peest see-klah-bluh

I don't like hills or traffic.	Je n'aime pas les côtes ni la circulation. zhuh nehm pah lay koht nee lah seer-kew-lah-see-ohn
I brake for bakeries.	Je m'arrête à chaque boulangerie. zhuh mah-reht ah shahk boo-lahn-zhuh-ree

Hiking

go hiking	faire de la randonnée fair duh lah rahn-doh-nay
a hike	une randonnée ewn rahn-doh-nay
a trail	un sentier uhn sahn-tee-ay
Where can I buy a...?	Où puis-je acheter...? oo pweezh ah-shuh-tay
...hiking map	...une carte de randonnée / carte IGN ewn kart duh rahn-doh-nay / kart ee zhay ehn
...compass	...une boussole ewn boo-sohl
Where's the trailhead?	Où commence le sentier? oo koh-mahns luh sahn-tee-ay
How do I get there?	Comment est-ce que j'y arrive? koh-mahn ehs kuh zhee ah-reev
Show me?	Vous pouvez me montrer? voo poo-vay muh mohn-tray
How is the trail marked?	Comment le sentier est-il balisé? koh-mahn luh sahn-tee-ay ay-teel bah-lee-zay

Most hiking trails are well-marked with signs listing the destination and the duration in hours ***(parcours de ____ heures)*** and minutes ***(parcours de ____ minutes).***

To reach the best views, consider taking advantage of the network of ***chemin de fer de montagne*** or ***trains de montagne*** (mountain railways).

Way to Go!

Whether you're biking or hiking, you'll want to know the best way to go.

Can you recommend a route / a hike that is...?	Pouvez-vous recommander un itinéraire / une randonnée qui est...? poo-vay-voo ruh-koh-mahn-day uhn ee-tee-nay-rair / ewn rahn-doh-nay kee ay
...easy	...facile fah-seel
...moderate	...modéré moh-day-ray
...strenuous	...difficile dee-fee-seel
...safe	...sans danger sahn dahn-zhay
...scenic	...panoramique / beau pah-noh-rah-meek / boh
...about ____ kilometers	...environ ____ kilomètres ahn-vee-rohn ____ kee-loh-meh-truh
How many hours / minutes?	Combien d'heures / de minutes? kohn-bee-an dur / duh mee-newt
uphill / level / downhill	montée / niveau / descente mohn-tay / nee-voh / day-sahnt

There are various types: ***train à crémaillère*** (cogwheel train—rack-and-pinion railway), ***funicular*** (an incline railway), ***téléphérique*** (cable car—one large car pulled up by cable), and ***télécabine*** (gondola—smaller compartments pulled up by cable).

Sports Talk

sports	sport spor
sports bar	un bar avec des sports à la télé uhn bar ah-vehk day spor ah lah tay-lay
game	match mahtch
team	équipe ay-keep
championship	championnat shahn-pee-oh-nah

field	terrain tuh-ran
court	court koor
fitness club	club de fitness kluhb duh feet-nehs
I like to play...	J'aime jouer à... zhehm zhoo-ay ah
I like to watch...	J'aime regarder... zhehm ruh-gar-day
American football	football américain foot-bohl ah-may-ree-kan
baseball	baseball bayz-bohl
basketball	basket bah-skeht
ice skating	patin sur glace pah-tan sewr glahs
golf	golf "golf"
miniature golf	golf miniature "golf" mee-nee-ah-tewr
rugby	rugby roog-bee
skiing	ski "ski"
snowboarding	snowboard "snowboard"
soccer	football foot-bohl
tennis	tennis tehn-ees
volleyball	volleyball voh-lay-bohl
Where can I play?	Où puis-je jouer? oo pweezh zhoo-ay
Where can I rent / buy equipment?	Où puis-je louer / acheter de l'équipment? oo pweezh loo-ay / ah-shuh-tay duh lay-keep-mahn
Where can I see a game?	Où puis-je voir un match? oo pweezh vwahr uhn mahtch

ENTERTAINMENT

What's Happening

event guide	guide des événements geed dayz ay-vay-nuh-mahn
What's happening tonight?	Qu'est-ce qui ce passe ce soir? kehs kee suh pahs suh swahr

What do you recommend?	Qu'est-ce que vous recommandez? kehs kuh voo ruh-koh-mahn-day
Where is it?	C'est où? say oo
How do I get there?	Comment est-ce que j'y arrive? koh-mahn ehs kuh zhee ah-reev
How do we get there?	Comment est-ce que nous y arrivons? koh-mahn ehs kuh nooz ee ah-ree-vohn
Is it free?	C'est gratuit? say grah-twee
Are there seats available?	Il y a des places disponibles? eel yah day plahs dee-spoh-nee-bluh
Where can I buy a ticket?	Où puis-je acheter un billet? oo pweezh ah-shuh-tay uhn bee-yay
Do you have tickets for today / tonight?	Avez-vous des billets pour aujourd'hui / ce soir? ah-vay-voo day bee-yay poor oh-zhoor-dwee / suh swahr
When does it start?	Ça commence à quelle heure? sah koh-mahns ah kehl ur
When does it end?	Ça se termine à quelle heure? sah suh tehr-meen ah kehl ur
Where do people stroll?	Les gens se balladent où? lay zhahn suh bah-lahd oo

For concerts and special events, ask at the local tourist office. Cafés, very much a part of the French social scene, are places for friends to spend the evening together. To meet new friends, the French look for ***pubs*** or ***bars américains.***

Music and Dance

Where's a good place for...?	Où se trouve un bon endroit pour...? oo suh troov uhn bohn ahn-drwah poor
...dancing	...danser dahn-say
...(live) music	...musique (en directe) mew-zeek (ahn dee-rehkt)

rock	rock rohk
jazz	jazz zhahz
blues	blues "blues"
classical	classique klah-seek
choir	de choeur duh kur
folk	folklorique fohk-loh-reek
folk dancing	danse folklorique dahns fohk-loh-reek
disco	disco dee-skoh
karaoke	karaoké kah-rah-oh-kay
singer	chanteur shahn-tur
band	groupe groop
bar with live band	bar avec un groupe musical bar ah-vehk uhn groop mew-zee-kahl
nightclub	boîte bwaht
cabaret	caberet kah-buh-ray
(no) cover charge	(pas de) admission (pah duh) ahd-mee-see-ohn
concert	concert kohn-sehr
opera	d'opéra doh-pay-rah
symphony	symphonique san-foh-neek
show	spectacle spehk-tah-kluh
performance	séance say-ahns
theater	théâtre tay-ah-truh
best seats	les meilleures places lay meh-yur plahs
cheap seats	les places bon marché lay plahs bohn mar-shay
sold out	complet kohn-play

Movies

movie	film feelm
Where is a movie theater?	Où est le cinema? oo ay luh see-nay-mah
Is this movie in English?	Est-ce que ce film est en anglais? ehs kuh suh feelm ayt ahn ahn-glay
original version	version originale (V.O.) vehr-see-ohn oh-ree-zhee-nahl (vay oh)
with subtitles	avec sous-titres ah-vehk soo-tee-truh
dubbed / "French version"	doublé / version française (V.F.) doo-blay / vehr-see-ohn frahn-sayz (vay "f")
3D	3D trwah-day
show times	l'horaire des séances loh-rair day say-ahns
matinee	matinée mah-tee-nay
ticket	billet bee-yay
discount	réduction ray-dewk-see-ohn
popcorn	popcorn "popcorn"
I liked it.	Je l'ai aimé. zhuh lay eh-may
The book is better.	Le roman est beaucoup mieux. luh roh-mahn ay boh-koo mee-uh

Paris has a great cinema scene, especially on the Champs-Élysées. Pick up a ***Pariscope,*** the periodical entertainment guide, and choose from hundreds of films. Those listed as ***V.O.*** are in their original language; ***V.F. (version française)*** means dubbed in French.

SHOPPING

These phrases will give you the basics on browsing and bargaining; help you shop for various items, including souvenirs, clothes, and jewelry; and assist you in shipping items home.

SHOP TILL YOU DROP

Bargain hunters keep an eye out for ***soldes*** (sales), ***liquidation de stock*** (liquidation sale), ***tout doit disparaître*** (everything must go), ***prix choc*** (a shockingly good price), or ***réductions*** (reduced). When the French go window shopping, they call it ***lèche-vitrines*** (window licking).

Shop Talk

opening hours	les heures d'ouverture layz ur doo-vehr-tewr
sale	solde sohld
discounted	prix réduit pree ray-dwee
big discounts	prix choc pree shohk
cheap	bon marché bohn mar-shay
affordable	abordable ah-bor-dah-bluh
(too) expensive	(trop) cher (troh) shehr
good value	bon rapport qualité prix bohn rah-por kah-lee-tay pree
window shopping	lèche-vitrines lehsh-vee-treen
Pardon me (for bothering you).	Excusez-moi (de vous déranger). ehk-skew-zay-mwah (duh voo day-rahn-zhay)
Where can I buy _____?	Où puis-je acheter _____? oo pweezh ah-shuh-tay _____
How much is it?	C'est combien? say kohn-bee-an
I'm just browsing.	Je regarde. zhuh ruh-gard
We're just browsing.	Nous regardons. noo ruh-gar-dohn
I'd like _____.	Je voudrais _____. zhuh voo-dray _____
Do you have...?	Vous avez...? vooz ah-vay
...more	...plus plew

Key Phrases: Shopping

How much is it?	C'est combien? say kohn-bee-an
I'm just browsing.	Je regarde. zhuh ruh-gard
Can I see more?	Je peux en voir d'autres? zhuh puh ahn vwahr doh-truh
I'll think about it.	Je vais réfléchir. zhuh vay ray-flay-sheer
I'll take it.	Je le prends. zhuh luh prahn
Do you accept credit cards?	Vous prenez les cartes? voo pruh-nay lay kart
Can I try it on?	Je peux l'essayer? zhuh puh lay-say-yay
It's too expensive / big / small.	C'est trop cher / grand / petit. say troh shehr / grahn / puh-tee

...something cheaper	...quelque chose de moins cher kehl-kuh shohz duh mwan shehr
...something nicer	...quelque chose plus agréable kehl-kuh shohz plew ah-gray-ah-bluh
Can I see more?	Je peux en voir d'autres? zhuh puh ahn vwahr doh-truh
May I see this more closely?	Pourrais-je voir de plus près? poo-rayzh vwahr duh plew preh
This one.	Celui ci. suhl-wee see
I'll think about it.	Je vais réfléchir. zhuh vay ray-flay-sheer
I'll take it.	Je le prends. zhuh luh prahn
What time do you close?	Vous fermez à quelle heure? voo fehr-may ah kehl ur
What time do you open tomorrow?	Vous allez ouvrir à quelle heure demain? vooz ah-lay oo-vreer ah kehl ur duh-man

Except in department stores, ask first before you pick up an item: ***Pourrais-je voir de plus près?*** (May I see this more closely?).

Pay Up

Where do I pay?	Où se trouve la caisse? oo suh troov lah kehs
cashier	caisse kehs
Do you accept credit cards?	Vous prenez les cartes? voo pruh-nay lay kart
VAT (Value-Added Tax)	TVA (Taxe sur la Valeur Ajoutée) tay vay ah (tahx sewr lah vah-lur ah-zhoo-tay)
Can I get...?	Je peux avoir...? zhuh puh ah-vwahr
I need the paperwork for...	J'ai besoin de remplir un formulaire pour... zhay buh-zwan duh rahn-pleer uhn for-mew-lair poor
...a VAT refund	...la détaxe lah day-tahx
Can you ship this?	Vous pouvez l'envoyer? voo poo-vay lahn-voy-ay

When you're ready to pay, look for a ***caisse*** (cashier). The cashier might ask you something like ***Auriez-vous quinze centimes?*** (Do you have 15 cents?), or ***Voulez-vous un sac?*** (Do you want a bag?).

If you make a major purchase from a single store, you may be eligible for a VAT refund; for details, see www.ricksteves.com/vat.

WHERE TO SHOP

Types of Shops

Where is a...?	Où est...? oo ay
antique shop	un magasin d'antiquités uhn mah-gah-zan dahn-tee-kee-tay
art gallery	une gallerie d'art ewn gah-luh-ree dar
bakery	une boulangerie ewn boo-lahn-zhuh-ree

barber shop	un salon de coiffeur pour hommes uhn sah-lohn duh kwah-fur poor ohm
beauty salon	un salon de coiffeur pour dames uhn sah-lohn duh kwah-fur poor dahm
bookstore...	une librairie... ewn lee-bray-ree
used bookstore...	une boutique de livres d'occasion... ewn boo-teek duh lee-vruh doh-kah-zee-ohn
...with books in English	...avec des livres en anglais ah-vehk day lee-vruh ahn ahn-glay
camera shop	un magasin de photo uhn mah-gah-zan duh foh-toh
call shop (for making cheap long-distance calls)	un centre d'appels téléphoniques uhn sahn-truh dah-pehl tay-lay-foh-neek
cheese shop	une fromagerie ewn froh-mah-zhuh-ree
clothing boutique	une boutique de vêtements ewn boo-teek duh veht-mahn
coffee shop	un café uhn kah-fay
computer store	un magasin informatique uhn mah-gah-zan an-for-mah-teek
crafts shop	un magasin d'artisanat uhn mah-gah-zan dar-tee-zahn-ah
delicatessen	une charcuterie-traiteur ewn shar-kew-tuh-ree-tray-tur
department store	un grand magasin uhn grahn mah-gah-zan
electronics store	un magasin d'équipements électroniques uhn mah-gah-zan day-keep-mahn ay-lehk-troh-neek
fabric store	un magasin de tissu uhn mah-gah-zan duh tee-sew
flea market	un marché aux puces uhn mar-shay oh pews

flower market	un marché aux fleurs	uhn mar-shay oh flur
grocery store	une épicerie	ewn ay-pee-suh-ree
hardware store	une quincaillerie	ewn kan-kī-yuh-ree
Internet café	un café internet	uhn kah-fay an-tehr-neht
jewelry shop (fine)	une boutique de joaillerie	ewn boo-teek duh zhoh-ī-ree
jewelry shop (cheap)	une bijouterie bon marché	ewn bee-zhoo-tuh-ree bohn mar-shay
launderette (self-service)	une laverie automatique	ewn lah-vuh-ree oh-toh-mah-teek
laundry (full-service)	une blanchisserie	ewn blahn-shee-suh-ree
liquor store	une caviste	ewn kah-veest
mobile phone shop	un magasin de portables	uhn mah-gah-zan duh por-tah-bluh
newsstand	une maison de la presse	ewn may-zohn duh lah prehs
office supply shop	une papeterie	ewn pah-peh-tuh-ree
open-air market	un marché en plein air	uhn mar-shay ahn plan air
optician	un opticien	uhn ohp-tee-see-an
pastry shop	une pâtisserie	ewn pah-tee-suh-ree
pharmacy	une pharmacie	ewn far-mah-see
photocopy shop	un magasin de photocopie	uhn mah-gah-zan duh foh-toh-koh-pee
shoe store	un magasin de chaussures	uhn mah-gah-zan duh shoh-sewr
shopping mall	un centre commercial	uhn sahn-truh koh-mehr-see-ahl
souvenir shop	une boutique de souvenirs	ewn boo-teek duh soo-vuh-neer

supermarket	une supermarché ewn sew-pehr-mar-shay
sweets shop	une confiserie ewn kohn-fee-suh-ree
toy store	un magasin de jouets uhn mah-gah-zan duh zhoo-ay
travel agency	une agence de voyages ewn ah-zhahns duh voy-yahzh
wine store	une caviste ewn kah-veest

In France, most small shops close for a long lunch (noon until about 2 p.m.), and all day on Sundays and Mondays. For tips and phrases on shopping for a picnic—at grocery stores or open-air markets—see page 173.

Shoppers in Paris enjoy browsing the characteristic stalls along the Seine riverbank called ***bouquinistes*** (boo-kan-neest), which sell used books, art, cards, and more.

Department Stores

department store	grand magasin grahn mah-gah-zan
floor	étage ay-tazh
Pardon me (for bothering you).	Excusez moi (de vous déranger). ehks-kew-say mwah (duh voo day-rahn-zhay)
Where is _____?	Où se trouve _____? oo suh troov _____
clothing for...	les vêtement de... lay veht-mahn duh
...men / women	...hommes / femmes ohm / fahm
...children	...enfants ahn-fahn
accessories	accessoires ahk-seh-swahr
books	livres lee-vruh
electronics	électroniques ay-lehk-troh-neek
fashion	mode mohd
footwear	chaussures shoh-sewr
groceries	épicerie ay-pee-suh-ree

housewares / kitchenware	bricolage / matériel de cusine bree-koh-lahzh / mah-tay-ree-ehl duh kwee-zeen
intimates	lingerie lan-zhuh-ree
jewelry	bijoux bee-zhoo
maternity (wear)	(vêtements de) femmes enceinte (veht-mahn duh) fahm ahn-sant
mobile phones	portables por-tah-bluh
stationery (office supplies, cards)	papeterie pah-peh-tuh-ree

Department stores, like the popular Printemps chain, sell nearly everything and are a good place to get cheap souvenirs and postcards. Most have a directory (often with English) by the escalator or elevator.

Street Markets

There are two types of street markets. The more common and colorful ***les marchés*** feature products from local farmers and artisans. ***Les marchés brocantes*** specialize in quasi-antiques and flea-market bric-a-brac.

Did you make this?	C'est vous qui l'avez fait? say voo kee lah-vay fay
Is this made in France?	C'est fabriqué en France? say fah-bree-kay ahn frahns
How much is it?	C'est combien? say kohn-bee-an
Cheaper?	Moins cher? mwan shehr
Will you take ____? (name price)	Est-ce que vous prendriez ____? ehs kuh voo prahn-dree-ay ____
Is it cheaper if I buy several?	C'est moins cher si j'en achète plusieurs? say mwan shehr see zhahn ah-sheht plewz-yur
Good price.	C'est un bon prix. say uhn bohn pree

My last offer.	Ma dernière offre. mah dehrn-yehr oh-fruh
I'll take it.	Je le prends. zhuh luh prahn
We'll take it.	Nous le prenons. noo luh pruh-nohn
I'm nearly broke.	Je suis presque fauché. zhuh swee prehsk foh-shay
We're nearly broke.	Nous sommes presque fauché. noo suhm prehsk foh-shay
My friend...	Mon ami... mohn ah-mee
My husband...	Mon mari... mohn mah-ree
My wife...	Ma femme... mah fahm
...has the money.	...a l'argent. ah lar-zhahn

It's OK to bargain at street markets, though not every vendor will drop prices. Expect to pay cash and be wary of pickpockets. For help with numbers, see page 26.

WHAT TO BUY

Here are some of the items you might buy, ranging from souvenirs to clothing to jewelry. For personal care items, see page 292. For electronics, see page 254.

Souvenirs

Do you have a...?	Vous avez...? vooz ah-vay
I'd like a...	Je voudrais... zhuh voo-dray
book	un livre uhn lee-vruh
guidebook	un guide uhn geed
children's book	un livre d'enfant uhn lee-vruh dahn-fahn
bookmark	un marque-page uhn mark-pahzh
calendar	un calendrier uhn kah-lahn-dree-ay
candle	une bougie ewn boo-zhee

doll	une poupée ewn poo-pay
journal	un journal uhn zhoor-nahl
magnet	un aimant uhn eh-mahn
notecards	des fiches day feesh
ornament	un ornament uhn or-nah-mahn
pen / pencil	un stylo / un crayon uhn stee-loh / uhn kray-ohn
postcard	une carte postale ewn kart poh-stahl
poster	une affiche ewn ah-feesh
print	une estampe / gravure ewn ehs-tahnp / grah-vewr
toy	un jouet uhn zhoo-ay
umbrella	un parapluie uhn pah-rah-plwee

Clothing

clothing	vêtement veht-mahn
This one.	Celui-ci. suhl-wee-see
Can I try it on?	Je peux l'essayer? zhuh puh lay-say-yay
Do you have a...?	Vous avez...? vooz ah-vay
...mirror	...un miroir uhn meer-wahr
...fitting room	...une salle d'essayage ewn sahl day-say-ahzh
It's too...	C'est trop... say troh
...expensive.	...cher. shehr
...big / small.	...grand / petit. grahn / puh-tee
...short / long.	...court / long. koor / lohn
...tight / loose.	...serré / grand. suh-ray / grahn
...dark / light.	...foncé / clair. fohn-say / klair
Do you have a different color / a different pattern?	Avez-vous une couleur différente / un motif différent? ah-vay-voo ewn koo-lur dee-fay-rahnt / uhn moh-teef dee-fay-rahn

What's this made of?	C'est en quoi ça? say ahn kwah sah
Is it machine washable?	C'est lavable en machine? say lah-vah-bluh ahn mah-sheen
Will it shrink?	Ça va rétrécir? sah vah ray-tray-seer
Will it fade in the wash?	Ça va déteindre au lavage? sah vah day-tan-druh oh lah-vahzh
Dry clean only?	Nettoyage à sec seulement? neh-twah-yahzh ah sehk suhl-mahn

For a list of colors, see page 248, and for fabrics, see page 249.

Types of Clothes and Accessories

For a...	Pour... poor
...man.	...un homme. uhn ohm
...woman.	...une femme. ewn fahm
...male teen.	...un adolescent. uhn ah-doh-luh-sahn
...female teen.	...une adolescente. ewn ah-doh-luh-sahnt
...male child.	...un petit garçon. uhn puh-tee gar-sohn
...female child.	...une petite fille. ewn puh-teet fee
...baby boy / girl.	...un bébé garçon / fille. uhn bay-bay gar-sohn / fee
I'm looking for a...	Je cherche... zhuh shehrsh
I want to buy a...	Je veux acheter... zhuh vuh ah-shuh-tay
bathrobe	un peignoir de bain uhn pehn-wahr duh ban
bib	un bavoir uhn bah-vwahr
belt	une ceinture ewn san-tewr
bra	un soutien-gorge uhn soo-tee-an-gorzh
dress	une robe ewn rohb
flip-flops	des tongs day tohn-guh
gloves	des gants day gahn

handbag	un sac à main uhn sahk ah man
hat	un chapeau uhn shah-poh
jacket	une veste ewn vehst
jeans	un jean uhn "jean"
leggings	un caleçon uhn kahl-sohn
nightgown	une chemise de nuit ewn shuh-meez duh nwee
nylons	des bas nylon day bah nee-lohn
pajamas	un pyjama uhn pee-zhah-mah
pants	un pantalon uhn pahn-tah-lohn
raincoat	un imperméable uhn an-pehr-may-ah-bluh
sandals	des sandales day sahn-dahl
scarf	un foulard uhn foo-lar
shirt...	une chemise... ewn shuh-meez
...long-sleeved	...à manches longues ah mahnsh lohn-guh
...short-sleeved	...à manches courtes ah mahnsh koort
...sleeveless	...sans manche sahn mahnsh
shoelaces	des lacets day lah-say
shoes	des chaussures day shoh-sewr
shorts	un short uhn short
skirt	une jupe ewn zhewp
sleeper (for baby)	une grenouillière / un pyjama (pour bébé) ewn gruh-noo-yehr / uhn pee-zhah-mah (poor bay-bay)
slip	un jupon uhn zhew-pohn
slippers	des chaussons day shoh-sohn
socks	des chaussettes day shoh-seht
sweater	un pull uhn pewl
swimsuit	un maillot de bain uhn mī-yoh duh ban
tank top	un débardeur uhn day-bar-dur

tennis shoes	des baskets day bahs-keht
tie	une cravate ewn krah-vaht
tights	un collant uhn koh-lahn
T-shirt	un T-shirt uhn "T-shirt"
underwear	des sous vêtements day soo veht-mahn
vest	un gilet uhn zhee-lay
wallet	un portefeuille uhn por-tuh-fuh-ee

Clothing Sizes

extra-small	extra-small "extra-small"
small	small "small"
medium	medium "medium"
large	large "large"
extra-large	extra-large "extra-large"
I need a bigger / smaller size.	J'ai besoin d'une plus grande / plus petite taille. zhay buh-zwan dewn plew grahnd / plew puh-teet tī
What's my size?	Quelle est ma taille? kehl ay mah tī

US-to-European Comparisons

When shopping for clothing, use these US-to-European comparisons as general guidelines (but note that no conversion is perfect).

Women's dresses and blouses: Add 30 (US size 10 = EU size 40)
Men's suits and jackets: Add 10 (US size 40 regular = EU size 50)
Men's shirts: Multiply by 2 and add about 8 (US size 15 collar = EU size 38)
Women's shoes: Add about 30 (US size 8 = EU size 38½)
Men's shoes: Add 32-34 (US size 9 = EU size 41; US size 11 = EU size 45)
Children's clothing: Small children, subtract 1 (US size 10 = EU size 9); juniors, subtract 4 (US size 14 = EU size 10)

Girls' shoes: Add 16–17 (US size 10 = EU size 26); over size 13 use women's sizes

Boys' shoes: Add 17.5–18 (US size 11 = EU size 29); over size 13 use men's sizes

Sew What?

Traveling is hard on clothes.

I need...	J'ai besoin... zhay buh-zwan
...a button.	...d'un bouton. duhn boo-tohn
...a needle.	...d'une aiguille. dewn ay-gwee
...thread.	...de fil. duh feel
...scissors.	...de ciseaux. duh see-zoh
...stain remover.	...d'un détachant. duhn day-tah-shahn
...a new zipper.	...d'une nouvelle fermeture à glissière. dewn noo-vehl fehr-muh-tewr ah glees-yehr
Can you fix it?	Pouvez-vous le réparer? poo-vay-voo luh ray-pah-ray

Colors

black	noir nwahr
blue	bleu bluh
brown	marron mah-rohn
gray	gris gree
green	vert vehr
orange	orange oh-rahnzh
pink	rose rohz
purple	violet vee-oh-lay
red	rouge roozh
white	blanc blahn
yellow	jaune zhohn

dark(er)	(plus) foncé (plew) fohn-say
light(er)	(plus) clair (plew) klair
bright(er)	(plus) coloré (plew) koh-loh-ray

Fabrics

What's this made of?	C'est en quoi ça? say ahn kwah sah
A mix of...	Un mélange de... uhn may-lahnzh duh
cashmere	cachemire kahsh-meer
cotton	cotton koh-tohn
denim	denim deh-neem
flannel	flanelle flah-nehl
fleece	laine polaire lehn poh-lair
lace	dentelle dahn-tehl
leather	cuir kweer
linen	lin lan
nylon	nylon nee-lohn
polyester	polyester poh-lee-ehs-tehr
silk	soie swah
velvet	velours vuh-loor
wool	laine lehn

Jewelry

jewelry	bijoux bee-zhoo
fine jewelry shop	une boutique de joaillerie ewn boo-teek duh zhoh-ī-ree
cheap fashion jewelry shop	une bijouterie bon marché ewn bee-zhoo-tuh-ree bohn mar-shay
bracelet	bracelet brahs-lay
brooch	broche brohsh

cuff links	des boutons de manchette day boo-tohn duh mahn-sheht
earrings	boucles d'oreille boo-kluh doh-ray
necklace	collier kohl-yay
ring	bague bahg
watch	montre mohn-truh
watch battery	pile de montre peel duh mohn-truh
silver / gold	argent / or ar-zhahn / or
Is this...?	C'est...? say
...sterling silver	...de l'argent duh lar-zhahn
...real gold	...de l'or véritable duh lor vay-ree-tah-bluh
...handmade	...fabriqué à la main fah-bree-kay ah lah man
...made in France	...fabriqué en France fah-bree-kay ahn frahns
...stolen	...volé voh-lay

SHIPPING AND MAIL

If you need to ship packages home, head for ***la Poste*** (post office), which is often marked ***PTT*** (for its old name, ***Postes, Télégraphes et Téléphones***). Otherwise, you can often get stamps at a ***tabac*** (tobacco shop).

At the Post Office

post office	la Poste / PTT lah pohst / pay tay tay
Where is the post office?	Où est la Poste? oo ay lah pohst
stamps	timbres tan-bruh
postcard	carte postale kart poh-stahl
letter	lettre leht-ruh
package	colis koh-lee

window / line	guichet / file gee-shay / feel
Which window for _____?	Quel guichet pour _____? kehl gee-shay poor _____
Is this the line for _____?	C'est la file pour _____? say lah feel poor _____
I need...	J'ai besoin... zhay buh-zwan
...to buy stamps.	...d'acheter des timbres. dah-shuh-tay day tan-bruh
...to mail a package.	...d'envoyer un colis. dahn-vwah-yay uhn koh-lee
to the United States	pour les Etats-Unis poor layz ay-tah-zew-nee
by air mail	par avion par ah-vee-ohn
by express mail	par express par ehk-sprehs
by surface mail	par surface par sewr-fahs
slow and cheap	lent et pas cher lahn ay pah shehr
How much is it?	C'est combien? say kohn-bee-an
How much to send a letter / postcard to _____?	Combien pour envoyer une lettre / carte postale pour _____? kohn-bee-an poor ahn-voh-yay ewn leht-ruh / kart poh-stahl poor _____
Pretty stamps, please.	De jolis timbres, s'il vous plaît. duh zhoh-lee tan-bruh see voo play
Can I buy a box?	Puis-je acheter une boîte? pweezh ah-shuh-tay ewn bwaht
This big.	De cette taille. duh seht tī
Do you have tape?	Avez-vous du scotch? ah-vay-voo dew skohtch
How many days will it take?	Ça va prendre combien de jours? sah vah prahn-druh kohn-bee-an duh zhoor
I always choose the slowest line.	Je choisis toujours la file la plus lente. zhuh shwah-zee too-zhoor lah feel lah plew lahnt

Bigger post offices may have windows labeled ***Timbres*** or ***Affranchissement*** for stamps, ***Envoi de Colis*** for packages, and ***Toutes Opérations*** for all services. If you need to ***prenez un numéro*** (take a number), watch the board listing the ***numéro appelé*** (number currently being served) and ***guichet*** (window) to report to.

Licking the Postal Code

to / from	à / de ah / duh
address	adresse ah-drehs
zip code	code postal kohd poh-stahl
envelope	enveloppe ahn-vuh-lohp
package	colis koh-lee
box	boîte bwaht
packing material	matériaux d'emballage mah-tay-ree-oh dahn-bah-lahzh
tape	scotch skohtch
string	ficelle fee-sehl
mailbox	boîte aux lettres bwaht oh leht-ruh
book rate	tarif-livres tah-reef-lee-vruh
weight limit	poids limite pwah lee-meet
registered	enregistré ahn-ruh-zhee-stray
insured	assuré ah-sew-ray
fragile	fragile frah-zheel
contents	contenu kohn-tuh-new
customs	douane doo-ahn
tracking number	numéro de suivi new-may-roh duh swee-vee

Post offices sell sturdy boxes, which you can assemble, fill with souvenirs, and mail home...so you can keep packing light.

TECHNOLOGY

This chapter covers phrases for your tech needs—from buying earbuds to taking photos, from making phone calls (using mobile or landline phones) to getting online (using your portable device or at a public Internet terminal).

TECH TERMS

Portable Devices and Accessories

I need a...	J'ai besoin de... zhay buh-zwan duh
Do you have a...?	Avez-vous...? ah-vay-voo
Where can I buy a...?	Où puis-je acheter...? oo pweezh ah-shuh-tay
battery (for my ____)	une pile (pour mon ____) ewn peel (poor mohn ____)
battery charger	un chargeur de piles uhn shar-zhur duh peel
charger	un chargeur uhn shar-zhur
computer	un ordinateur uhn or-dee-nah-tur
convertor	un convertisseur uhn kohn-vehr-tee-sur
CD / DVD	un CD / DVD uhn say day / day vay day
ebook reader	un ereader uhn ee-ree-dehr
electrical adapter	un adaptateur électrique uhn ah-dahp-tah-tur ay-lehk-treek
flash drive	une carte mémoire flash ewn kart may-mwahr flahsh
headphones / earbuds	un casque / les écouteurs uhn kahsk / layz ay-koo-tur
iPod / MP3 player	iPod / un balladeur MP3 "iPod" / uhn bah-lah-dur ehm pay trwah
laptop	un ordinateur portable / laptop uhn or-dee-nah-tur por-tah-bluh / "laptop"
memory card	une carte mémoire ewn kart may-mwahr

mobile phone	un portable uhn por-tah-bluh
SIM card	une carte SIM ewn kart seem
speakers (for my ____)	des haut-parleurs (pour mon ____) dayz oh-par-lur (poor mohn ____)
tablet	une tablette ewn tah-bleht
(mini) USB cable	un (petit) câble USB uhn (puh-tee) kah-bluh ew ehs bay
USB key	clé USB klay ew ehs bay
video game	un jeu vidéo uhn zhuh vee-day-oh
Wi-Fi	Wi-Fi wee-fee

Familiar brands (like iPad, Facebook, YouTube, Instagram, or whatever the latest craze is) are just as popular in Europe as they are back home. Invariably, these go by their English names (sometimes with a French accent).

Cameras

camera	un appareil-photo uhn ah-pah-ray-foh-toh
digital camera	un appareil-photo numérique uhn ah-pah-ray-foh-toh new-may-reek
video camera	une caméra vidéo ewn kah-may-rah vee-day-oh
lens cap	un bouchon d'objectif uhn boo-shohn dohb-zhehk-teef
film (for cameras)	la pellicule lah peh-lee-kewl
Can I / Can you download my photos onto a CD?	Puis-je / Pouvez-vous graver mes photos sur un CD? pweezh / poo-vay-voo grah-vay may foh-tohs sewr uhn say day
Will you take my / our photo?	Vous pouvez prendre ma / notre photo? voo poo-vay prahn-druh mah / noh-truh foh-toh

Can I take a photo of you?	Je peux prendre votre photo? zhuh puh prahn-druh voh-truh foh-toh
Smile!	Souriez! soo-ree-ay

You'll find words for batteries, chargers, and more in the previous list.

TELEPHONES

Travelers have several phoning options. A mobile phone provides the best combination of practicality and flexibility. Public pay phones are available, but increasingly rare (and often require buying an insertable phone card). You can also make calls online (using Skype or a similar program) and from your hotel room. As this is a fast-changing scene, check my latest tips at www.ricksteves.com/phoning.

Telephone Terms

telephone	téléphone tay-lay-fohn
phone call...	appel téléphonique... ah-pehl tay-lay-foh-neek
...local	...local loh-kahl
...domestic	...national nah-see-oh-nahl
...international	...international an-tehr-nah-see-oh-nahl
...toll-free	...gratuit grah-twee
...with a credit card	...avec une carte de crédit ah-vehk ewn kart duh kray-dee
...collect	...en PCV ahn pay say vay
mobile phone	un portable uhn por-tah-bluh
mobile number	numéro de portable new-may-roh duh por-tah-bluh
landline	numéro fixe new-may-roh feeks
fax	fax fahks
operator	standardiste stahn-dar-deest

Key Phrases: Telephones

telephone	téléphone tay-lay-fohn
phone call	appel téléphonique ah-pehl tay-lay-foh-neek
mobile phone	un portable uhn por-tah-bluh
Where is the nearest phone?	Où est le téléphone le plus proche? oo ay luh tay-lay-fohn luh plew prohsh
May I use your phone?	Je peux téléphoner? zhuh puh tay-lay-foh-nay
Where is a mobile phone shop?	Où est un magasin de portables? oo ay uhn mah-gah-zan duh por-tah-bluh

directory assistance	les renseignements lay rahn-sehn-yuh-mahn
phone book	bottin / annuaire boh-tan / ah-new-air

France has a direct-dial 10-digit phone system (no area codes). For phone tips—including a calling chart for dialing European numbers—see the Appendix chapter (page 423).

Making Calls

Where is the nearest phone?	Où est le téléphone le plus proche? oo ay luh tay-lay-fohn luh plew prohsh
May I use your phone?	Je peux téléphoner? zhuh puh tay-lay-foh-nay
Can you talk for me?	Vous pouvez parler pour moi? voo poo-vay par-lay poor mwah
It's busy.	C'est occupé. say oh-kew-pay
This doesn't work.	Ça ne marche pas. sah nuh marsh pah

out of service	hors service or sehr-vees
Try again?	Essayez de nouveau? ay-say-yay duh noo-voh

If the number you're calling is out of service, you'll likely hear this recording: ***Le numéro que vous demandez n'est pas attribué.***

On the Phone

Hello, this is ____.	Âllo, c'est ____. ah-loh say ____
My name is ____.	Je m'appelle ____. zhuh mah-pehl ____
Do you speak English?	Parlez-vous anglais? par-lay-voo ahn-glay
Sorry, I speak only a little French.	Désolé, je parle seulement un petit peu de français. day-zoh-lay zhuh parl suhl-mahn uhn puh-tee puh duh frahn-say
Speak slowly, please.	Parlez lentement, s'il vous plaît. par-lay lahnt-mahn see voo play
Wait a moment.	Un moment. uhn moh-mahn

The French answer a call by saying simply ***Allô*** (Hello).

In this book, you'll find the phrases you need to reserve a hotel room (page 80) or a table at a restaurant (page 105). To spell your name over the phone, refer to the code alphabet on page 17.

Mobile Phones

Your US mobile phone should work in Europe if it's GSM-enabled, tri-band or quad-band, and on a calling plan that includes international service. Alternatively, you can buy a phone in Europe.

mobile phone	un portable uhn por-tah-bluh
smartphone	un smartphone uhn "smartphone"
roaming	itinérance / roaming ee-teen-ehr-ahns / "roaming"

text message	SMS / texto "SMS" / tehk-stoh
Where is a mobile phone shop?	Où est un magasin de portables? oo ay uhn mah-gah-zan duh por-tah-bluh
I'd like to buy...	Je voudrais acheter... zhuh voo-dray ah-shuh-tay
...a (cheap) mobile phone.	...un portable (pas cher). uhn por-tah-bluh (pah shehr)
...a SIM card.	...une carte SIM. ewn kart seem
prepaid credit	unités prépayées ew-nee-tay pray-pay-ay
calling time	temps d'appel tahn dah-pehl
contract	abonnement ah-buhn-mahn
band	bande bahnd
tri-band / quad band	tri-bande / quatri-bande tree-bahnd / kah-tree-bahnd
locked	bloqué bloh-kay
unlocked	debloqué day-bloh-kay
Is this phone unlocked?	Est-ce que ce téléphone est débloqué? ehs kuh suh tay-lay-fohn ay day-bloh-kay
Can you unlock this phone?	Pouvez-vous débloquer ce téléphone? poo-vay-voo day-bloh-kay suh tay-lay-fohn
How do I...?	Comment puis-je...? koh-mahn pweezh
...make calls	...appeler ah-puh-lay
...receive calls	...recevoir les appels ruh-suh-vwahr layz ah-pehl
...send a text message	...envoyer un SMS / texto ahn-vwoh-yay uhn "SMS" / tehk-stoh
...check my voicemail	...vérifier ma boîte vocale vehr-ee-fee-ay mah bwaht voh-kahl
...set the language to English	...paramétrer la langue en anglais pah-rah-may-tray lah lahng ahn ahn-glay

...mute the ringer	...appuyer sur la touche sourdine ah-pwee-yay sewr lah toosh soor-deen
...change the ringer	...changer la sonnerie shahn-zhay lah suhn-ree
...turn it on	...allumer ah-lew-may
...turn it off	...éteindre ay-tan-druh

Buying a Mobile Phone SIM Card

The simplest (but potentially most expensive) solution is to roam with your US phone in Europe. If your phone is unlocked ***(debloqué),*** you can save money by buying a cheap European SIM card (which usually comes with some calling credit) at a mobile-phone shop or a newsstand. After inserting a SIM card in your phone, you'll have a European number and pay lower European rates.

Where can I buy...?	Où puis-je acheter...? oo pweezh ah-shuh-tay
I'd like to buy...	Je voudrais acheter... zhuh voo-dray ah-shuh-tay
...a SIM card.	...une carte SIM. ewn kart seem
...more calling time.	...plus de temps. plew duh tahn
Will this SIM card work in my phone?	Est-ce que cette carte SIM va fonctionner avec mon téléphone? ehs kuh seht kart seem vah fohnk-see-oh-nay ah-vehk mohn tay-lay-fohn
Which SIM card is best for my phone?	Quelle carte SIM est la meilleure pour mon téléphone? kehl kart seem ay lah meh-ur poor mohn tay-lay-fohn
How much per minute for...?	Combien par minute pour...? kohn-bee-an par mee-newt poor
...making...	...émettre... ay-meh-truh
...receiving...	...recevoir... ruh-suh-vwahr

...domestic calls	...appels nationaux ah-pehl nah-see-oh-noh
...international calls	...appels internationaux ah-pehl an-tehr-nah-see-oh-noh
...calls to the US	...appels vers les Etats-Unis ah-pehl vehr layz ay-tah-zew-nee
How much for text messages?	Combien par SMS / texto? kohn-bee-an par "SMS" / tehk-stoh
How much credit is included?	Combien y-a-til d'unités incluses? kohn-bee-an yah-teel dew-nee-tay an-klewz
Can I roam with this card in another country?	Puis-je passer des appels depuis un pays étranger? pweezh pah-say dayz ah-pehl duh-pwee uhn pay-ee ay-trahn-zhay
Do you have a list of rates?	Avez-vous une liste des tarifs? ah-vay-voo ewn leest day tah-reef
How do I...?	Comment puis-je...? koh-mahn pweezh
...insert this into the phone	...insérer ceci dans mon téléphone an-say-ray suh-see dahn mohn tay-lay-fohn
...check the credit balance	...vérifier le nombre d'unités restantes vehr-ee-fee-ay luh nohn-bruh dew-nee-tay rehs-tahnt
...buy more time	...acheter des unités ah-shuh-tay dayz ew-nee-tay
...change the language to English	...paramétrer la langue sur anglais pah-rah-may-tray lah lahng sewr ahn-glay
...turn off the SIM PIN	...invalider la sécurité code PIN an-vahl-ee-day lah say-kew-ree-tay kohd peen

Each time you turn on your phone, you'll be prompted to punch in the **SIM PIN** (the numerical code that came with your SIM card). Before leaving the shop, have the clerk help you set up your new SIM card. Ask to have the prompts and messages changed to English; find out if it's possible to turn off the SIM PIN feature; and be sure you know how to check your balance and add more time (typically you can buy top-ups at mobile-phone shops, newsstands, and grocery stores wherever you see the symbol of your mobile-phone company).

Pay Phones and Hotel-Room Phones

If you want to use a phone booth or your hotel-room phone, buy a phone card at a newsstand or tobacco shop. There are two types. The insertable card (***télécarte,*** tay-lay-kart) is designed to stick directly into a slot in a public pay phone. The cheap international "code card" (***carte à code,*** kart ah kohd) comes with a toll-free access number and a PIN that work from any phone.

Where is a public pay phone?	Où y-a-t-il un téléphone public payant? oo yah-teel uhn tay-lay-fohn pew-bleek pay-yahn
Can I call from my room?	Est-ce que je peux appeler depuis ma chambre? ehs kuh zhuh puh ah-peh-lay duh-pwee mah shahn-bruh
How do I dial out?	Comment puis-je passer un appel vers l'extérieur? koh-mahn pweezh pah-say uhn ah-pehl vehr lehks-tay-ree-ur
How much per minute for a...?	Combien la minute pour un...? kohn-bee-an lah mee-newt poor uhn
...local call	...appel local ah-pehl loh-kahl
...domestic call	...appel national ah-pehl nah-see-oh-nahl
...international call	...appel international ah-pehl an-tehr-nah-see-oh-nahl
Can I dial this number for free?	Puis-je appeler ce numéro gratuitement? pweezh ah-puh-lay suh new-may-roh grah-tweet-mahn

GETTING ONLINE

To get online in Europe, you can bring your own portable device or use public Internet terminals (such as the ones at an Internet café, library, or your hotel).

Internet Terms

Internet access	accès à l'internet ahk-seh ah lan-tehr-neht
Wi-Fi	Wi-Fi wee-fee
email	email ee-mehl
computer	ordinateur or-dee-nah-tur
Internet café	café internet kah-fay an-tehr-neht
surf the Web	surfer le web sewr-fay luh wehb
username	nom d'utilisateur nohn dew-tee-lee-zah-tur
password	mot de passe moh duh pahs
network key	mot de passe pour le réseau moh duh pahs poor luh ray-zoh
secure network	un réseau sûr / un réseau en sécurité uhn ray-zoh sewr / uhn ray-zoh ahn say-kew-ree-tay
website	site web seet wehb
homepage	page d'accueil pahzh dah-kuh-ee
download	télécharger tay-lay-shar-zhay
print	imprimer an-pree-may
My email address is ____.	Mon adresse email est ____. mohn ah-drehs ee-mehl ay ____
What's your email address?	Quelle est votre adresse email? kehl ay voh-truh ah-drehs ee-mehl

Note that a few terms look the same as in English, but are pronounced differently: ***www*** (doo-bluh-vay, doo-bluh-vay, doo-bluh-vay); ***Wi-Fi*** (wee-fee); ***CD*** (say day); ***DVD*** (day vay day); ***MP3*** (ehm pay trwah); and ***USB*** (ew ehs bay).

Key Phrases: Getting Online

Where is a Wi-Fi hotspot?	Où se trouve un point Wi-Fi? oo suh troov uhn pwan wee-fee
Where can I get online?	Où puis-je me connecter? oo pweezh muh koh-nehk-tay
Where is an Internet café?	Où se trouve un café internet? oo suh troov uhn kah-fay an-tehr-neht
Can I check my email?	Je peux regarder mon email? zhuh puh ruh-gar-day mohn ee-mehl

Tech Support

Help me, please.	Aidez-moi, s'il vous plaît. eh-day-mwah see voo play
How do I...?	Comment je...? koh-mahn zhuh
...start this	...démarre ça day-mar sah
...get online	...me connecte muh koh-nehkt
...get this to work	...fais marcher ça fay mar-shay sah
...stop this	....arrête ça ah-reht sah
...send this	...envoie ça ahn-vwah sah
...print this	...imprime ça an-preem sah
...make this symbol	...fais ce symbole fay suh san-bohl
...copy and paste	...fais un copier-coller fay uhn kohp-yay-koh-lay
...type @	...tape arobase tahp ah-roh-bahz
This doesn't work.	Ça ne marche pas. sah nuh marsh pah

Using Your Own Portable Device

If you have a smartphone, tablet computer, laptop, or other wireless device, you can get online at many hotels, cafés, and public hotspots.

Most Internet access is Wi-Fi (pronounced wee-fee), but occasionally you'll connect by plugging an Ethernet cable directly into your laptop. While Internet access is often free, sometimes you'll have to pay.

laptop	ordinateur portable / laptop or-dee-nah-tur por-tah-bluh / "laptop"
tablet	tablette tah-bleht
smartphone	smartphone "smartphone"
Where is a Wi-Fi hotspot?	Où se trouve un point Wi-Fi? oo suh troov uhn pwan wee-fee
Do you have Wi-Fi?	Avez-vous le Wi-Fi? ah-vay-voo luh wee-fee
What is the...?	C'est quoi le...? say kwah luh
...network name	...nom du réseau nohn dew ray-zoh
...username	...nom d'utilisateur nohn dew-tee-lee-zah-tur
...password	...mot de passe moh duh pahs
Do I need a cable?	J'ai besoin d'un câble? zhay buh-zwan duhn kah-bluh
Do you have a...?	Vous avez un...? vooz ah-vay uhn
Can I borrow a...?	Je peux emprunter un...? zhuh puh ahn-pruhn-tay uhn
...charging cable	...câble pour charger kah-bluh poor shar-zhay
...Ethernet cable	...câble ethernet kah-bluh "ethernet"
...USB cable	...câble USB kah-bluh ew ehs bay
Free?	Gratuit? grah-twee
How much?	Combien? kohn-bee-an
Do I have to buy something to use the Internet?	J'ai besoin d'acheter quelque chose pour utiliser l'internet? zhay buh-zwan dah-shuh-tay kehl-kuh shohz poor ew-tee-lee-zay lan-tehr-neht

Using a Public Internet Terminal

Many hotels have terminals in the lobby for guests to get online; otherwise, an Internet café is usually nearby.

Where can I get online?	Où puis-je me connecter? oo pweezh muh koh-nehk-tay
Where is an Internet café?	Où se trouve un café internet? oo suh troov uhn kah-fay an-tehr-neht
Can I use this computer to...?	Je peux utiliser cet ordinateur pour...? zhuh puh ew-tee-lee-zay seht or-dee-nah-tur poor
...get online	...me connecter muh koh-nehk-tay
...check my email	...regarder mon email ruh-gar-day mohn ee-mehl
...download photos	...télécharger des photos tay-lay-shar-zhay day foh-toh
...print (something)	...imprimer (quelque chose) an-pree-may (kehl-kuh shohz)
boarding passes	cartes d'embarquement kart dahn-bar-kuh-mahn
tickets	billets bee-yay
reservation confirmation	confirmer une réservation kohn-feer-may ewn ray-zehr-vah-see-ohn
Free?	Gratuit? grah-twee
How much (for... minutes)?	C'est combien (pour... minutes)? say kohn-bee-an (poor... mee-newt)
...10	...dix dees
...15	...quinze kanz
...30	...trente trahnt
...60	...soixante swah-sahnt
I have a...	J'ai... zhay
Do you have a...?	Avez-vous...? ah-vay-voo
...webcam	...une webcam ewn "webcam"

...headset	...des écouteurs dayz ay-koo-tur
...USB cable	...un câble USB uhn kah-bluh ew ehs bay
...memory card	...une carte mémoire ewn kart may-mwahr
...flash drive	...une carte mémoire flash ewn kart may-mwahr flahsh
...USB key	...une clé USB ewn klay ew ehs bay
Can you switch the keyboard to American?	Vous-pourriez changer le clavier au format américain? vooz-poo-ree-ay shahn-zhay luh klah-vee-ay oh for-maht ah-may-ree-kan

If you're using a public Internet terminal, the keyboard, menus, and on-screen commands will likely be designed for French speakers. Some computers allow you to make the French keyboard work as if it were an American one (ask the clerk if it's possible).

French Keyboards

On French keyboards, most command keys differ, and some keys are in a different location. For example, the **M** key is where the semicolon is on American keyboards. The **A** and **Q** keys and the **Z** and **W** keys are reversed from American keyboards. Here's a rundown of how major commands are labeled on a French keyboard:

YOU'LL SEE...	IT MEANS...	YOU'LL SEE...	IT MEANS...
Entrée	Enter	**Suppr**	Delete
Maj	Shift	←	Backspace
Ctrl	Ctrl	**Inser**	Insert
Alt	Alt	↖	Home
Verr Maj	Shift Lock	**Fin**	End
Verr Num	Num Lock	**Page Haut**	Page Up
Tab	Tab	**Page Bas**	Page Down
Echap	Esc		

The Alt key to the right of the space bar is actually a different key, called **Alt Gr** (for "Alternate Graphics"). Press this key to insert the extra symbol that appears on some keys (such as the € in the corner of the E key).

A few often-used keys look the same, but have different names in French:

@ sign	signe arobase	seen-yuh ah-roh-bahz
dot	point	pwan
hyphen (-)	tiret	tee-ray
underscore (_)	souligne	soo-leen-yuh
slash (/)	barre oblique / "slash"	bar oh-bleek / "slahsh"

French speakers have several names for the @ sign, but the most common is ***arobase.*** When saying an email address, you say ***arobase*** in the middle.

To type @, press **Alt Gr** and the **à/0** key. Belgian keyboards may require pressing **Alt Gr** and the **é/2** key. If that doesn't work, try copying-and-pasting the @ sign from elsewhere on the page.

On Screen

YOU'LL SEE...	IT MEANS...	YOU'LL SEE...	IT MEANS...
Réseau	Network	**Aperçu**	View
Utilisateur (nom)	User (name)	**Insérer**	Insert
Mot de passe	Password	**Format**	Format
Clef / Clé	Key	**Outils**	Tools
Dossier	Folder	**Aide**	Help
Fichier	File	**Options**	Options
Nouveau	New	**Mail**	Mail
Ouvrir	Open	**Message**	Message
Fermer	Close	**Répondre à tous**	Reply All
Sauver	Save	**CC**	CC
Imprimer	Print	**Réexpédier**	Forward
Annuler	Delete	**Envoyer**	Send

YOU'LL SEE...	IT MEANS...	YOU'LL SEE...	IT MEANS...
Rechercher	Search	**Recevoir**	Receive
Éditer	Edit	**Boîte de réception**	Inbox
Couper	Cut	**Pièces jointes / Document joints / Joindre**	Attach
Copier	Copy	**Expédier**	Upload
Coller	Paste	**Télécharge**	Download
Paramétres	Settings		

HELP!

These phrases will help you in case of a medical emergency, theft, loss, fire, or—if you're a woman—harassment. France's medical emergency phone number is 15; for police, dial 17. ***SOS médecins*** are doctors who make emergency house calls. If you need help, someone will call an ***SOS médecin*** for you. If you're lost, see the phrases on page 74.

EMERGENCIES

Medical Help

Help!	Au secours! oh suh-koor
Help me, please.	Aidez-moi, s'il vous plaît. eh-day-mwah see voo play
emergency	urgence ewr-zhahns
accident	accident ahk-see-dahn
medical clinic / hospital	clinique médicale / hôpital klee-neek may-dee-kahl / oh-pee-tahl
Call...	Appelez... ah-puh-lay
...a doctor.	...un docteur. uhn dohk-tur
...the police.	...la police. lah poh-lees
...an ambulance.	...le SAMU. luh sah-moo
I need / We need...	J'ai besoin / Nous avons besoin... zhay buh-zwan / nooz ah-vohn buh-zwan
...a doctor.	...un docteur. uhn dohk-tur
...to go to the hospital.	...d'aller à l'hôpital. dah-lay ah loh-pee-tahl
It's urgent.	C'est urgent. say ewr-zhahn
injured	blessé bleh-say
bleeding	saigne sehn-yuh
choking	étouffe ay-toof
unconscious	inconscient an-kohn-see-ahn
not breathing	ne respire pas nuh rehs-peer pah

Key Phrases: Help!

Help!	Au secours! oh suh-koor
emergency	urgence ewr-zhahns
clinic / hospital	clinique médicale / hôpital klee-neek may-dee-kahl / oh-pee-tahl
Call a doctor.	Appelez un docteur. ah-puh-lay uhn dohk-tur
ambulance	SAMU sah-moo
police	police poh-lees
thief	voleur voh-lur
Stop, thief!	Arrêtez, au voleur! ah-reh-tay oh voh-lur

Thank you for your help.	Merci pour votre aide. mehr-see poor voh-truh ehd
You are very kind.	Vous êtes très gentil. vooz eht treh zhahn-tee

If you need someone to come and get you because you're having a heart attack, you need the ***SAMU,*** which stands for ***Service d'Aide Médicale Urgente. Ambulance*** is also a word in French, but not for emergencies. ***Les ambulances*** are for transporting people without cars to doctor's visits. For other health-related words, see the Personal Care and Health chapter.

Theft and Loss

thief	voleur voh-lur
pickpocket	pickpocket peek-poh-keht
police	police poh-lees
embassy	ambassade ahn-bah-sahd

Stop, thief!	Arrêtez, au voleur!	ah-reh-tay oh voh-lur
Call the police!	Appelez la police!	ah-puh-lay lah poh-lees
I've been robbed.	On m'a volé.	ohn mah voh-lay
We've been robbed.	Nous avons été volé.	nooz ah-vohn ay-tay voh-lay
A thief took...	Un voleur à pris...	uhn voh-lur ah pree
Thieves took...	Des voleurs ont pris...	day voh-lur ohn pree
I've lost my...	J'ai perdu mon...	zhay pehr-dew mohn
We've lost our...	Nous avons perdu nos...	nooz ah-vohn pehr-dew noh
money	argent	ar-zhahn
credit card	carte de crédit	kart duh kray-dee
passport	passeport	pahs-por
ticket	billet	bee-yay
railpass	passe Eurail	pahs "Eurail"
baggage	bagages	bah-gahzh
purse	sac	sahk
wallet	portefeuille	por-tuh-fuh-ee
watch	montre	mohn-truh
jewelry	bijoux	bee-zhoo
camera	appareil-photo	ah-pah-ray-foh-toh
mobile phone	téléphone portable	tay-lay-fohn por-tah-bluh
iPod / iPad	iPod / iPad	"iPod" / "iPad"
tablet	tablette	tah-bleht
computer	ordinateur	or-dee-nah-tur
laptop	ordinateur portable / laptop	or-dee-nah-tur por-tah-bluh / "laptop"
faith in humankind	foi en l'humanité	fwah ahn lew-mah-nee-tay

I want to contact my embassy.	Je veux contacter mon ambassade. zhuh vuh kohn-tahk-tay mohn ahn-bah-sahd
I need to file a police report (for my insurance).	Je veux porter plainte à la police (pour mon assurance). zhuh vuh por-tay plahnt ah lah poh-lees (poor mohn ah-sewr-rahns)
Where is the police station?	Où se trouve la gendarmerie? oo suh troov lah zhahn-dar-muh-ree

To replace a passport, you'll need to go in person to your embassy (see page 425). Cancel and replace your credit and debit cards by calling your credit-card company (as of this printing, these are the 24-hour US numbers that you can call collect: Visa—tel. 303/967-1096, MasterCard—tel. 636/722-7111, American Express—tel. 336/393-1111). If you'll want to submit an insurance claim for lost or stolen gear, be sure to file a police report, either on the spot or within a day or two. For more info, see www.ricksteves.com/help. Precautionary measures can minimize the effects of loss—back up your photos and other files frequently.

Fire!

fire	feu fuh
smoke	fumée few-may
exit	sortie sor-tee
emergency exit	sortie de secours sor-tee duh suh-koor
fire extinguisher	extincteur ehks-tank-tur
Call the fire department.	Appelez les pompiers. ah-puh-lay lay pohn-pee-yay

HELP FOR WOMEN

Generally the best way to react to unwanted attention is loudly and quickly.

No!	Non! nohn
Stop it!	Arrêtez! ah-reh-tay
Enough!	Ça suffit! sah sew-fee
Don't touch me.	Ne me touchez pas. nuh muh too-shay pah
Leave me alone.	Laissez-moi tranquille. lay-say-mwah trahn-keel
Go away.	Allez-vous en. ah-lay-vooz ahn
Get lost!	Dégagez! day-gah-zhay
Drop dead!	Foutez-moi la paix! foo-tay-mwah lah pay
Police!	Police! poh-lees

Safety in Numbers

If a guy is bugging you, approach a friendly-looking couple, family, or business for a place to stay safe.

A man is bothering me.	Un homme est en train de me harceler. uhn ohm ayt ahn tran duh muh ar-suh-lay
May I...?	Est-ce que je peux...? ehs kuh zhuh puh
...join you	...vous joindre voo zhwan-druh
...sit here	...m'asseoir ici mah-swahr ee-see
...wait here until he's gone	...attendez ici jusqu'à ce qu'il parte ah-tahn-day ee-see zhew-skah skeel part

You Want to Be Alone

I want to be alone.	Je veux être seule. zhuh vuh eh-truh suhl
I'm not interested.	Ça ne m'intéresse pas. sah nuh man-tay-rehs pah
I'm married.	Je suis mariée. zhuh swee mah-ree-ay
I'm waiting for my husband.	J'attends mon mari. zhah-tahn mohn mah-ree
I'm a lesbian.	Je suis lesbienne. zhuh swee lehz-bee-ehn
I have a contagious disease.	J'ai une maladie contagieuse. zhay ewn mah-lah-dee kohn-tah-zhee-uhz

SERVICES

Whether you're getting a haircut, going to a spa, getting something fixed, or doing laundry, you'll find the phrases you need in this chapter.

HAIR AND BODY

At the Hair Salon

haircut	une coupe ewn koop
Where is...?	Où se trouve...? oo suh troov
...a hair salon	...un salon de coiffure pour femmes uhn sah-lohn duh kwah-fur poor fahm
...a barber	...un salon de coiffure pour hommes uhn sah-lohn duh kwah-fur poor ohm
...the price list	...la liste des prix lah leest day pree
I'd like...	J'aimerais... zheh-may-ray
...a haircut.	...une coupe. ewn koop
...a shampoo.	...un shampooing. uhn shahn-pwan
...a wash and dry.	...un brushing. uhn "brushing"
...highlights.	...des mèches. day mehsh
...my hair colored.	...mes cheveux colorés. may shuh-vuh koh-loh-ray
...a permanent.	...une permanente. ewn pehr-mah-nahnt
...just a trim.	...juste rafraîchir. zhewst rah-freh-sheer
How much?	Combien? kohn-bee-an
Cut about this much off.	Coupez ça à peu près. koo-pay sah ah puh preh
Here. (gesturing)	Ici. ee-see
Short.	Court. koor
Shorter.	Plus court. plew koor
Shave it all off.	Rasez les tous. rah-zay lay too

As long as possible.	Aussi long que possible. oh-see lohn kuh poh-see-bluh
Longer.	Plus long. plew lohn
layered cut	une coupe dégradée ewn koop day-grah-day
bangs	franges frahnzh
Cut my bangs here.	Coupez ma frange ici. koo-pay mah frahnzh ee-see
front	devant duh-vahn
top	au dessus oh deh-sew
back	derrière dehr-ee-ehr
sides	sur les côtés sewr lay koh-tay
sideburns	pattes paht
beard / moustache	barbe / moustache bahrb / moo-stahsh
hair color	couleur de cheveux koo-lur duh shuh-vuh
blonde (m / f)	blond / blonde blohn / blohnd
brown (m / f)	brun / brune bruhn / brewn
black (m / f)	noir / noire nwahr / nwahr
red (m / f)	roux / rousse roo / roos
Please touch up my roots.	S'il vous plaît, retouchez-moi les racines. see voo play ruh-too-shay-mwah lay rah-seen
I'd like my hair...	J'aimerais mes cheveux... zheh-may-ray may shuh-vuh
...blow-dried.	...séchés. say-shay
...styled.	...stylés. stee-lay
...straightened.	...redressés. ruh-dreh-say
...wavy.	...ondulé. ohn-dew-lay
I want to look like I just got out of bed.	Je veux ressembler à quelqu'un qui sort du lit. zhuh vuh ruh-sahn-blay ah kehl-kuhn kee sor dew lee

hairspray	laque lahk
hair gel	gel à cheveux zhehl ah shuh-vuh
It looks good.	C'est bien. say bee-an
A tip for you.	Un pourboire pour vous. uhn poor-bwahr poor voo

French women often go to a salon to simply get their hair washed and dried, using the English word "brushing." ***Un brushing*** is less risky than a haircut and an affordable luxury for women visiting France.

At the Spa

spa	un spa uhn spah
spa treatment	un traitement au spa uhn treht-mahn oh spah
Where can I get...?	Où puis-je me faire...? oo pweezh muh fair
I'd like a...	Je voudrais... zhuh voo-dray
...massage.	...un modelage. uhn moh-duh-lahzh
...manicure.	...une manucure. ewn mah-new-kewr
...pedicure.	...un pédicure. ewn pay-dee-kewr
...facial.	...un masque facial. uhn mahsk fah-see-ahl
...wax.	...l'épilation à la cire. lay-pee-lah-see-ohn ah lah seer
eyebrows	les cils lay seel
upper lip	la moustache lah moo-stahsh
legs	les jambes lay zhahnb
bikini zone	le maillot luh mī-yoh
Brazilian	brésilien bray-zee-lee-an

Massage

In France, the word ***massage*** by law can only be used by physical therapists. ***Modelage*** is the term that spas use to describe a massage given by a masseuse who doesn't have a medical degree.

Where can I get a...?	Où puis-je me faire...? oo pweezh muh fair
...massage (at a spa)	...un modelage uhn moh-duh-lahzh
...massage (from physical therapist)	...un massage uhn mah-sahzh
30 minutes / 1 hour / 1½ hours	trente minutes / une heure / une heure et demie trahnt mee-newt / ewn ur / ewn ur ayd-mee
How much?	Combien? kohn-bee-an
Spend more / less time on my...	Passez plus / moins de temps sur... pah-say plews / mwan duh tahn sewr
...back.	...le dos. luh doh
...neck.	...le cou. luh koo
...shoulders.	...les épaules. layz ay-pohl
...head.	...la tête. lah teht
...arms.	...les bras. lay brah
...hands.	...les mains. lay man
...legs.	...les jambes. lay zhahnb
...feet.	...les pieds. lay pee-ay
It hurts.	Ça fait mal. sah fay mahl
Ouch!	Aïe! ī-yuh
Light / Medium / Firm pressure.	Pression légère / moyenne / ferme. preh-see-ohn lay-zhehr / moh-yehn / fehrm
Less / More pressure.	Moins de / Plus de pression. mwan duh / plew duh preh-see-ohn

Stop.	Arrêtez. ah-reh-tay
Don't stop.	N'arrêtez pas. nah-reh-tay pah
That feels good.	Ça me fait du bien. sah muh fay dew bee-an

REPAIRS

These handy lines can apply to various repairs, whether you tackle them yourself or go to a shop.

This is broken.	C'est cassé. say kah-say
Can I borrow a...?	Puis-je emprunter...? pweezh ahn-pruhn-tay
I need a...	J'ai besoin... zhay buh-zwan
screwdriver (Phillips / straight edge)	d'un tournevis (cruciforme / plat) duhn toor-nuh-vee (krew-see-form / plah)
pliers	de pinces duh pans
wrench	d'une clé dewn klay
hammer	d'un marteau duhn mar-toh
scissors	de ciseaux duh see-zoh
needle	d'une aiguille dewn ay-gwee
thread	de fil duh feel
string	de ficelle duh fee-sehl
duct tape	de ruban adhésif duh rew-bahn ah-day-zeef
Can you fix it?	Vous pouvez le réparer? voo poo-vay luh ray-pah-ray
Just do the essentials.	Ne faites que le minimum. nuh feht kuh luh mee-nee-muhm
How much will it cost?	Ça coutera combien? sah koo-tuh-rah kohn-bee-an
When will it be ready?	Ce sera prêt quand? suh suh-rah preh kahn

I need it by ____.	Il me le faut avant ____. eel muh luh foh ah-vahn ____
Without it, I'm lost.	Sans, je suis perdu. sahn zhuh swee pehr-dew

LAUNDRY

Laundry Locator

Where is a...?	Où est une...? oo ay ewn
...full-service laundry	...blanchisserie blahn-shee-suh-ree
...self-service laundry	...laverie automatique lah-vuh-ree oh-toh-mah-teek
Do you offer laundry service? (ask hotelier)	Avez-vous un service de linge? ah-vay-voo uhn sehr-vees duh lanzh
How much?	Combien? kohn-bee-an
At what time does this open / close?	À quelle heuere c'est ouvert / fermé? ah kehl ur say oo-vehr / fehr-may

Full-Service Laundry

At some launderettes, you can pay extra to have the attendant wash, dry, and fold your clothes. Be sure to clearly communicate the time you will pick it up.

full-service laundry	blanchisserie blahn-shee-suh-ree
Same-day service?	Lavé le même jour? lah-vay luh mehm zhoor
By when do I need to drop off my clothes?	Je dois déposer mon linge quand? zhuh dwah day-poh-zay mohn lanzh kahn
When will my clothes be ready?	Mon linge sera prêt quand? mohn lanzh suh-rah preh kahn

Could I get them sooner?	Je pourrais les avoir plus tôt? zhuh poo-ray layz ah-vwahr plew toh
Dried?	Séché? say-shay
Folded?	Plié? plee-ay
Ironed?	Repassé? ruh-pah-say
Please don't dry this.	Ne séchez pas ceci, s'il vous plait. nuh say-shay pah suh-see see voo play
I'll come back...	Je reviendrai... zhuh ruh-vee-an-dray
...later today.	...plus tard aujourd'hui. plew tar oh-zhoor-dwee
...tomorrow.	...demain. duh-man
...at ____ o'clock.	...à ____ heures. ah ____ ur
This isn't mine.	Ce n'est pas à moi. suh nay pah ah mwah
I'm missing a ____.	Il me manque un ____. eel muh mahnk uhn ____

For a list of clothes and colors, see pages 245 and 248.

Self-Service Laundry

self-service laundry	laverie automatique lah-vuh-ree oh-toh-mah-teek
washer / dryer	machine à laver / machine à sécher mah-sheen ah lah-vay / mah-sheen ah say-shay
soap	savon sah-vohn
laundry detergent	lessive leh-seev
softener	adoucissant ah-doo-see-sahn
stain remover	détachant day-tah-shahn
money	argent ar-zhahn
coins	pièces pee-ehs
token	jeton zhuh-tohn

Help me, please.	Aidez-moi, s'il vous plaît. eh-day-mwah see voo play
Where do I pay?	Où faut-il payer? oo foh-teel pay-ay
I need change.	J'ai besoin de monnaie. zhay buh-zwan duh moh-nay
Where is the detergent?	Où se trouve la lessive? oo suh troov lah leh-seev
Where do I put the detergent?	Où est-ce qu'il faut mettre la lessive? oo ehs keel foh meh-truh lah leh-seev
This isn't working.	Ça ne marche pas. sah nuh marsh pah
How do I start this?	Comment faut-il faire pour démarre? koh-mahn foh-teel fair poor day-mar
How long will it take?	Ca va durer combien de temps? sah vah dew-ray kohn-bee-an duh tahn
Are these yours?	C'est à vous? sayt ah voo
This stinks.	Ça pue. sah pew
This smells like...	Ça sent comme... sah sahn kohm
...springtime.	...le printemps. luh pran-tahn
...a locker room.	...un vestiaire. ewn vehs-tee-air
...cheese.	...le fromage. luh froh-mahzh
Hey there, what's spinning?	Pardon, qu'est-ce qui tourne? par-dohn kehs kee toorn

Don't begin a load too soon before closing time—or you might get evicted with a damp pile of partly washed laundry. Look for a sign telling you the last time you're allowed to start a load ***(dernier lavage autorisé à 20 heures),*** or what time the machines stop working, such as ***Ne pas faire fonctionner les machines après 21 heures*** (The machines stop working at 9 p.m.).

Laundry Instructions Decoder

Many launderettes are unstaffed. Every launderette has clearly posted instructions, but they're not always in English. Use this decoder to figure things out.

mode d'emploi / instructions	instructions
machine à laver	washer
linge	clothes
remplir	load
lavage / sechage	wash / dry
lessive / détergent	laundry detergent
assouplissant	softener
eau de javel / javel	bleach
liquide / poudre	liquid / powder
bac	reservoir (for adding soap)
à vos risques et périls	at your own risk
déposer / insérer	insert (clothes) / insert (money)
pièce / jeton	coin / token
fente	coin slot
faites l'appoint	exact change required
pas de monnaie	no change given
ouvrir / fermez porte	open / close door
appuyer bouton	press button
sélectionner / composer	choose / enter
démarrer / programme	start / program
pressage permanent	permanent press
linge délicat	delicates
chaud / froid	hot / cold
lavage en cours	in use
prelavage / cycle de lavage	pre-wash / main wash cycle
cycle d'essorage / cycle de rinçage	spin cycle / rinse cycle
séchoir	dryer
par _____ minutes de séchage	per _____ minutes of drying
vider / retirer	empty / remove
terminé	finished

Wash Temperatures

When choosing your wash cycle, you might see a series of numbers, such as:

45° / 90° / 55 m	whites
45° / 60° / 50 m	colors
45° / 45° / 40 m	permanent press / mixed
– / 30° / 30 m	warm
– / 17° / 25 m	cold / delicates

The first two numbers are the temperatures in Celsius for the pre-wash cycle, then the main-wash cycle; the third number shows how many minutes the cycle takes. (For a rough conversion from Celsius to Fahrenheit, double the number and add 30.)

You'll likely buy drying time in small units (5- or 10-minute increments) rather than a full cycle. The choice of temperatures are ***doux*** (low and slow), ***moyen*** (medium), and ***fort*** (high).

PERSONAL CARE AND HEALTH

This chapter will help keep you supplied with toiletries and guide you in getting treatment if you're not feeling well. Along with words for ailments, body parts, and medications, you'll find sections on eye and ear care, dental needs, reproductive health, women, babies, allergies, mental health, disabilities, and various medical conditions. For medical emergencies, see page 272 in the Help! chapter.

PERSONAL CARE

aftershave lotion	lotion d'après rasage loh-see-ohn dah-preh rah-zahzh
antiperspirant	anti-transpirant ahn-tee-trahn-spee-rahn
breath freshener / mints	rafraîchisseurs d'haleine / bonbons à la menthe rah-freh-shee-sur dah-lehn / bohn-bohn ah la mahnt
cologne	cologne koh-lohn-yuh
comb	peigne pehn-yuh
conditioner for hair	après-shampoing ah-preh-shahn-pwan
dental floss	fil dentaire feel dahn-tair
deodorant	déodorant day-oh-doh-rahn
face cleanser	lait nettoyant lay neh-twah-yahn
facial tissue	kleenex "kleenex"
fluoride rinse	rince-bouche fluoré rans-boosh flew-oh-ray
hair dryer	sèche-cheveux sehsh-shuh-vuh
hairbrush	brosse à cheveux brohs ah shuh-vuh
hand lotion	crème pour les mains krehm poor lay man
hand sanitizer	désinfectant pour les mains day-zan-fehk-tahn poor lay man
lip balm	beaume pour les lèvres bohm poor lay leh-vruh

lip gloss	gloss à lèvres "gloss" ah leh-vruh
lipstick	rouge à lèvres roozh ah leh-vruh
makeup	maquillage mah-kee-ahzh
mirror	miroir meer-wahr
moisturizer (with sunblock)	crème hydratante (avec protection solaire) krehm ee-drah-tahnt (ah-vehk proh-tehk-see-ohn soh-lair)
nail clipper	coupe-ongles koop-ohn-gluh
nail file	lime à ongles leem ah ohn-gluh
nail polish	vernis à ongles vehr-nee ah ohn-gluh
nail polish remover	dissolvant dee-sohl-vahn
perfume	parfum par-fuhn
Q-tips (cotton swabs)	coton-tiges koh-tohn-teezh
razor	rasoir rahz-wahr
sanitary pads	serviettes hygiéniques sehrv-yeht ee-zhay-neek
scissors	ciseaux see-zoh
shampoo	shampoing shahn-pwan
shaving cream	mousse à raser moos ah rah-zay
soap	savon sah-vohn
sunscreen	crème solaire krehm soh-lair
tampons	tampons tahn-pohn
tissues	mouchoirs en papier moosh-wahr ahn pahp-yay
toilet paper	papier hygiénique pahp-yay ee-zhay-neek
toothbrush	brosse à dents brohs ah dahn
toothpaste	dentifrice dahn-tee-frees
tweezers	pince à épiler pans ah ay-pee-lay

HEALTH

Throughout Europe, people with a health problem go first to the pharmacist, who can diagnose and prescribe remedies for most simple ailments. Pharmacists are usually friendly and speak English. If necessary, the pharmacist will send you to a doctor or a clinic.

After 7:00 p.m., most pharmacies are closed, but you'll find the name, address, and phone number on their front door of the nearest after-hours ***pharmacie de garde.*** In an emergency, go to the police station, which will call ahead to the pharmacist. At the pharmacy, ring the doorbell and the pharmacist will open the door. ***Voilà.***

Getting Help

Where is a...?	Où est...? oo ay
...(24-hour) pharmacy	...une pharmacie (de garde) ewn far-mah-see (duh gard)
...clinic	...une clinique médicale ewn klee-neek may-dee-kal
...hospital	...l'hôpital loh-pee-tahl
I am sick.	Je suis malade. zhuh swee mah-lahd
He / She is sick.	Il / Elle est malade. eel / ehl ay mah-lahd
I need a doctor...	J'ai besoin d'un docteur... zhay buh-swan duhn dohk-tur
We need a doctor...	Nous avons besoin d'un docteur... nooz ah-vohn buh-swan duhn dohk-tur
...who speaks English.	...qui parle anglais. kee parl ahn-glay
Please call a doctor.	S'il vous plaît appelez un docteur. see voo play ah-puh-lay uhn dohk-tur
Could a doctor come here?	Un docteur pourrait venir? uhn dohk-tur poo-ray vuh-neer
It's urgent.	C'est urgent. say ewr-zhahn
ambulance	SAMU sah-moo

Key Phrases: Health

I am sick.	Je suis malade. zhuh swee mah-lahd
I need a doctor (who speaks English).	J'ai besoin d'un docteur (qui parle anglais). zhay buh-swan duhn dohk-tur (kee parl ahn-glay)
pain	douleur doo-lur
It hurts here.	J'ai mal ici. zhay mahl ee-see
medicine	médicament may-dee-kah-mahn
Where is a pharmacy?	Où est une pharmacie? oo ay ewn far-mah-see

health insurance	assurance maladie ah-sew-rahns mah-lah-dee
Receipt, please.	Une facture, s'il vous plait. ewn fahk-tewr see voo play

Ailments

I have...	J'ai... zhay
He / She has...	Il / Elle a... eel / ehl ah
I need medicine for...	J'ai besoin d'un médicament pour... zhay buh-swan duhn may-dee-kah-mahn poor
bee sting	une piqûre d'abeille ewn pee-kewr dah-bay
bite(s) from...	morsure(s)... mor-sewr
...bedbugs	...des punaises de lit day pew-nehz duh lee
...dog	...de chien duh shee-an

...mosquitoes	...des moustiques day moos-teek
...spider	...d'araignée dar-ayn-yay
...tick	...de tique duh teek
blisters	des ampoules dayz ahn-pool
body odor	l'odeur corporelle loh-dur kor-por-ehl
burn	une brûlure ewn brew-lewr
chapped lips	les lèvres gerçées lay lehv-ruh zhehr-say
chest pains	maux de poitrine moh duh pwah-treen
chills	des frissons day free-sohn
a cold	un rhume uhn rewm
congestion	la congestion lah kohn-zheh-stee-ohn
constipation	la constipation lah kohn-stee-pah-see-ohn
cough	la toux lah too
cramps...	des crampes... day krahnp
...muscle	...musculaires mew-skew-lair
...stomach	...d'estomac deh-stoh-mah
...menstrual	...menstruelles mahn-strew-ehl
diarrhea	la diarrhée lah dee-ah-ray
dizziness	le vertige luh vehr-teezh
earache	l'otite loh-teet
eczema	l'eczéma lehk-zay-mah
fever	une fièvre ewn fee-eh-vruh
flu	la grippe lah greep
food poisoning	empoisonement alimentaire ahn-pwah-zohn-mahn ah-lee-mahn-tair
gas	le gaz luh gahz
hay fever	le rhume des foins luh rewm day fwan
headache	mal à la tête mahl ah lah teht
heartburn	le reflux gastrique luh ruh-flew gah-streek

hemorrhoids	hémorroïdes ay-mor-wahd
hot flashes	bouffées de chaleur boo-fay duh shah-lur
indigestion	une indigestion ewn an-dee-zheh-stee-ohn
infection	une infection ewn an-fehk-see-ohn
inflammation	une inflammation ewn an-flah-mah-see-ohn
insomnia	de l'insomnie duh lan-sohm-nee
lice	des poux day poo
lightheaded	tête légère teht lay-zhehr
migraine	une migraine ewn mee-grehn
motion sickness	mal des transports mahl day trahns-por
nausea	la nausée lah noh-zay
numbness	engourdissement ahn-goor-dees-mahn
pain	la douleur lah doo-lur
pimples	des boutons day boo-tohn
pneumonia	la pneumonie lah pnuh-moh-nee
pus	pus pews
rash	boutons boo-tohn
sinus problems	problèmes de sinus proh-blehm duh see-news
sneezing	l'éternuement lay-tehr-new-mahn
sore throat	mal à la gorge mahl ah lah gorzh
splinter	écharde ay-shard
stomachache	mal à l'estomac mahl ah leh-stoh-mah
(bad) sunburn	un (méchant) coup de soleil uhn (may-shahn) koo duh soh-lay
swelling	une enflure ewn ahn-flewr
tendonitis	tendinite tahn-dee-neet
toothache	mal aux dents mahl oh dahn

urinary tract infection	une infection urinaire ewn an-fehk-see-ohn ew-ree-nair
frequent urination	fréquente envie d'uriner fray-kahnt ahn-vee dew-ree-nay
painful urination	miction douloureuse meek-see-ohn doo-loor-uhz
vomiting	le vomissement luh voh-mees-mahn
wart(s)	verrue(s) veh-rew
I'm going bald.	Je deviens chauve. zhuh duh-vee-an shohv

For major illnesses, see "Medical Conditions" on page 312.

It Hurts

pain	douleur doo-lur
painful	douloureux doo-loo-ruh
It hurts here.	J'ai mal ici. zhay mahl ee-see
My ____ hurts. (body parts listed on next page)	Mon ____ me fait mal. mohn ____ muh fay mahl
aching (soreness)	courbaturé koor-bah-tew-ray
bleeding	saignement sehn-yuh-mahn
blocked	bloqué bloh-kay
broken	cassé kah-say
bruise	contusion kohn-tew-zee-ohn
chafing	irritations ee-ree-tah-see-ohn
cracked	fêlé feh-lay
fractured	fracturé frahk-tew-ray
infected	infecté an-fehk-tay
inflamed	enflammé ahn-flah-may
punctured (a rusty nail)	entaillé (un clou rouillé) ahn-tī-yay (uhn kloo roo-yay)
scraped	éraflé ay-rah-flay

sore	irrité ee-ree-tay
sprained	foulé foo-lay
swollen	gonflé gohn-flay
weak (no energy)	faible feh-bluh
diagnosis	diagnostic dee-ahg-noh-steek
What can I do?	Que puis-je faire? kuh pweezh fair
Is it serious?	C'est sérieux? say say-ree-uh
Is it contagious?	C'est contagieux? say kohn-tah-zhee-uh

Body Parts

ankle	cheville shuh-vee
appendix	appendice ah-pahn-dees
arm	bras brah
back	dos doh
bladder	vessie veh-see
blood	sang sahn
body	corps kor
bone	os oh
bowel movement	selle sehl
brain	cerveau sehr-voh
breast	seins san
chest	poitrine pwah-treen
ear	oreille oh-ray
elbow	coude kood
eye	oeil oy
face	visage vee-zahzh
fingers	doigts dwah
fingernail	ongle de doigt ohn-gluh duh dwah
foot	pied pee-ay
hand	main man
head	tête teht

heart	coeur	kur
hip	hanche	ahnsh
intestines	intestins	an-tehs-tan
kidney	reins	ran
knee	genou	zhuh-noo
leg	jambe	zhahmb
lips	lèvres	leh-vruh
liver	foie	fwah
lung	poumon	poo-mohn
mouth	bouche	boosh
muscles	muscles	mew-skluh
neck	cou	koo
nose	nez	nay
ovary	ovaire	oh-vair
penis	pénis	pay-nee
poop	ka-ka	kah-kah
shoulder	épaule	ay-pohl
skin	peau	poh
stomach	estomac	eh-stoh-mah
teeth	dents	dahn
testicles	testicules	teh-stee-kewl
throat	gorge	gorzh
toes	doigts de pied	dwah duh pee-ay
toenail	ongle de pied	ohn-gluh duh pee-ay
tongue	langue	lahng
urine	urine	ew-reen
uterus	utérus	ew-tay-rew
vagina	vagin	vah-zhan
waist	taille	tī-yuh
wrist	poignet	pwahn-yay
right / left	droite / gauche	drwaht / gohsh

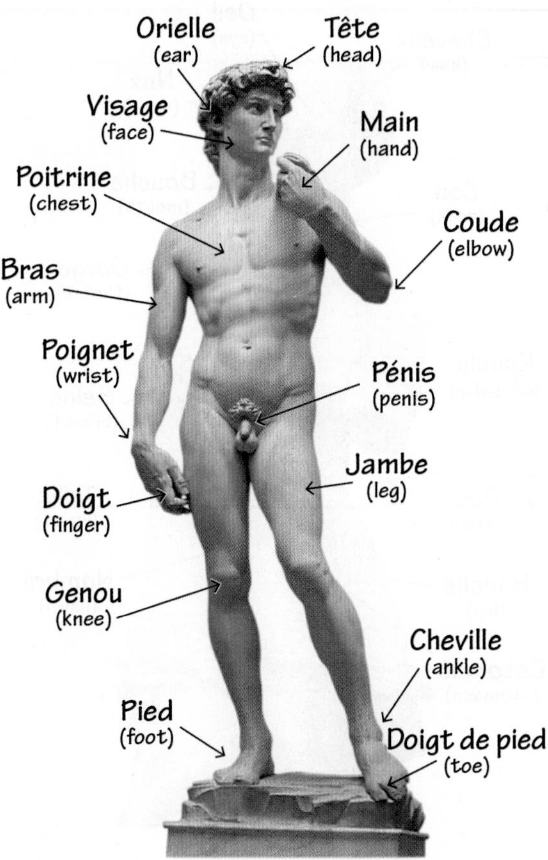
Orielle
(ear)
Tête
(head)
Visage
(face)
Main
(hand)
Poitrine
(chest)
Coude
(elbow)
Bras
(arm)
Poignet
(wrist)
Pénis
(penis)
Jambe
(leg)
Doigt
(finger)
Genou
(knee)
Cheville
(ankle)
Pied
(foot)
Doigt de pied
(toe)

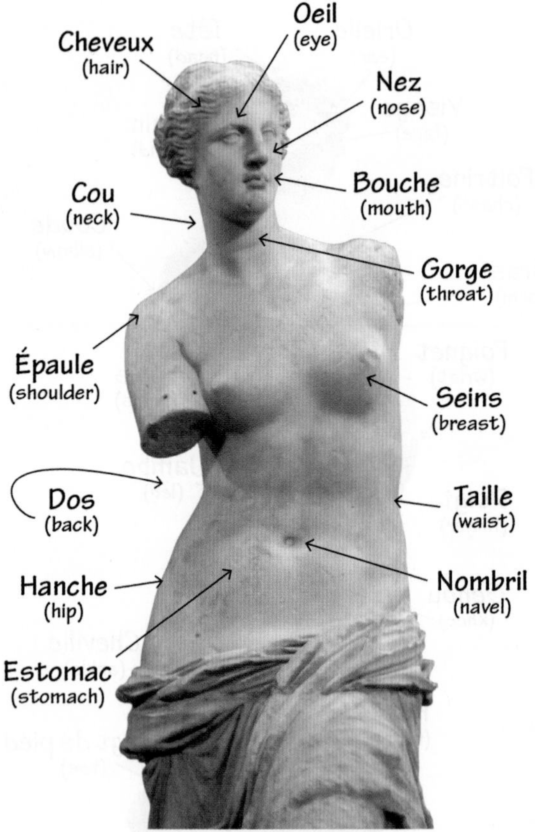
Oeil
(eye)
Cheveux
(hair)
Nez
(nose)
Bouche
(mouth)
Cou
(neck)
Gorge
(throat)
Épaule
(shoulder)
Seins
(breast)
Dos
(back)
Taille
(waist)
Nombril
(navel)
Hanche
(hip)
Estomac
(stomach)

First-Aid Kit and Medications

American name-brand medications are rare in Europe, but you'll find equally good local equivalents. Rather than looking for Sudafed, ask for Actifed (decongestant). Instead of Nyquil, request Vicks or Dolirhume (cold medicine). For prescription drugs, ask your doctor for the generic name (for example, atorvastatin instead of Lipitor), which is more likely to be understood internationally. If using a European thermometer, see page 428 for help with temperature conversions.

medicine	médicament may-dee-kah-mahn
pill	comprimé kohn-pree-may
prescription	ordonnance or-doh-nahns
to refill	remplir de nouveau rahn-pleer duh noo-voh
pharmacy	pharmacie far-mah-see
24-hour pharmacy	pharmacie de garde far-mah-see duh gard
antacid	anti-acide ahn-tee-ah-seed
anti-anxiety medicine	anxiolytique (Xanax) ahnk-see-oh-lee-teek ("Xanax")
antibiotic	antibiotique ahn-tee-bee-oh-teek
antihistamine (like Benadryl)	antihistaminique (Cetirizine) ahn-tee-ees-tah-mee-neek (suh-tee-ree-zeen)
aspirin	aspirine ah-spee-reen
non-aspirin substitute	Tylenol tee-leh-nohl
adult diapers (like Depends)	couches pour adultes koosh poor ah-dewlt
bandage	bandage bahn-dahzh
Band-Aids	pansements pahn-suh-mahn
cold medicine	remède contre le rhume ruh-mehd kohn-truh luh rewm

cough drops	pastilles pour la toux pah-stee poor lah too
decongestant (like Sudafed)	décongestant day-kohn-zhehs-tahn
diarrhea medicine	médicament pour la diarrhée may-dee-kah-mahn poor lah dee-ah-ray
disinfectant	désinfectant day-zan-fehk-tahn
first-aid cream	crème antiseptique krehm ahn-tee-sehp-teek
gauze / tape	gaze / sparadra gahz / spah-rah-drah
hemorrhoid medicine	Préparation H (no kidding) pray-pah-rah-see-ohn ahsh
hydrogen peroxide	eau oxygénée oh ohk-see-zhay-nay
ibuprofen (like Advil)	ibuprofène ee-bew-proh-fehn
inhaler	inhalateur an-ahl-ah-tur
insulin	insuline an-sew-leen
itch reliever	quelque chose pour soulager des démangeaisons kehl-kuh shohz poor soo-lah-zhay day day-mahn-zhay-zohn
laxative	laxatif lahk-sah-teef
moleskin (for blisters)	pansement ampoules pahns-mahn ahn-pool
mosquito repellant	anti-moustique ahn-tee moos-teek
pain killer	calmant kahl-mahn
stomachache medicine	médicament pour les maux d'estomac may-dee-kah-mahn poor lay moh deh-stoh-mah
support bandage	pansement élastique pahns-mahn ay-lah-steek
syringe	seringue suh-rang
tetanus shot	vaccin contre le tétanos vahk-san kohn-truh luh tay-tah-nohs
thermometer	thermomètre tehr-moh-meh-truh

Vaseline	Vaseline vah-zuh-leen
vitamins	vitamines vee-tah-meen
Does it sting?	Est-ce que ça pique? ehs kuh sah peek
Take one pill every ____ hours for ____ days.	Prendre un comprimé toutes les ____ heures pendant ____ jours. prahn-druh uhn kohn-pree-may toot lay ____ ur pahn-dahn ____ zhoor

SPECIFIC NEEDS

The Eyes Have It

optician	opticien ohp-tee-see-an
eye / eyes	oeil / yeux uh-ee / yuh
eye drops (for inflammation)	gouttes pour les yeux (pour l'inflammation) goot poor layz yuh (poor lan-flah-mah-see-ohn)
artificial tears	larmes artificielles larmz ar-tee-fee-see-ehl
glasses	lunettes lew-neht
sunglasses	lunettes de soleil lew-neht duh soh-lay
reading glasses	lunettes de vue lew-neht duh vew
glasses case	étui à lunettes ay-twee ah lew-neht
(broken) lens	verre (cassé) vehr (kah-say)
to repair	réparer ray-pah-ray
replacement	remplacement rahn-plahs-mahn
prescription	ordonnance or-doh-nahns
contact lenses...	lentilles de contact... lahn-tee duh kohn-tahkt
...soft	...souples soop-luh
...hard	...dures dewr

all-purpose solution	solution pour tout soh-lew-see-ohn poor too
contact lens case	boîte à lentilles de contact bwaht ah lahn-tee duh kohn-tahkt
I don't see well.	Je ne vois pas bien. zhuh nuh vwah pah bee-an
nearsighted	myope mee-yohp
farsighted	presbyte prehs-beet
20 / 20 vision	vision vingt sur vingt veez-yohn van sewr van

All Ears

ear(s)	oreille(s) oh-ray
right / left	droite / gauche drwaht / gohsh
earache	otite oh-teet
ear infection	infection de l'oreille an-fehk-see-ohn duh loh-ray
ear wax (removal)	cérumen (nettoyage) say-rew-mahn (neh-twah-yahzh)
I don't hear well.	Je n'entends pas bien. zhuh nahn-tahn pah bee-an
hearing aid	protèse auditive proh-tehz oh-dee-teev
batteries	piles peel

Tooth Trouble

dentist	dentiste dahn-teest
tooth / teeth	dent / dents dahn
toothache	mal aux dents mahl oh dahn
braces	appareil dentaire ah-pah-ray dahn-tair
crown	couronne koo-rohn

dentures	prothèse proh-tehz
filling	plombage plohn-bahzh
gums	gencives zhahn-seev
broken	cassé kah-say
cracked	fissurée fee-sew-ray
The filling / The tooth fell out.	Le plombage / La dent est tombé. luh plohn-bahzh / lah dahnt ay tohn-bay
Ouch! It hurts!	Aïe! Ça fait mal! ī / sah fay mahl

Dental products (such as toothpaste) appear in the "Personal Care" list at the beginning of this chapter.

On Intimate Terms

personal lubricant (like KY Jelly)	lubrifiant personnel / sexuel lew-bree-fee-ahn pehr-soh-nehl / sehk-sew-ehl
contraceptives	contraceptifs kohn-trah-sehp-teef
condoms	préservatifs / capotes pray-zehr-vah-teef / kah-poht
birth-control pills	les pilules lay pee-lewl
prescription refill	renouvellement d'ordonnance ruh-noo-vehl-mahn dor-doh-nahns
morning-after pill	pilule du lendemain pee-lewl dew lahn-duh-man
herpes (inactive)	herpès (inactif) ehr-pehs (an-ahk-teef)
HIV / AIDS	VIH / SIDA vay ee ahsh / see-dah
STD (sexually transmitted disease)	MST (maladie sexuellement transmissible) ehm ehs tay (mah-lah-dee sehk-sew-ehl-mahn trahns-mee-see-bluh)

For Women

menstruation	menstruation mahn-strew-ah-see-ohn
period	les règles lay reh-gluh
tampons	tampons tahn-pohn
sanitary pads	serviettes hygiéniques sehrv-yeht ee-zhay-neek
I need medicine for...	J'ai besoin d'un médicament pour... zhay buh-zwan duhn may-dee-kah-mahn poor
...menstrual cramps.	...des crampes menstruelles. day krahnp mahn-strew-ehl
...a yeast infection.	...une candidose. ewn kahn-dee-dohz
...a urinary tract infection.	...une infection urinaire. ewn an-fehk-see-ohn ew-ree-nair
cranberry juice	jus d'airelles zhew dair-ehl
I'd like to see a female...	Je voudrais voir une femme... zhuh voo-dray vwahr ewn fahm
...doctor.	...docteur. dohk-tur
...gynecologist.	...gynécologue. zhee-nay-koh-lohg
I've missed a period.	J'ai du retard dans mes règles. zhay dew ruh-tar dahn may reh-gluh
pregnancy test	test de grossesse tehst duh groh-sehs
ultrasound	écographie ay-koh-grah-fee
I am / She is... pregnant.	Je suis / Elle est... enceinte. zhuh swee / ehl ay... ahn-sant
... ___ weeks / months	...de ___ semaines / mois duh ___ suh-mehn / mwah
miscarriage	fausse couche fohs koosh
abortion	avortement ah-vor-tuh-mahn
menopause	ménopause may-noh-pohz

For Babies

baby	bébé bay-bay
baby carrier	porte-bébé port-bay-bay
baby food	nourriture pour bébé noo-ree-tewr poor bay-bay
bib	bavoir bah-vwahr
booster seat	réhausseur ray-oh-sur
bottle	biberon bee-buh-rohn
breastfeeding	allaitement maternel ah-leht-mahn mah-tehr-nehl
Where can I breastfeed?	Où puis-je allaiter mon bébé? oo pweezh ah-leh-tay mohn bay-bay
car seat	siège voiture see-ehzh vwah-tewr
crib	lit d'enfant lee dahn-fahn
diapers	couches koosh
diaper wipes	lingettes de couche lan-zheht duh koosh
diaper ointment	pommade de couche poh-mahd duh koosh
formula...	lait pour bébé... lay poor bay-bay
...powdered	...en poudre ahn poo-druh
...liquid	...liquide lee-keed
...soy	...soja soh-zhah
high chair	chaise haute shehz oht
medication for...	médicament pour... may-dee-kah-mahn poor
...diaper rash	...l'érythème fessier lay-ree-tehm feh-see-ay
...ear infection	...une infection de l'oreille ewn an-fehk-see-ohn duh loh-ray
...teething	...la poussée des dents lah poo-say day dahn

pacifier	tétine tay-teen
playpen	parc park
stroller	poussette poo-seht
Is this safe for children? (point to item)	C'est sans danger pour les enfants? say sahn dahn-zhay poor layz ahn-fahn
He / She is ___ weeks / months / years old.	Il / Elle a ___ semaines / mois / ans. eel / ehl ah ___ suh-mehn / mwah / ahn
Will you refrigerate this?	Vous pouvez mettre ça au frigo? voo poo-vay meh-truh sah oh free-goh
Will you warm... for a baby?	Vous pouvez réchauffer... pour un bébé? voo poo-vay ray-shoh-fay... poor uhn bay-bay
...this	...ça sah
...some water	...un peu d'eau uhn puh doh
...some milk	...un peu de lait uhn puh duh lay
Not too hot, please.	Pas trop chaud, s'il vous plaît. pah troh shoh see voo play

Allergies

If you need to explain which specific food you're allergic to, look it up in this book's Menu Decoder.

I am...	Je suis... zhuh swee
He / She is...	Il / Elle est... eel / ehl ay
...allergic to...	...allergique à... ah-lehr-zheek ah
...lactose / dairy products.	...lactose / produits laitiers. lahk-tohs / proh-dwee layt-yay
...nuts.	...noix. nwah
...penicillin.	...pénicilline. pay-nee-see-leen
...cat / dog fur.	...poil de chat / chien. pwahl duh shah / shee-an

...pollen.	...pollen. poh-lehn
...shellfish.	...fruits de mer. frwee duh mehr
...sulfa.	...sulfamides. sewl-fah-meed
...wheat.	...farine. fah-reen
epipen	adrénaline auto-injectable ah-dray-nah-leen oh-toh-an-zhehk-tah-bluh

Mental Health

anxiety	l'anxiété lahnks-yay-tay
bipolar disorder	le trouble bipolaire luh troo-bluh bee-poh-lair
confusion	la confusion mentale lah kohn-few-zee-ohn mahn-tahl
depression	la dépression lah day-preh-see-ohn
panic attacks	des crises de panique day kreez duh pah-neek
I feel suicidal.	Je me sens suicidaire. zhuh muh sahn swee-see-dair
I need...	J'ai besoin... zhay buh-swan
...medicine to calm down.	...de médicaments pour me calmer. duh may-dee-kah-mahn poor muh kahl-may
...to call home.	...d'appeler chez moi. dah-puh-lay shay mwah
...a psychologist.	...d'un psychothérapeute. duhn see-koh-tay-rah-puht
...a psychiatrist.	...d'un psychiatre. duhn see-kee-ah-truh

Disabilities

cane	canne kahn
disabled	handicapé ahn-dee-kah-pay
elevator	ascenseur ah-sahn-sur
ramp	rampe rahnp
stairs	des escaliers dayz ehs-kahl-yay
walker	déambulateur day-ahn-bew-lah-tur
wheelchair	fauteuil roulant foh-tuh-ee roo-lahn
I am disabled.	Je suis handicapé. zhuh swee ahn-dee-kah-pay
He / She is disabled.	Il / Elle est handicapé. eel / ehl ay ahn-dee-kah-pay
Stairs are difficult / impossible.	Les escaliers sont difficiles / impossible. layz ehs-kahl-yay sohn dee-fee-seel / an-poh-see-bluh
Do you have...?	Avez-vous...? ah-vay-voo
...an elevator	...un ascenseur uhn ah-sahn-sur
...an adapted entrance...	...un accès adapté... uhn ahk-seh ah-dahp-tay
...an adapted room...	...une chambre adaptée... oon shahn-bruh ah-dahp-tay
...for people with mobility problems	...aux personnes à mobilité réduite oh pehr-suhn ah moh-bee-lee-tay ray-dweet

MEDICAL CONDITIONS

If you have a condition that's not listed here, find out the French word and keep it handy.

I have...	J'ai... zhay
He / She has...	Il / Elle a... eel / ehl ah
Alzheimer's disease	maladie d'Alzheimer mah-lah-dee dahlt-sī-mehr

arthritis	l'arthrite	lar-treet
asthma	l'asthme	lahz-muh
cancer	cancer	kahn-sehr
cancer of the ____ (body parts listed earlier)	cancer du / des ____	kahn-sehr dew / day ____
leukemia	leucémie	lew-say-mee
lymphoma	lymphone	lan-fohn
I have been in remission for ____ months / years.	J'ai été en période de rémission pendant ____ mois / années.	zhay ay-tay ahn pay-ree-ohd duh ray-mee-see-ohn pahn-dahn ____ mwah / ah-nay
chronic pain	douleur chronique	doo-lur kroh-neek
diabetes	diabète	dee-ah-beht
epilepsy	l'épilepsie	lay-pee-lehp-see
heart attack	crise cardiaque	kreez kar-dee-ahk
heart condition	problème cardiaque	proh-blehm kar-dee-ahk
heart disease	maladie cardiaque	mah-lah-dee kar-dee-ahk
I have a pacemaker.	J'ai un stimulateur cardiaque.	zhay uhn stee-mew-lah-tur kar-dee-ahk
high blood pressure	l'hypertension	lee-pehr-tahn-see-ohn
high cholesterol	taux de cholestérol élevé	toh duh koh-leh-stay-rohl ay-luh-vay
incontinence	incontinence	an-kohn-tee-nahns
multiple sclerosis	sclérose en plaque	sklay-rohz uhn plahk
stroke	accident cérébral vasculaire	ahk-see-dahn say-ray-brahl vah-skew-lair
Aging sucks. ("Aging is rotten luck.")	Vieillir c'est la poisse.	vee-yay-yeer say lah pwahs

CHATTING

When it comes time to connect with locals, these phrases can help you strike up a conversation, talk to children, chat about the weather, or ignite a French romance.

SMALL TALK

Introductions

My name is ____.	Je m'appelle ____.	zhuh mah-pehl ____
What's your name?	Quel est votre nom?	kehl ay voh-truh nohn
Pleased to meet you.	Enchanté.	ahn-shahn-tay
This is ____.	C'est ____.	say ____
How are you?	Comment allez-vous?	koh-mahnt ah-lay-voo
Very well, thanks.	Très bien, merci.	treh bee-an mehr-see
May I sit here?	Je pourrais m'asseoir?	zhuh poo-ray mah-swahr
May we sit here?	Nous pourrions nous asseoir ici?	noo poo-ree-ohn nooz ah-swahr ee-see
Where are you from?	D'où venez-vous?	doo vuh-nay-voo
What...?	Quel / Quelle...?	kehl
...city	...ville	veel
...country	...pays	pay-ee
...planet	...planète	plah-neht
I come from...	Je viens...	zhuh vee-an
...America (the United States).	...d'Amérique (des États-Unis).	dah-mehr-eek (dayz ay-tah-zew-nee)
...Canada.	...du Canada.	dew kah-nah-dah
Where are you going? (formal / familiar)	Où allez-vous? / Où vas-tu?	oo ah-lay voo / oo vah-tew
I'm going to ____.	Ja vais à ____.	zhuh vay ah ____
We're going to ____.	Nous allons à ____.	nooz ah-lohn ah ____

Key Phrases: Chatting

My name is ____.	Je m'appelle ____. zhuh mah-pehl ____
What's your name?	Quel est votre nom? kehl ay voh-truh nohn
Where are you from?	D'où venez-vous? doo vuh-nay-voo
I come from ____.	Je viens de ____. zhuh vee-an duh ____
I like ____.	J'aime ____. zhehm ____
Do you like ____?	Vous aimez ____? vooz eh-may ____
I'm going to ____.	Je vais à ____. zhuh vay ah ____
Where are you going?	Où allez-vous? oo ah-lay-voo
Happy travels!	Bon voyage! bohn voy-yahzh

Nothing More than Feelings

I am / You are...	Je suis / Vous êtes... zhuh swee / vooz eht
He / She is...	Il / Elle est... eel / ehl ay
...happy. (m / f)	...content / contente. kohn-tahn / kohn-tahnt
...excited.	...ravi. rah-vee
...sad.	...triste. treest
...tired.	...fatigué. fah-tee-gay
...angry.	...fâché. fah-shay
...jealous. (m / f)	...jaloux / jalouse. zhah-loo / zhah-looz
...frustrated.	...frustré. frew-stray
I am...	J'ai... zhay
...hungry.	...faim. fan
...thirsty.	...soif. swahf
...hot.	...trop chaud. troh shoh

...cold.	...froid. frwah
...homesick.	...le mal du pays. luh mahl dew pay-ee
...lucky.	...de la chance. duh lah shahns

Who's Who

This is my (m / f)...	C'est mon / ma... say mohn / mah
friend	ami ah-mee
boyfriend / girlfriend	petit ami / petite amie puh-teet ah-mee / puh-teet ah-mee
husband / wife	mari / femme mah-ree / fahm
male partner / female partner	copain / copine koh-pan / koh-peen
son / daughter	fils / fille fees / fee
brother / sister	frère / soeur frehr / sur
father / mother	père / mère pehr / mehr
uncle / aunt	oncle / tante ohn-kluh / tahnt
nephew / niece	neveu / nièce nuh-vuh / nee-ehs
cousin (m / f)	cousin / cousine koo-zan / koo-zeen
grandfather / grandmother	grand-père / grand-mère grahn-pehr / grahn-mehr
grandson / granddaughter	petit-fils / petite-fille puh-tee-fees / puh-teet-fee
great-____	arrière-____ ah-ree-ehr-____

Family Matters

Are you...?	Vous êtes...? vooz eht
I am / We are...	Je suis / Nous sommes... zhuh swee / noo suhm
...married	...marié mah-ree-ay
...engaged	...fiancé fee-ahn-say

We are friends.	Nous sommes amis. noo suhm ah-mee
We are partners.	Nous sommes partenaires. noo suhm par-tuh-nair
Do you have...?	Vous avez...? vooz ah-vay
I have / We have...	J'ai / Nous avons... zhay / nooz ah-vohn
...children	...des enfants dayz ahn-fahn
...grandchildren	...des petits-enfants day puh-teet ahn-fahn
...photos	...des photos day foh-toh
boy / girl	garçon / fille gahr-sohn / fee
How many boys / girls?	Combien de garçons / filles? kohn-bee-an duh gar-sohn / fee
Beautiful baby!	Quel beau bébé! kehl boh bay-bay
Beautiful boy / girl!	Quel beau garçon / belle fille! kehl boh gar-sohn / behl fee
Beautiful children!	Quels beaux enfants! kehl bohz ahn-fahn
How old is your child?	Quel âge a votre enfant? kehl ahzh ah voh-truh ahn-fahn
age / ages	âge / âges ahzh / ahzh
grown-up	adulte ah-dewlt

Chatting with Children

What's your name?	Quel est ton prénom? kehl ay tohn pray-nohn
My name is ____.	Je m'appelle ____. zhuh mah-pehl ____
How old are you?	Quel âge as-tu? kehl ahzh ah-tew
How old am I?	Quel âge est-ce que j'ai? kehl ahzh ehs kuh zhay
I'm ____ years old.	J'ai ____ ans. zhay ____ ahn
Do you have siblings?	Tu as des frères et soeurs? tew ah day frehr ay sur
Do you like school?	Tu aimes l'école? tew ehm lay-kohl

What are you studying?	Tu étudies quoi? tew ay-tew-dee kwah
What's your favorite subject?	Quel est ton sujet préféré? kehl ay tohn sew-zhay pray-fay-ray
Will you teach me / Will you teach us some French words?	Tu m'apprends / Tu nous apprends quelques mots en français? tew mah-prahn / tew nooz ah-prahn kehl-kuh moh ahn frahn-say
Do you have pets?	As-tu un animal chez toi? ah-tew uhn ah-nee-mahl shay twah
I have a...	J'ai un... zhay uhn
We have a...	Nous avons un... nooz ah-vohn uhn
...cat / dog / fish / bird.	...chat / chien / poisson / oiseau. shah / shee-an / pwah-sohn / wah-zoh
Gimme five.	Tape là. tahp lah

Equivalent to our word "kids," the French say ***les gamins*** or ***les gosses.*** Snot-nosed kids are ***les morveux*** and brats are called ***les mômes.***

If you want to do a high five with a kid, hold up your hand and say ***Tape là*** (Hit me here). For a French sing-along, you'll find the words for "Happy Birthday" on page 40.

Work

What is your occupation?	Quel est votre métier? kehl ay voh-truh may-tee-yay
Do you like your work?	Aimez-vous votre métier? eh-may-voo voh-truh may-tee-yay
I am...	Je suis... zhuh swee
...retired.	...à la retraite. ah lah ruh-treht
...unemployed.	...au chômage. oh shoh-mahzh
...a student. (m / f)	...un étudiant / une étudiante. uhn ay-tewd-yahn / ewn ay-tewd-yahnt
...a professional traveler.	...un voyageur professionnel. uhn voy-ah-zhur proh-feh-see-oh-nehl

I'm studying to work in...	J'étudie pour travailler dans... zhay-tew-dee poor trah-vah-yay dahn
I work in...	Je travaille dans... zhuh trah-vī dahn
I used to work in...	Je travaillais dans... zhuh trah-vī-yay dahn
I want a job in...	Je veux un travail dans... zhuh vuh uhn trah-vī dahn
accounting	la comptabilité lah kohn-tah-bee-lee-tay
the arts	les arts layz ar
banking	le secteur bancaire luh sehk-tur bahn-kair
business	le commerce luh koh-mehrs
engineering	l'ingéniérie lan-zhay-nee-yay-ree
a factory	une usine ewn ew-zeen
government	le gouvernement luh goo-vehrn-mahn
home construction	la construction de maisons lah kohn-strewk-see-ohn duh may-zohn
information technology	l'informatique lan-for-mah-teek
journalism	le journalisme luh zhoor-nah-leez-muh
the legal profession	le secteur légal luh sehk-tur lay-gahl
the medical field	le secteur médical luh sehk-tur may-dee-kahl
the military	le militaire luh mee-lee-tair
public relations	les relations publiques lay ruh-lah-see-ohn pewb-leek
a restaurant	un restaurant uhn rehs-toh-rahn
science	les sciences lay see-ahns
social services	le secteur social luh sehk-tur soh-see-ahl
a store	un magasin uhn mah-gah-zan
teaching	l'enseignement lahn-sehn-yuh-mahn
the travel industry	le tourisme luh too-reez-muh

Travel Talk

I am / Are you...?	Je suis / Vous êtes...? zhuh swee / vooz eht
...on vacation	...en vacances ahn vah-kahns
...on business	...en voyage d'affaires ahn voy-yahzh dah-fair
How long have you been traveling?	Il y a longtemps que vous voyagez? eel yah lohn-tahn kuh voo voy-yah-zhay
day(s) / week(s)	jour(s) / semaine(s) zhoor / suh-mehn
month(s) / year(s)	mois / année(s) mwah / ah-nay
When are you going home?	Quand allez-vous rentrer? kahn ah-lay-voo rahn-tray
This is my / our first time in ____.	C'est ma / notre première fois en ____. say mah / noh-truh pruhm-yehr fwah ahn ____
It is / It's not a tourist trap.	C'est / Ce n'est pas un piège à touristes. say / suh nay pah uhn pee-ehzh ah too-reest
This is paradise.	Ceci est le paradis. suh-see ay luh pah-rah-dee
France is wonderful.	La France est belle. lah frahns ay behl
The French are friendly / rude.	Les Français sont gentils / impolis. lay frahn-say sohn zhahn-tee / an-poh-lee
What is your favorite...?	Quel est votre... préféré? kehl ay voh-truh... pray-fay-ray
...country	...pays pay-ee
...place	...endroit ahn-drwah
...city	...ville veel
My favorite is ____.	Mon préféré est ____. mohn pray-fay-ray ay ____
I've / We've traveled to ____.	J'ai / Nous avons voyagé à ____. zhay / nooz ah-vohn voy-yah-zhay ah ____

Next I'll / we'll go to ____.	Et puis je vais / nous allons à ____. ay pwee zhuh vay / nooz ah-lohn ah ____
I'd like / We'd like...	Je voudrais / Nous voudrions... zhuh voo-dray / noo voo-dree-ohn
...to go to ____.	...aller à ____. ah-lay ah ____
...to return to ____.	...rentrer à ____. rahn-tray ah ____
My / Our vacation is ____ days long, starting in ____ and ending in ____.	Mon / Notre voyage est de ____ jours, qui commencent à ____ et qui finissent à ____. mohn / noh-truh voy-yahzh ay duh ____ zhoor kee koh-mahns ah ____ ay kee fee-nees ah ____
Travel is enlightening.	Voyager ouvre l'esprit. voy-yah-zhay oo-vruh leh-spree
I wish all (American) politicians traveled.	Je souhaite que tous les politiciens (américains) voyagent. zhuh sweht kuh too lay poh-lee-tee-see-an (ah-may-ree-kan) voy-yahzh
Happy travels!	Bon voyage! bohn voy-yahzh
Keep on travelin'!	N'arrêtez pas de voyager! nah-reh-tay pah duh voy-ah-zhay

Staying in Touch

What is your...?	Quel est votre...? kehl ay voh-truh
Here is my / our...	C'est ma / notre... say mah / noh-truh
...email address	...adresse email ah-drehs ee-mehl
...home address	...adresse de domicile ah-drehs duh doh-mee-seel
...phone number	...numéro de téléphone new-may-roh duh tay-lay-fohn
I am / Are you on Facebook?	Je suis / Êtes-vous sur Facebook? zhuh swee / eht-voo sewr "Facebook"

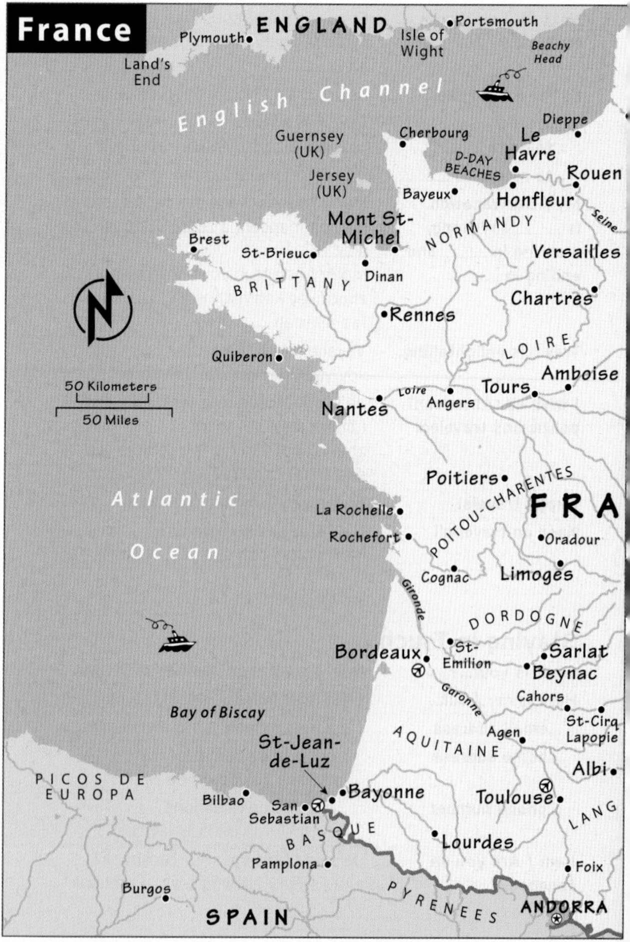
France
ENGLAND
Plymouth
Portsmouth
Isle of Wight
Beachy Head
Land's End
English Channel
Dieppe
Guernsey (UK)
Cherbourg
Le Havre
D-DAY BEACHES
Rouen
Jersey (UK)
Bayeux
Honfleur
Seine
Mont St-Michel
NORMANDY
Brest
St-Brieuc
Versailles
Dinan
BRITTANY
Chartres
Rennes
LOIRE
Quiberon
Amboise
50 Kilometers
50 Miles
Loire
Tours
Angers
Nantes
Poitiers
POITOU-CHARENTES
Atlantic Ocean
La Rochelle
FRA
Rochefort
Oradour
Cognac
Limoges
Gironde
DORDOGNE
St-Emilion
Sarlat
Bordeaux
Beynac
Garonne
Cahors
Bay of Biscay
St-Cirq Lapopie
Agen
AQUITAINE
St-Jean-de-Luz
Albi
PICOS DE EUROPA
Bayonne
Bilbao
Toulouse
San Sebastian
LANG
BASQUE
Lourdes
Pamplona
Foix
Burgos
PYRENEES
ANDORRA
SPAIN

Calais
Ghent
Brussels
Köln
BELGIUM
Rhine
GERMANY
Lille
Meuse
La Roche
Namur
Abbeville
Mosel
Frankfurt
Main
PICARDY
LUXEMBOURG
Luxembourg City
Laon
Rothenburg
Heidelberg
Reims
Metz
CHAMPAGNE
Verdun
LORRAINE
Paris
Baden-Baden
Nancy
Seine
Moselle
ALSACE
Strasbourg
Danube
Laroche
Culmont
Colmar
Rhine
Loire
BURGUNDY
JURA MTNS.
Basel
Zürich
LIECHT.
Dijon
Bourges
Beaune
AUST.
Bern
SWITZERLAND
NCE
Cluny
Lausanne
Geneva
Zermatt
Annecy
Lyon
Rhône
Chamonix
Aosta
Milan
Dordogne
AUVERGNE
Loire
Vienne
SAVOIE
Grenoble
LOMBARDY
Turin
Po
Valence
ITALY
PROVENCE
CINQUE TERRE
Genoa
Orange
Vaison la Romaine
Millau
Avignon
MONACO
Ligurian Sea
Pisa
UEDOC
Nîmes
Arles
Nice
Cannes
Livorno
Minerve
COTE D'AZUR
Marseille
Toulon
Carcassonne
Cassis
CORSICA (France)
Bastia
Collioure
Mediterranean Sea
Calvi

Europe

200 Kilometers
200 Miles
Bergen
SCOTLAND
Belfast
Edinburgh
N. IRE.
North Sea
Galway
Dublin
York
IRELAND
ENGLAND
NETH.
Dingle Peninsula
WALES
Cardiff
London
Amsterdam
Bath
Bruges
Brussels
BELG.
Mont St-Michel
NORMANDY
LUX.
Paris
BRITTANY
ALSACE
Atlantic Ocean
LOIRE
Colmar
FRANCE
SWITZ.
Chamonix
DORDOGNE
Lyon
PROVENCE
Santiago de Compostela
Monaco
San Sebastián
Arles
Carcassonne
Nice
Andorra
Porto
Salamanca
PORTUGAL
Barcelona
Nazaré
Madrid
Lisbon
Toledo
SPAIN
Córdoba
Sevilla
Granada
Mediterranean
ALGARVE
ANDALUCÍA
Algiers
Tangier
Gibraltar (UK)
MOROCCO
ALGERIA

FINLAND
NORWAY
Helsinki
Turku
SWEDEN
Oslo
Tallinn
Stockholm
ESTONIA
Baltic Sea
RUSSIA
LATVIA
To Moscow →
Riga
DENMARK
LITHUANIA
Copenhagen
RUSS.
Vilnius
Minsk
Gdansk
Hamburg
POLAND
BELARUS
Berlin
Warsaw
GERMANY
Kiev
RHINE VALLEY
Prague
Kraków
UKRAINE
Frankfurt
CZECH REP.
SLOVAK.
Munich
Vienna
Brat.
MOL.
BAVARIA
Salzburg
Budapest
Bern
TIROL
AUST.
ROMANIA
HUNG.
DOLOMITES
SLOV.
Bucharest
Black Sea
Milan
CROATIA
Belgrade
CINQUE TERRE
Venice
Zag.
BOSNIA-HERZ.
Florence
Sara.
SERBIA
Mostar
Sofia
TUSCANY
Dubrovnik
SAN MARINO
MONT.
KOS.
BULGARIA
CORSICA (FRANCE)
Adriatic Sea
Istanbul
Rome
MAC.
ITALY
ALB.
Naples
TURKEY
SARDINIA (ITALY)
GREECE
AMALFI COAST
CORFU
Athens
Sea
SICILY
PELOPONNESE
TUNISIA
CRETE

Weather

Is it going to rain...?	Il va pleuvoir...? eel vah pluh-vwahr
What will the weather be like...?	Quel temps fera-t-il...? kehl tahn fuh-rah-teel
...today	...aujourd'hui oh-joor-dwee
...tomorrow	...demain duh-man
cloudy	nuageux new-ah-zhuh
cold	froid frwah
foggy	brumeux brew-muh
hot	chaud shoh
muggy	humide ew-meed
rainy	pluvieux plew-vee-uh
snowy	neigeux neh-zhuh
stormy	orageux oh-rah-zhuh
sunny	ensoleillé ahn-soh-lay-yay
warm	assez chaud ah-say shoh
windy	venteux vahn-tuh
Like today?	Comme aujourd'hui? kohm oh-zhoor-dwee
Should I bring a jacket / an umbrella?	Je devrais apporter une veste / un parapluie? zhuh duh-vray ah-por-tay ewn vehst / uhn pah-rah-plwee
It's raining like cow's piss. (French saying)	Il pleut comme une vâche qui pisse. eel pluh kohm ewn vahsh kee pees
The fog is like pea soup.	C'est vraiment de la purée de pois. say vray-mahn duh lah pew-ray duh pwah
The wind could blow your ears off.	Le vent pourrait vous enlever les oreilles. luh vahn poo-ray vooz ahn-luh-vay layz oh-ray
A rainbow!	Un arc en ciel! uhn ark ahn see-ehl

To figure out temperature conversions, see page 428.

Thanks a Million

Thank you very much.	Merci beaucoup. mehr-see boh-koo
This is great fun.	C'est vraiment amusant. say vray-mahn ah-mew-zahn
You are...	Vous êtes... vooz eht
...kind.	...gentil. zhahn-tee
...wonderful.	...magnifique. mahn-yee-feek
...generous. (m / f)	...généreux / généreuse. zhay-nay-ruh / zhay-nay-ruhz
You've been a great help!	Vous m'avez beaucoup aidé! voo mah-vay boh-koo eh-day
I will remember you...	Je me souviendrai de vous... zhuh muh soov-yan-dray duh voo
We will remember you...	Nous nous souviendrons de vous... noo noo soov-yan-drohn duh voo
...always.	...toujours. too-zhoor
...till Tuesday.	...jusqu'à mardi. zhews-kah mar-dee

Responses for All Occasions

I / We like that.	Ça me / nous plaît. sah muh / noo play
I like you.	Je vous aime bien. zhuh vooz ehm bee-an
We like you.	Nous vous aimons bien. noo vooz ehm-ohn bee-an
I trust you.	Je vous fais confiance. zhuh voo fay kohn-fee-ahns
I will miss you.	Vous me manquerez. voo muh mahn-kuh-ray
That's cool.	C'est chouette. say shweht
Excellent!	Excellent! ehk-say-lahn
What a nice place.	Quel endroit sympa. kehl ahn-drwah san-pah

Perfect.	Parfait. par-fay
Funny.	Amusant. ah-mew-zahn
Interesting.	Intéressant. an-tay-reh-sahn
I see.	Je vois. zhuh vwah
Why not?	Pourquoi pas? poor-kwah pah
Really?	Vraiment? vray-mahn
Wow!	Wow! "wow"
Congratulations!	Félicitations! fay-lee-see-tah-see-ohn
Well done!	Bien joué! bee-an zhoo-ay
You're welcome.	Je vous en prie. zhuh vooz ahn pree
It's nothing.	De rien. duh ree-an
Bless you! (sneeze)	À vos souhaits! ah voh sway
Enjoy your meal!	Bon appétit! bohn ah-pay-tee
What a pity.	Quel dommage. kehl doh-mahzh
That's life.	C'est la vie. say lah vee
No problem.	Pas de problème. pah duh proh-blehm
OK.	D'accord. dah-kor
I'll be right back.	Je reviens tout de suite. zhuh ruh-vee-an tood sweet
I hope so.	J'espère que oui. zhehs-pehr kuh wee
I hope not.	J'espère que non. zhehs-pehr kuh nohn
This is the good life!	Que la vie est belle! kuh lah vee ay behl
Have a good day!	Bonne journée! buhn zhoor-nay
Good luck!	Bonne chance! buhn shahns
Let's go!	Allons-y! ah-lohn-zee

Favorite Things

What is your favorite...?	Quel est votre... préféré? kehl ay voh-truh... pray-fay-ray
My favorite... is_____.	Mon... préféré c'est _____. mohn... pray-fay-ray say _____

art	art ar
book	livre lee-vruh
food	nourriture noo-ree-tewr
hobby	hobby oh-bee
ice cream	glace glahs
movie	films feelm
music	musique mew-zeek
sport	sports spor
team	équipe ay-keep
TV show	programme de télé proh-grahm duh tay-lay
vice	vices vees
video game	jeu vidéo zhuh vee-day-oh
Who is your favorite...?	Qui est votre... préféré? kee ay voh-truh... pray-fay-ray
...actor	...acteur ahk-tur
...singer	...chanteur shahn-tur
...artist	...artiste ar-teest
...author	...auteur oh-tur
...director	...réalisateur ray-ah-lee-zah-tur
...athlete	...athlète aht-leht

For sports words, see page 229.

GRUNTS AND CURSES, SMOKES AND TOKES

Conversing with Animals

rooster / cock-a-doodle-doo	coq / cocorico kohk / koh-koh-ree-koh
bird / tweet tweet	oiseau / cui cui wah-zoh / kwee kwee
cat / meow	chat / miaou shah / mee-ah-oo
dog / woof woof	chien / ouah ouah shee-an / wah wah

duck / quack quack	canard / coin coin kah-nar / kwan kwan
cow / moo	vache / meu vahsh / muh
pig / oink oink	cochon / groin groin koh-shohn / grwan grwan

Profanity

People make animal noises, too. These words will help you understand what the more colorful locals are saying.

Go to hell!	Va te faire voir! vah tuh fair vwahr
Damn! (Good God!)	Bon Dieu! bohn dee-uh
breasts (colloq.)	nichons nee-shohn
penis (colloq.)	bite beet
drunk	bourré boo-ray
This sucks.	C'est dégueulasse. say day-guh-lahs
Fuck off.	Je t'en merde. zhuh tahn mehrd
Fuck you.	Va te faire foutre. vah teh fair foo-trah
Dumb fuck.	Espèce d'enculé. es-pehs dahn-kew-lay
Shit.	Merde. mehrd
You are a...	Vous êtes un... vooz eht uhn
Don't be a...	Ne soyez pas un... nuh soh-yay pah uhn
...bastard.	...salaud. sah-loh
...bitch.	...salope. sah-lohp
...asshole. (m / f)	...con / conne. kohn / kuhn
...idiot.	...idiot. ee-dee-oh
...jerk.	...connard. koh-nar
...imbecile.	...imbécile. an-bay-seel
...stupid.	...stupide. stew-peed

Con—which literally is part of the female anatomy—is commonly used profanity meaning idiot, asshole, and/or jerk. You can also say ***C'est con*** meaning "It's stupid." The female version, ***conne,*** is used just as often.

Neither version is as vulgar as the English equivalent. ***Je t'en merde*** and ***Va te faire foutre*** both basically are saying "fuck off" or "fuck you," but the first expression is less intense.

Sweet Curses

My goodness.	Mon Dieu. mohn dee-uh
Goodness gracious.	Mon bon Dieu. mohn bohn dee-uh
Oh, my gosh.	Oh la la. oo lah lah
Shoot.	Zut. zewt
Darn it!	Mince! mans
Too bad.	C'est dommage / Tant pis. say doh-mahzh / tahn pee

Smokes and Tokes

Do you smoke?	Vous fumez? voo few-may
Do you smoke pot?	Vous fumez de l'herbe? voo few-may duh lehrb
I (don't) smoke.	Je (ne) fume (pas). zhuh (nuh) fewm (pah)
We (don't) smoke.	Nous (ne) fumons (pas). noo (nuh) few-mohn (pah)
I don't have any.	Je n'en ai pas. zhuh nahn ay pah
lighter	briquet bree-kay
cigarettes	cigarette see-gah-reht
cigar	cigare see-gar
marijuana	de l'herbe / marijuana duh lehrb / mah-ree-wah-nah
hash	hachisch ah-sheesh
joint	joint "joint"
stoned	stoned "stoned"
Wow!	Wow! "wow"

For drinking phrases, see page 160 in the Eating chapter.

A FRENCH ROMANCE

Words of Love

I / me / you / we	je / moi / tu / nous zhuh / mwah / tew /noo
love	amour ah-moor
kiss	bisou bee-zoo
date	rendez-vous rahn-day-voo
to flirt	draguer drah-gay
to kiss	embrasser ahn-brah-say
to cuddle with	se blottir contre suh bloh-teer kohn-truh
to make love	faire l'amour fair lah-moor
single	célibataire say-lee-bah-tair
married	marié mah-ree-ay
engaged	fiancé fee-ahn-say
anniversary	anniversaire de mariage ah-nee-vehr-sair duh mah-ree-ahzh
faithful	fidèle fee-dehl
sexy	sexy "sexy"
cozy	douillet doo-yay
romantic	romantique roh-mahn-teek
my angel	mon ange mohn ahnzh
my doe	ma biche mah beesh
my love	mon amour mohn ah-moor
my little cabbage	mon petit chou mohn puh-tee shoo
my flea (endearing)	ma puce mah pews
my treasure	mon trésor mohn tray-sor
baby	bébé bay-bay

Ah, l'Amour

For words related to birth control and STDs, see page 307.

What's the matter?	Qu'est-ce qu'il y a? kehs keel yah
Nothing.	Rien. ree-an
I am / Are you...?	Je suis / Vous êtes...? zhuh swee / vooz eht
...single	...célibataire say-lee-bah-tair
...straight	...hétéro ay-tay-roh
...gay	...homosexuel / gay oh-moh-sehk-sew-ehl / "gay"
...bisexual	...bisexuel bee-sehk-sew-ehl
...undecided	...indécis an-day-see
...prudish (m / f)	...pudibond / pudibonde pew-dee-bohn / pew-dee-bohnd
I have...	J'ai... zhay
Do you have...?	Vous avez...? vooz ah-vay
...a boyfriend	...un petit ami uhn puh-teet ah-mee
...a girlfriend	...une petite amie ewn puh-teet ah-mee
We are on our honeymoon.	C'est notre lune de miel. say noh-truh lewn duh mee-ehl
I'm married.	Je suis marié. zhuh swee mah-ree-ay
I'm married, but...	Je suis marié, mais... zhuh swee mah-ree-ay may
I'm not married.	Je ne suis pas marié. zhuh nuh swee pah mah-ree-ay
I am adventurous.	Je suis aventureux. zhuh sweez ah-vahn-tew-ruh
I'm lonely (tonight).	Je me sens seul (ce soir). zhuh muh sahn suhl (suh swahr)
I am rich and single.	Je suis riche et célibataire. zhuh swee reesh ay say-lee-bah-tair

Do you mind if I sit here?	Ça vous embête si je m'assois ici? sah vooz ahn-beht see zhuh mah-swah ee-see
Would you like a drink?	Vous voulez un verre? voo voo-lay uhn vehr
Will you go out with me?	Vous voulez sortir avec moi? voo voo-lay sor-teer ah-vehk mwah
Would you like to go out tonight for...?	Vous voulez m'accompagner ce soir pour...? voo voo-lay mah-kohn-pahn-yay suh swahr poor
...a walk	...une promenade ewn proh-muh-nahd
...dinner	...dîner dee-nay
...a drink	...boire un pot bwahr uhn poh
Where can we go dancing?	Où pouvons-nous aller danser? oo poo-vohn-noo ah-lay dahn-say
Do you want to dance?	Vous voulez danser? voo voo-lay dahn-say
Again?	De nouveau? duh noo-voh
Let's celebrate!	Faisons la fête! feh-zohn lah feht
Let's just be friends.	Soyons amis. swah-yohn ah-mee
I have many diseases.	J'ai plusieurs maladies. zhay plewz-yur mah-lah-dee
I have only safe sex.	Je pratique que le safe sex. zhuh prah-teek kuh luh "safe sex"
Can I take you home?	Tu veux venir chez moi? tew vuh vuh-neer shay mwah
Kiss me.	Embrasse-moi. ahn-brahs-mwah
May I kiss you?	Je peux t'embrasser? zhuh puh tahn-brah-say
Kiss me more.	Embrasse-moi plus. ahn-brahs-mwah plew
Can I see you again?	On peut se revoir? ohn puh suh ruh-vwahr

Your place or mine?	Chez toi ou chez moi? shay twah oo shay mwah
You are my most beautiful souvenir.	Tu es mon plus beau souvenir. tew ay mohn plew boh soo-vuh-neer
Oh my God.	Mon Dieu. mohn dee-uh
I love you.	Je t'aime. zhuh tehm
Darling, will you marry me?	Chéri, tu veux m'épouser? shay-ree tew vuh may-poo-zay

DICTIONARY

A FRENCH / ENGLISH

A

à to; at
à bord aboard
à côté de next to
à elle hers
à la retraite retired
à l'envers upside-down
à l'heure on time
à lui his
à moi mine
à travers through
à vous yours
abordable affordable
abstrait abstract
abuser to abuse
accepter to accept
accès access; entrance
accès internet Internet access
accessible à un fauteuil roulant wheelchair-accessible
accrocher to hang
acheter to buy
adaptateur électrique electrical adapter
addition restaurant bill
admission cover charge
adolescent teenager
adresse address
adresse email email address
adulte adult
aéroport airport
affaires business
affiche poster
Afrique Africa
âge age
agence de location de voiture car rental agency
agence de voyage travel agency
âgés, personnes seniors
agneau lamb
agnostique agnostic
agrafeuse stapler
agressif aggressive
aider to help
aigre sour
aiguille needle
aile wing
aimable kind
aimer to love
aimer bien to like
air air
aire de jeux park playground
alarme incendie fire alarm
alcool alcohol
allaitement maternel breastfeeding
allaiter to breastfeed
Allemagne Germany
aller to go
aller simple one way (ticket)
allergique allergic
aller-retour round trip (ticket)
allumer to light; to turn on
allumette match; matchstick
amant lover
ambassade embassy
amende fine (penalty)
amer bitter
Amérique America
ami friend

French Dictionary Rules

Here are a few tips for using this dictionary:

- Remember that all French nouns have a grammatical **gender** (masculine or feminine). Even inanimate objects are assigned a gender. In general, words ending in ***e*** relate to females or feminine words—though there are many exceptions. Because casual visitors aren't expected to get this perfect, I haven't listed the gender for each noun.
- To make words plural, for most words just add **s.** However, there are some words where you add ***x,*** such as ***châteaux.***
- **Nouns** that can describe either a man or a woman (such as professions) are usually listed in the dictionary under the male form. If the words vary dramatically by gender, they are both listed: A male singer is a ***chanteur***, while a female singer is a ***chanteuse***.
- **Adjectives** must match their nouns. For simplicity, I've listed most adjectives with the masculine ending. In many cases, to change it to feminine, just add an ***e.*** (A happy man is ***content,*** while a happy woman is ***contente.***) If a basic adjective varies dramatically by gender, they are both listed: A handsome man is ***beau***, while a beautiful woman is ***belle***.
- Verbs are listed in their infinitive form (most verbs end in ***er, re,*** or ***ir***). This loosely translates to the English form "to ____" (for example, ***parler*** is "to talk"). To use a verb correctly in a sentence, you'll have to conjugate it (for example, if ***parler*** is "to speak," then ***je parle*** means "I speak"). For examples of conjugated verbs, see page 416.
- For specific food terms, look them up in the Menu Decoder, starting on page 179.

amical friendly
amitié friendship
amour love (n)
ampoule bulb; lightbulb; blister
amusement fun (n, adj)
ancêtre ancestor
ancien ancient
âne donkey
angine strep throat
anglais English
Angleterre England
angoisse anxiety
animal domestique pet
année year
anniversaire birthday
anniversaire de mariage anniversary
annonce announcement
annuaire telephone book
annuler to cancel; to delete
antiacide antacid
antibiotique antibiotic
antiquité antique (n)
août August
appareil photo camera
appareil photo numérique digital camera
appartement apartment
appel téléphonique phone call
appeler to call
apporter to bring
apprécier to enjoy
apprendre to learn
après after; afterwards
après demain day after tomorrow
après rasage aftershave
après-midi afternoon
après-shampoing conditioner (hair)
araignée spider
arbre tree
arc-en-ciel rainbow
argent money; silver
arobase "at" sign (@)
arrêt stop (n)
arrêt de bus bus stop
arrêt de Métro subway stop
arrêter to stop
arrivées arrivals
arriver to arrive
art art
arthrite arthritis
artiste artist
arts crafts
ascenseur elevator
aspirine aspirin
asseoir to sit
assez enough
assiette plate
assiette d'enfant children's plate
assister to attend
assurance insurance
assurance maladie health insurance
assuré insured
asthme asthma
athée atheist
attacher to attach
attendre to wait
attirant attractive
attraper to catch
au chômage unemployed

au lieu de instead
au revoir goodbye
aube sunrise
auberge de jeunesse youth hostel
aucun none
au-dessus above
aujourd'hui today
autel altar
auteur author
authentique genuine
automatique automatic
automne fall; autumn
autoportrait self-portrait
autorisé allowed
autoriser to authorize
autoroute toll road; expressway
autostop, faire de l' to hitchhike
autre other
Autriche Austria
aux urgences emergency room
avaler to swallow
avant before
avec with
avenir future
avion plane
avion, par air mail
avis opinion
avocat lawyer; avocado
avoir to have
avoir besoin de to need
avoir les courbatures sore
avoir l'intention de to intend
avoir peur de to be afraid of
avoir sommeil sleepy
avortement abortion
avril April

B

bac ferry
bagage baggage; luggage
bagage de cabine carry-on luggage
bague ring (n)
baignoire bathtub
bain bath
baiser kiss (n)
balader to stroll
baladeur MP3 MP3 player
balcon balcony
balle ball
banane banana
bandage adhésif Band-Aid
banque bank
bar bar
barbe beard
barquette container
bas low
bas, en down
basket basketball
baskettes tennis shoes
bateau boat
bateau de croisière cruise ship
bâtiment building
batterie battery (auto)
baume pour les lèvres lip balm
bavoir bib
beau (m) handsome
beaucoup much; many
beau-père father-in-law
bébé baby
Belgique Belgium
belle (f) beautiful
belle-mère mother-in-law
berceau crib

besoin need (n)
besoin de, avoir to need
beurre butter
bibliothèque library
bien good; well
bientôt soon
bienvenue welcome
bière beer
bijouterie jewelry shop
bijoux jewelry
billet ticket
biologique organic
bisou kiss (n)
bizarre strange
blague joke (n)
blanc white
blé wheat
blessé hurt; injured
blesser to hurt
blessure injury
bleu blue
blond blond
bloqué locked (mobile phone)
blush blush (makeup)
boeuf beef
boire to drink
bois wood
boisson drink (n)
boîte box
boîte automatique automatic transmission
boîte aux lettres mailbox
boîte de conserve can (n)
boîte de nuit nightclub
boîte manuelle manual transmission
boîte vocale voicemail
bol bowl
bombe bomb
bon good; valid
bon marché cheap
bonbon candy
bonheur happiness
bonjour hello; good day
bonne affaire good deal
bonne santé healthy
bottes boots
bottin telephone book
bouche mouth
boucherie butcher
bouchon cork; traffic jam
bouchon d'objectif lens cap
bouchon pour le lavabo sink stopper
boucle d'oreille earrings
bouffées de chaleur hot flashes
bougie candle; sparkplug
bouilli boiled
bouillir to boil
bouilloire kettle
boulangerie bakery
boules quiès earplugs
boulot job
bouteille bottle
boutique shop
boutique de souvenirs souvenir shop
boutique de vêtements clothing shop
bouton button
boutons rash; pimples
bras arm
break station wagon
briquet lighter (n)

broche brooch
bronzage suntan (n)
bronzer sunbathe
brosse hairbrush
brosse à dents toothbrush
brouillard fog
brûlure burn (n)
brume mist
brun brown
brushing wash and dry (hair salon)
bruyant noisy; loud
buffet salade salad bar
bureau office; desk
bureau des objets trouvés lost and found office
bus city bus

C

ça that (thing)
Ça va? How are you?
Ça va. OK; fine; I'm fine
cabine téléphonique phone booth
câble cable
câble USB USB cable
caca poop
caché hidden
cachot dungeon
cadeau gift
cafard cockroach
café coffee; coffee shop
café internet Internet café
caisse cashier
calcul rénal kidney stone
calendrier calendar
calepin notebook
calmant painkiller
calme calm (adj)
caméra vidéo video camera
camion van
camp, lit de cot
camping-car R.V.
canard duck
canne cane
canoë canoe
canot rowboat
capitaine captain
car long-distance bus
carafe carafe
carafe d'eau carafe of tap water (restaurant)
carrousel des bagages baggage claim
carré square (shape)
carrefour intersection
carte card; map; menu
carte bancaire debit card
carte d'embarquement boarding pass
carte de crédit credit card
carte de membre membership card (hostel)
carte de randonné hiking map
carte de visite business card
carte mémoire memory card
carte postale postcard
carte SIM SIM card
carte téléphonique telephone card
cascade waterfall
casque headphones; helmet
casquette cap
cassé broken

cathédrale cathedral
catholique Catholic (adj)
caution deposit
cave cellar
caviste wine and liquor store
ce this (m)
ce soir tonight
ceci this
céder le passage to yield
ceinture belt (n)
cela that
célèbre famous
célébrer to celebrate
célibataire single (unmarried)
cendrier ashtray
cent hundred
centre center
centre commercial shopping mall
centre-ville downtown
céramique ceramic
cercle circle
cerveau brain
cette this (f)
chaîne chain
chair flesh; meat
chaire pulpit
chaise chair
chaise haute high chair
chaise roulante wheelchair
chambre room
chambre d'hôte room in a private home; B&B
chambre libre vacancy (hotel)
champ field
championnat championship
chance luck; chance
chanceux lucky
chandelle candle
change change (n); exchange (n)
changer to change
chanson song
chanter to sing
chanteur (m) / chanteuse (f) singer
chapeau hat
chapelle chapel
chaque each; every
charcuterie delicatessen
chargeur charger
chargeur de piles battery charger
charmant charming
chat cat
château castle
chaud hot
chauffage heat
chauffer to heat
chauffeur driver
chaussettes socks
chaussons slippers
chaussures shoes
chaussures de tennis tennis shoes
chef boss
chef-d'oeuvre masterpiece
chemin de fer railway
chemise shirt
chemise de nuit nightgown
chemisier blouse
chèque check
chèque de voyage travelers check
cher expensive

chercher to look for; to search
cheval horse
chevalier knight
cheveux hair
cheveux, coupe de haircut
cheville ankle
chèvre goat
chien dog
chien méchant beware of the dog
chinois Chinese
chirurgie surgery
chocolat chocolate
choeur choir
chômage, au unemployed
chose thing
chose, quelque something
chrétien Christian (adj)
ciel sky; heaven
cinéma movie theater
cinq five
cintre coat hanger
circulation traffic
ciseaux scissors
cité city (fortified; medieval)
clair clear (adj)
classe class
classe, deuxième second class
classe, première first class
classique classical
clavier keyboard
clé key
clé USB flash drive
clef key
clignotant turn signal
climatisé air-conditioned
clinique médicale medical clinic
cloche bell
cloître cloister
clou nail
cochon pig
code PIN PIN code
code postal zip code
code régional area code
coeur heart
coiffeur barber; barber shop
coiffeur pour dames beauty salon
coin corner
coincé stuck
col mountain pass
colis package
collants nylons (pantyhose)
coller to paste
collier necklace
colline hill
combattre to fight
combien how many; how much
combien de temps how long
commander to order
commencer to begin; to start
comment how
compagnie company
compagnon companion
compartiment privé sleeper (train)
complet no vacancy; sold out; full
compliqué complicated
composter to validate
comprendre to understand
comptable accountant
compter to count
compteur taxi meter

conditions d'annulation cancellation policy
conducteur conductor
conduire to drive
confirmer to confirm
confiserie candy shop
confortable comfortable; cozy
congestion congestion (sinus)
conjoint partner
connaissance knowledge
connecter to connect (log on)
consigne baggage check (left luggage)
consigne automatique locker
construire to build
contagieux contagious
content happy
continuer to continue
contraceptif contraceptive; birth control
contrôle baggage check-in (for a flight); inspection
contrôler to control
convertisseur convertor
copier to copy
copieux filling (adj)
coquillage shellfish
coquille shell
corde rope
corde à linge clothesline
corps body
correct right; correct
correspondance connection; transfer (train)
correspondance, prendre une to transfer (train)
côte coast; rib (body part)
côté side
coton cotton
coton-tiges cotton swabs (Q-Tips)
cou neck
couche diaper
coucher de soleil sunset
couchette berth (train)
coude elbow
coudre to sew
couleur color (n)
couloir corridor; hall
coup de soleil sunburn
coupable guilty
coupe de cheveux haircut
couper to cut
couper en tranches to slice up
coupure cut (injury)
cour de récréation school playground
courir to run
courrier mail (n)
courroie du ventilateur fan belt
court short
coussin cushion
coût cost (n)
couteau knife
coûter to cost
couverts silverware
couverture blanket
couvre-feu curfew
couvrir to cover
craindre to fear
crampe cramp
crampe d'estomac stomach cramp

crampes menstruelles menstrual cramps
cravate tie (clothing)
crayon pencil
crayon de cire crayon
crayon pour les yeux eyeliner
crème cream
crème à raser shaving cream
crème anti-démangeaison itch reliever
crème antiseptique first-aid cream
crème chantilly whipped cream
crème hydratante moisturizer
crème pour les mains hand lotion
croire (en) to believe (in)
croix cross
cru raw
crustacés crustaceans (lobster, shrimp, crab)
crypte crypt
cuillère spoon
cuir leather
cuisine kitchen
cuisiner to cook
cuisse thigh
cuit cooked
cuivre copper
cuivre jaune brass
cure-dent toothpick

D

d'accord agree; OK
dames women (formal)
dangereux dangerous
dans in; into
danser to dance
date date (calendar, romantic)
date limite de validité expiration (validity)
de of; from
de l'herbe marijuana
déambulateur walker (for disabled)
débloquer to unlock (mobile phone)
début beginning
déca / décaféiné decaf / decaffeinated
décalage horaire jet lag
décapsuleur bottle opener
décembre December
déclarer to declare (customs)
décongestant decongestant
dedans inside
défoncé stoned; high (drugs)
dehors outside
déjà already
déjeuner lunch
délai delay
délicat delicate
délicieux delicious
demain tomorrow
demain, après day after tomorrow
demander to ask
demander pour to ask for
démangeaison itch (n)
demi half
demi-journée half day
demi-portion half portion (food)
démocratie democracy
dent tooth

dentelle lace
dentifrice toothpaste
dentiste dentist
dents teeth
dents, mal aux toothache
déodorant deodorant
dépanneur tow truck
départs departures
dépêcher to hurry
dépenser to spend
déplacer to move
dépression depression
depuis since
déranger to disturb
dernier last (adj)
derrière behind (n, prep)
désastre disaster
descente downhill
désespéré desperate
désinfectant disinfectant
désinfectant pour les mains hand sanitizer
désolé sorry
dessous, en below
dessus, au above
détachant stain remover
détaxe tax refund
déteindre to fade
détester to hate
deux two
deuxième second
deuxième classe second class
déverrouiller to unlock (door)
déviation detour (n)
diabète diabetes
diabétique diabetic
diamant diamond
diapositive slide (photo)
diarrhée diarrhea
dictionnaire dictionary
Dieu God
difficile strenuous; difficult
dimanche Sunday
dinde turkey
dîner dinner; to dine
dire to say; to tell
direct direct
directeur manager
direction direction; management
diriger to lead; to steer; to guide
discuter to discuss
disponible available
disque compact compact disc
dissolvant nail polish remover
distributeur automatique cash machine; ATM
divertissement entertainment
divorcé divorced
dix ten
docteur doctor
doigt finger
dôme dome
domestique domestic
dommage, quel it's a pity
donner to give
dormir to sleep
dortoir dormitory
dos back
dos, sac à backpack
douane customs
douche shower
douleur pain
douter to doubt
doux sweet; mild; soft

douzaine dozen
drapeau flag
draps sheets
drogue drug (medicine)
droit straight; right (legal)
droite right (direction)
droitiste conservative (n)
drôle funny
dur hard; tough

E

eau water
eau du robinet tap water
eau gazeuse sparkling water
eau minérale mineral water
eau plate still water
eau potable drinkable water
eau, carafe de carafe of tap water (restaurant)
échanger to exchange
écharpe scarf
échelle ladder
école school
économique economical
écouter to listen
écouteurs earbuds
écran screen (n)
écrire to write
eczéma eczema
éducation education
effacer to erase
efficace effective
égal equal
église church
elle she; her
elles they (f)
emballer to wrap
embarquement boarding (transportation)
embarquer to board
embêter to bother
embouteillage traffic jam
embrasser to kiss
emplacement campsite
emploi occupation
employé employee
empoisonement alimentaire food poisoning
emporter to take out (food)
emprunter to borrow
en in; by (train, car, etc.)
en bas down
en haut up; upstairs
en panne broken
en plus extra
en retard delayed; late
en sécurité safe
en surpoids overweight (person)
enceinte pregnant
encore again; more; another
endormi asleep
endroit place (site)
enfant child
enfin finally
enflure swelling (n)
engourdissement numbness
ennuyeux boring
enquête investigation
enregistrement check-in (baggage)
enseigner to teach
ensemble together
ensoleillé sunny
entendre to hear

E

enterrement funeral
enthousiasme enthusiasm
entraîner to practice
entre between
entrée entrance; entry; first course (meal)
entrer to enter
enveloppe envelope
environnement environment (nature)
envoyer to send; to ship
épais thick
épaule shoulder
épice spice (seasoning)
épicerie grocery store
épilation à la cire wax (spa)
épilepsie epilepsy
épingle pin (n)
épingle à nourrice safety pin
épouse (f) / époux (m) spouse
épuisé exhausted
épuisé de to run out of
équipe team
équitation horse riding
erreur mistake (n)
érythème fessier diaper rash
escalier stairs
Espagne Spain
espoir hope (n); to hope
essayer to try (attempt)
essence gasoline
essuie-glace windshield wiper
essuyer to wipe
est is; east
estomac stomach
estomac, mal à l' stomachache
et and
étage story; floor
étain pewter
état state (n)
États-Unis United States
été summer
éteindre to turn off (lights; devices)
éternuer to sneeze
étoile star (in sky)
étourdi lightheaded; dizzy
étrange strange
étranger foreigner; stranger
étroit narrow
étudiant student
étui à lunettes glasses case
exact exact
exactement exactly
examiner to examine
excuse apology
exemple example
exiger to require
explication explanation
expliquer to explain
exposition exhibit; exhibition
expression expression (facial; phrase)

F

façade facade
fâché angry
facile easy
facturer to charge (amount)
fade bland
faible weak
faim hungry
faire to make; to do

faire de la randonnée to go hiking
faire du shopping to shop
faire du ski to ski
faire du sport to exercise
faire le bagage to pack
faire le tour to go around
faire une folie to splurge
fait maison homemade
falaise cliff
fameux famous
familier familiar
famille family
fantastique fantastic
fatigué tired
fausse couche miscarriage
fauteuil roulant wheelchair
faux false
favori favorite
félicitations congratulations
femelle female
femme woman; wife
fenêtre window
ferme farm (n)
fermé closed
fermer to close
fermer à clef to lock
fermeture closing (n)
fermeture éclair zipper
fermier farmer; farm-raised
fesses buttocks
festival / fête festival
feu fire; stoplight; lighter
feu arrière taillight
feux d'artifices fireworks
février February
fiancé engaged; fiancé
ficelle string (n)
fichier file (computer)
fièvre fever
fil thread (n)
fil dentaire dental floss
fille girl; daughter
film movie
fils son
fin end (n)
finale final
fini over; finished
finir to finish
fixer to set (a schedule or date)
flash flash (camera)
fleur flower
fleuve river
fois, une once
folle (f) crazy
fond bottom; back
fond de teint foundation (makeup)
fond de teint compact face powder
fontaine fountain
football soccer
football américain American football
forêt forest
formulaire form (document)
fort strong
fossé moat
fou (m) crazy
foulard scarf
foule crowd (n)
four oven
fourchette fork
fourmi ant

F

fraîche fresh
frais cool; fresh (adj); fee (n)
français French
France France
frange bangs (hair)
freins brakes
fréquence frequency
fréquent frequent; common
frère brother
frire to fry
frissons chills
frites French fries
froid cold (adj)
fromage cheese
fromagerie cheese shop
frontière border (n)
fruit fruit
fruits de mer seafood
frustré frustrated
fumée smoke (n)
fumeur smoking
fusible fuse
fusil gun

G

galerie gallery
galerie d'art art gallery
gant de toilette washcloth
gants gloves
garantie guarantee (n)
garantie dommages collisions CDW (collision damage waiver)
garçon boy
garder to keep; to save
gare train station
gare routière bus station
garer to park
gasoil diesel
gaspiller to waste
gauche left
gauchiste liberal (n)
gaz gas (vapor)
gaze gauze
gazole diesel
gênant embarrassing
gencive gum (mouth)
généreux generous
genou knee
gens people
gentil nice
gérer to manage
gilet vest; sweater
gîte country home rental
glace ice cream
glacé frozen; glazed
glaçon ice cube
glissant slippery
gluten gluten
gomme eraser
gorge throat
gorge, mal à la sore throat
gothique Gothic
goût taste
goûter to taste; afternoon snack
gouttes pour les yeux eye drops
gouvernement government
grain de beauté mole
graisseux greasy
grammaire grammar
grand big; tall; large
grand lit double bed
grand magasin department store

grande route highway
Grande-Bretagne Great Britain
grand-mère grandmother
grand-père grandfather
gras fatty
grasse, matière fat (n)
gratuit free (no cost); toll-free
grave serious
Grèce Greece
grillé toasted
grippe flu
gris gray
gros fat (adj)
grossesse pregnancy
grotte cave
groupe group
groupe de musique band (musical)
guerre war
guichet ticket window
guide guide; guidebook
guider to guide
guitare guitar
gymnastique gymnastics
gynécologue gynecologist

H

habitude habit
hachisch hash (drug)
haleine breath
hanche hip (body part)
handicapé handicapped
haut high
haut, en up; upstairs
hémorroïdes hemorrhoids
hépatite hepatitis
herbe grass; herb; marijuana
heure hour
heure, à l' on time
heure de pointe rush hour
heures d'ouverture opening hours
heureuse (f) / heureux (m) happy
hier yesterday
histoire history; story
hiver winter
homme man
hommes men
homosexuel homosexual
honnête honest
honte shame
hôpital hospital
horaire timetable; schedule
horloge clock
hors-d'oeuvre appetizer
hors taxe duty free
hôtel hotel
huile oil
huile solaire tanning oil
huit eight
humain human
humide humid
hypertension high blood pressure

I

ibuprofène ibuprofen
ici here
idéal ideal
idée idea
ignorer to ignore
il he
île island

I

illégal illegal
illimité unlimited
illuminer to light up (illuminate)
ils they (m)
immangeable inedible
immédiatement immediately
immigration immigration
immigré immigrant
imperméable raincoat
impoli rude
important important; significant
importé imported
impôts taxes
impressionniste Impressionist
imprimante printer
imprimer to print (computer)
inclure to include
inclus included
inconscient unconscious
incorrect incorrect
incroyable incredible
indépendant independent
indigestion indigestion
indiquer to point
industrie industry
infection infection
infection urinaire urinary tract infection
infirmière nurse
information information
informer to inform
ingénieur engineer
inquiéter to worry
insecte insect
insectifuge insect repellant
insolation sunstroke
insomnie insomnia
inspecter to inspect
inspection des bagages baggage inspection (security)
instructions instructions (directions)
insuline insulin
insulte insult (n)
interdit prohibited
intéressant interesting
intérieur indoors
international international
intestin intestine
intolérant au lactose lactose intolerant
invité guest
inviter to invite
Irlande Ireland
islamique Islamic
Italie Italy
ivre drunk

J

jalouse (f) / jaloux (m) jealous
jamais never
jambe leg
jambon ham
janvier January
jardin garden
jardinage gardening
jaune yellow
je I
jeter to throw
jeton token
jeu game
jeu de cartes cards (deck)
jeu vidéo videogame
jeudi Thursday

jeune young
jeunes youths
jeunesse, auberge de youth hostel
joint joint (marijuana)
joli pretty
jouer to play; to act; athlete (n)
jouet toy
jour day
jour férié holiday
journal newspaper
juger to judge
juif Jewish
juillet July
juin June
jumeaux twins
jupe skirt
jupon slip (clothing)
jus juice
jusqu'à until
juste fair (just)

K

kasher kosher
kayak kayak
kilo kilogram
kilométrage mileage (in kilometers)
kilomètre kilometer

L

là there
là-bas over there
lac lake
lacet shoelace
laid ugly
laine wool
laisser to allow
lait milk
lait nettoyant face cleanser
lait pour bébé baby formula
lampe lamp
lampe de poche flashlight
langue language; tongue
lapin rabbit
lavabo sink (n)
laver to wash
laver à la main to hand wash
laver, machine washing machine
laverie launderette
laxatif laxative
le meilleur best
le moins least
le pire worst
le plus most
légal legal
léger light (weight)
légume vegetable
lent slow
lentilles de contact contact lenses
lesbienne lesbian
lessive laundry detergent
lettre letter
leur their
lever to lift
lèvre lip
l'heure time (clock)
l'heure, à on time
l'heure d'arriver arrival time; check-in time
l'heure de départ departure time
libérer to liberate; to free

L

libérer la chambre to check-out (hotel)
librairie book shop
libre free; available
libre-service self-service
lieu de, au instead
ligne line
ligne aérienne airline
lime à ongles nail file
limite de vitesse speed limit
lin linen
lingerie intimates
lingette de couche diaper wipe
liquide liquid (adj); cash (n)
liquide de transmission transmission fluid
lire to read
liste list
lit bed
lit, grand double bed
lit de camp cot
lit jumeau twin bed
lit pliant roll-away bed
lit superposé bunk bed
litre liter
livre book (n)
location rental
loin far
long long
lotion solaire suntan lotion
louer to rent
lourd heavy
lumière light (n)
lundi Monday
lune moon
lune de miel honeymoon
lunettes eyeglasses
lunettes de lecture reading glasses
lunettes de soleil sunglasses
lutte fight (n)
luxueux luxurious

M

ma my
mâcher to chew
machine à laver washing machine
machine à sécher dryer
mâchoire jaw
Madame Mrs.
Mademoiselle Miss
magasin shop; store
magasin d'antiquités antiques shop
magasin de photo camera shop
magasin de photocopie photocopy shop
magasin de portables cell phone shop
magasin de vêtements clothing boutique
magasin de jouets toy store
mai May
maigre skinny
maillot de bain swimsuit
main hand
maintenant now
mais but
maison house
maison de la presse newsstand
maison, fait homemade
mal à la gorge sore throat
mal à l'estomac stomachache

mal aux dents toothache
mal aux oreilles earache
mal de mer seasickness
mal de tête headache
mal du pays homesickness
malade sick
maladie disease
mâle male
malentendu misunderstanding
malheureusement unfortunately
manche sleeve
Manche, la English Channel
manger to eat
manquer to miss (long for)
manteau coat
manucure manicure
maquillage makeup
marbre marble (material)
marchand de vin wine shop
marché market
marché alimentaire farmer's market
marché aux fleurs flower market
marché en plein air open-air market
marché aux puces flea market
marché, bon cheap
marcher to walk
mardi Tuesday
mari husband
mariage wedding; marriage
marié married
mars March
marteau hammer
masque facial facial (spa)
massage massage (medical)
match game (sports)
matière material
matière grasse fat (n)
matin morning
mauvais bad
maux de poitrine chest pains
mécanicien mechanic
méchant mean
médias media
médicament medicine
médiéval medieval
meilleur better
meilleur, le best
mélange mix (n)
mélanger to mix
membre member
même same
mensonge lie (untruth)
mer sea
merci thanks
mercredi Wednesday
mère mother
mesdames ladies
messe church service; Mass
métal metal
météo weather forecast
méthode method
Métro subway
meubles furniture
micro-onde microwave
midi noon
mien, le mine
mignon cute
milieu, au middle
militaire military
mille thousand
mince thin

M

minorité minority
minuit midnight
minute minute (time)
miroir mirror
mixte mixed
mode fashion; style
modelage massage (spa)
modéré moderate
moderne modern
modifier to change
moi me
moins less; minus
moins cher cheaper
mois month
moment time (occasion)
mon my
monastère monastery
monde world
monsieur gentleman; sir
montagne mountain
montée uphill
montre watch (jewelry)
montrer to show
moquette carpet
morceau piece
mort dead
mosquée mosque
mot word; note
mot de passé password
moteur engine
moto / motocyclette motorcycle
mouchoirs en papier facial tissue
mouillé wet
moulin windmill
mourir to die
moustique mosquito
moyen medium
MST (maladie sexuellement transmissible) STD (sexually transmitted disease)
mur wall (room)
mûr ripe
mural mural
musée museum
musicien musician
musique music
musulman Muslim (n, adj)
mycose athlete's foot
myope nearsighted

N

nager to swim
natation swimming
national national
nationalité nationality
nature nature
naturel natural
naturiste nudist
nausée nausea
navette shuttle bus
navire ship (n)
né born
nécessaire necessary
neige snow (n)
néoclassique Neoclassical
nerveux nervous
neuf nine
neveu nephew
nez nose
ni neither
nièce niece
n'importe le quel anything
n'importe où anywhere

n'importe qui anyone
n'importe quoi whatever
Noël Christmas
noir black
noix nuts; walnuts
nom last name
non no
non-fumeur non-smoking
nord north
normale normal
notre, le ours
nouer to tie (in a knot)
nourrir to feed
nourrisson infant
nourriture food
nourriture pour bébé baby food
nous we; us
nouveau new
nouvelles news
novembre November
nu nude
nuageux cloudy
nuit night
nulle part nowhere
numéro de suivi tracking number
numéro de téléphone telephone number

O

objet object; purpose
obligatoire required
obtenir to get (obtain)
occasion opportunity
occupé busy; occupied
océan ocean
octobre October
odeur odor
oeil eye
oeuf egg
officiel official
offre offer
offrir to offer
oiseau bird
Olympiques Olympics
ombre shade (noun)
ombre à paupières eye shadow
oncle uncle
ongle fingernail
onglet hanger steak
opéra opera
opération operation (medical)
opticien optician
optimiste optimistic
or gold
ordinaire common
ordinateur computer
ordinateur portable laptop
ordonnance prescription
oreille ear
oreiller pillow
oreilles, mal aux earache
orgue organ
orteil toe
os bone
ou or
où where
oublier to forget
ouest west
oui yes
ouvert open (adj)
ouvre-boîte can opener
ouvrir to open

P

page page (n)
page d'accueil home page
paille straw (drinking)
pain bread
paire pair
paix peace
palais palace
panne, en broken
panneau sign
panier basket
panoramique, beau scenic
pansement bandage
pansement élastique support bandage
pantalon pants
papa dad
papeterie office supplies store
papier paper
papier hygiénique toilet paper
Pâques Easter
par avion air mail
paradis paradise; heaven
paramètres settings (computer)
parapluie umbrella
parc park (n)
parc aquatique water park
parc d'amusement amusement park
parce que because
pardon excuse me
pare-brise windshield
paresseuse (f) / paresseux (m) lazy
parfait perfect
parfum flavor (n); perfume
parking parking lot
parler to talk; to speak
partager to share
partir to leave; to depart
partout everywhere
pas not
passage piéton pedestrian crossing
passager passenger
passé past
passe Eurail railpass
passeport passport
passer to go through
pastille cough drop; lozenge
pâté de maisons block (street)
patient patient (n, adj)
patinage skating
patins à roulettes roller skates
pâtisserie pastry shop; pastry
pause break (rest) (n)
pauvre poor
payer to pay
pays country
pays, mal du homesickness
Pays-Bas Netherlands
péage toll
peau skin
péché sin
pêcher to fish
pédalo paddleboat
peigne comb (n)
peignoir de bain bathrobe
peindre to paint
pellicule film (camera)
pelouse grass (lawn)
pénicilline penicillin
pénis penis
penser to think

pension small hotel
perdre to lose
perdu missing (lost)
père father
Père Noël Santa Claus
période period (time)
périphérique ring road; beltway
permanente permanent
personne person; nobody
personnes âgés seniors
pessimiste pessimistic
pétillant fizzy
petit small; little
petit ami boyfriend
petit déjeuner breakfast
petit lit single bed
petite amie girlfriend
petite-fille granddaughter
petit-fils grandson
petits-enfants grandchildren
petits gâteaux cookies
peu few
peur fear (n)
peut-être maybe
phare headlight; lighthouse
pharmacie pharmacy
photocopie photocopy (n)
pièce coin
pied foot
piéton pedestrian
pile battery (electronics)
pile de montre watch battery
pilule pill
pilule, la birth control pill
pince à épiler tweezers
pince à linge clothes pins
pince à ongles nail clipper
pinces pliers
piquant spicy (hot)
pique-nique picnic
piquets de tente tent pegs
pire worse
pire, le worst
piscine swimming pool
piste cyclable bicycle path
placard closet
place square (town); seat; parking space
placer to place
plage beach
plage naturiste nude beach
plaindre to complain
plaire to please; to make happy
plaisant pleasant
plaît, s'il vous please
plan map
plan du Métro subway map
planche à voile windsurfing
planche de surf surfboard
plante plant
plastique plastic
plat flat (adj); plate; dish (n)
plat du jour special (plate of the day)
plat principal main course (meal)
plein full
plein air, en outdoors; cage-free
pleurer to cry
pleuvoir to rain
pluie rain (n)
plus tard later
plus tranquille quieter
pneu tire

pneumonie pneumonia
poche pocket
poids weight
poids limite weight limit
poignée handle (n)
poignet wrist
point point; dot (computer)
point de vue point of view; viewpoint
poisson fish (n)
poitrine chest
poitrine, maux de chest pains
poivre pepper (spice)
police police
politicien politician
politique political
pomme apple
pomme de terre potato
pompe pump (n)
pompiers fire department
pont bridge
populaire popular
porc pork
porcelaine porcelain
port harbor
portable cell phone
porte door
portefeuille wallet
porter to carry; to wear
portion portion
portrait portrait
poser to set down; to put down
position position
posséder to own
poste post; job
poste, la post office; postal service
poster to mail
potable, eau drinkable water
poubelle trash; trashcan
pouce thumb
poudre powder
poule chicken (animal)
poulet chicken (meat)
pouls pulse
poumons lungs
poupée doll
pour for
pourboire tip (gratuity)
pourcentage percent
pourquoi why
pourri rotten
poussée des dents teething (baby)
pousser to push
poussette stroller (baby)
poussière dust
pouvoir can (v); power (n)
poux lice
pratique practical
précieux precious
préférer to prefer
premier first
première classe first class
premiers secours first aid
prendre to take
prendre une correspondance to transfer (train)
prénom first name
près near
préservatif condom
président president
presque approximately; almost
presser to urge; to press

prêt ready
prêter to lend
prêtre priest
primeur produce stand
prince prince
princesse princess
principal main
principe principle
printemps spring
prise electrical outlet
privé private
prix price
problème problem
problème cardiaque heart condition
problème de sinus sinus problem
prochain next
produire to produce
produit product
produits artisanaux handicrafts
produits laitiers dairy products
professeur teacher
promener to stroll
promettre to promise
propre clean (adj)
propriétaire owner
prospérer to prosper
protéger to protect
prudence caution
prudent careful
publique public
puce flea; chip (mobile phone)
puer to stink; to smell bad
puis then
puissant powerful
pull sweater
punaises de lit bedbugs
pyjama pajamas

Q

quad-bande quad-band
quai platform (train); stall (bus station); quay; embankment
qualité quality
quand when
quantité quantity
quart quarter (¼)
quatre four
que what
quel dommage it's a pity
quelque chose something
quelque part somewhere
quelques some
quelqu'un someone
queue line (queue); tail
qui who
quiès, boules earplugs
quincaillerie hardware store

R

racisme racism
radeau raft
radiateur radiator
radio radio; X-ray
rafraîchir to trim; to refresh
raisonnable sensible
Ralentissez! Slow down!
rampe ramp
randonnée hike (n)
randonnée à vélo bike ride
rapide quick
rappeler to remind
raser to shave

R

rasoir razor
rater to miss (fail to reach)
ravi excited
réaliser to realize
récent recent
réceptionniste receptionist
recette recipe
recevoir to receive
recharger to recharge
réclamation complaint
reçu receipt
réduction discount (n)
reflux gastrique heartburn
réfugié refugee
regarder to look; to watch
régional local
règle policy; rule (n)
règles rules; period (menstruation)
rehausseur booster seat
reine queen
relier to connect
relique relic
remboursement refund (n)
remède remedy
remède contre le rhume cold medicine
remparts fortified wall
remplir to fill
remplir de nouveau to refill
rencontrer to meet
rendez-vous appointment
rendre to return (bring something back)
renseignements directory assistance
rentrer to return (go back); to re-enter
réparer to repair; to fix
repas meal
repassé ironed
répéter to repeat
répondeur answering machine
répondre to answer
réponse answer (n)
reposer to relax; to rest
reproduction copy (n)
République Tchèque Czech Republic
réseau network
réservation reservation
réserver to reserve
réservoir d'essence gas tank
résoudre to resolve
respirer to breathe
restaurant restaurant
restauré restored
rester to stay
retard, en delayed; late
retardement delay (n)
retirer to remove
retourner to return (go back)
retraite, à la retired
rétrécir to shrink
rêve dream (n)
réveille alarm clock
réveiller to wake up
rêver to dream
revoir, au goodbye
rez-de-chaussée ground floor
rhume cold (n)
rhume des foins hay fever
riche rich

rideaux curtains
rien nothing
rien, de you're welcome
rince-bouche mouthwash
rire to laugh
rivière river
robe dress (n)
robinet faucet
robuste sturdy
rocade ring road; bypass
rocher rock (n)
roi king
roller rollerblades
romantique romantic
rondpoint roundabout
ronfler to snore
rose pink
rosé pink wine
roue wheel
rouge red
rouge à joues blush (makeup)
rouge à lèvres lipstick
route road
route nationale national highway
ruban adhésif duct tape
rue street
ruelle little street; passage
ruines ruins
ruisseau stream (n)
Russie Russia

S

sac bag; purse
sac à dos backpack
sac à main handbag; purse
sac de couchage sleeping bag
sac en plastique plastic bag
sachet bag
sacré holy
sage wise
saignement bleeding
saison season
salade salad; lettuce
salaud bastard
sale dirty (adj)
salé salty
salle hall (room)
salle d'attente waiting room
salle de bains bathroom
salon de coiffure hair salon
salope bitch
salut hi
samedi Saturday
SAMU ambulance (emergency)
sandales sandals
sang blood
sans without
sans fil wireless
sans issue dead end
sans plomb unleaded (gasoline)
santé health
Santé! Cheers!
santé, en bonne healthy
saucisse sausage
sauf except
sauter to jump
sauvage wild
sauver to save (computer)
sauvetage rescue (n)
savoir to know
savon soap
savoureux tasty
scandaleux scandalous

Scandinavie Scandinavia
scientifique scientist
scooter motor scooter
scotch tape (Scotch)
sculpteur sculptor
sculpture sculpture
seau bucket; pail
sec dry (adj)
sèche-cheveux hair dryer
sécher to dry
secours help (n)
secours, au Save me!
secret secret
sécurité, en safe
seins breasts
sel salt
selle stool (poop)
semaine week
semblable similar
sembler to seem
sens unique one way (street)
sentier trail; path
sentir to feel (touch); to smell
séparé separate (adj)
sept seven
septembre September
sérieux serious
serré tight
serrure lock (n)
serveur waiter
serveuse waitress
serviable helpful
service favor (n)
service de babysitting babysitting service
service rapide fast food
serviette napkin
serviette de bain towel
serviettes hygiéniques sanitary pads
servir to serve
seul alone
seulement only
sexe gender; sex; genitalia
sexy sexy
shampooing shampoo
short shorts
si if; yes (in response to a negative)
SIDA AIDS
siècle century
siège auto (pour bébé) car seat (for baby)
sieste nap (n)
signe arobase "at" sign (@)
s'il vous plaît please
single single (for one person)
site web website
six six
ski skiing
ski nautique waterskiing
slip underpants
smartphone smartphone
SMS text message
SNCF French State Railways
snowboard snowboarding
soeur sister
soie silk
soif thirsty
soigner to treat; to tend; to care for
soir evening
soir, ce tonight
soirée party (n); evening

soja soy
sol floor
soldat soldier
solde sale
soleil sun; sunshine
solution solution
solution de lentille multifonction all-purpose solution (contacts)
solution de lentille nettoyante cleaning solution (contacts)
solution de lentille trempage soaking solution (contacts)
sombre dark
sommeil, avoir sleepy
sortie exit (n)
sortie de secours emergency exit
sortie du Métro subway exit
soudain suddenly
souffrir to suffer
souhaiter to wish
souligne underscore (_)
soulignement underline (n)
soupe soup
sourcil eyebrow
sourire to smile; smile (n)
souris mouse; mice
sous under; below
sous-sol basement
sous-titres subtitles
sous-vêtements underwear
soutien-gorge bra
souvenir to remember; memory
spa spa
spécial special
spécialement especially
spécialité specialty
spectacle show (n)
standardiste operator
station station
station de Métro subway station
station de service gas station
station de taxi taxi stand
stationnement interdit no parking
stupide stupid
stylo pen
sucre sugar
sucré sweet
sud south
suffisant sufficient
suggérer to recommend
Suisse Switzerland
suivre to follow
super great
supermarché supermarket
supplément supplement
sur on
surfer to surf
surfeur surfer
surnom nickname
surprise surprise (n)
symbole symbol
sympa nice; friendly
synthétique synthetic

T

table table
tableau painting
tablette tablet computer
taille size; waist
talc talcum powder
tant pis too bad
tante aunt

taper to type
tapis rug
tard late
tarif réduit reduced fare
tasse cup
tatouage tattoo
taxe tax
teinture d'iode iodine
télécharger to download
téléphone telephone
téléphone payant pay phone
télévision television
température temperature
tempête storm
temporaire temporary
temps weather; time (duration)
tendinite tendinitis
tendre tender (adj)
tente tent
TER (train express régional) local train
terminé done; finished
terminer to finish
terrasse terrace
terre earth; soil; land
terroriste terrorist
test de grossesse pregnancy test
tester to test
testicules testicles
tête head
tête légère lightheaded
tétine pacifier
texto text message
TGV (train à grande vitesse) high-speed train
thé tea
théâtre theater; play (n)
thermomètre thermometer
thon tuna
tiède lukewarm
timbre stamp
timide shy
tique tick (insect)
tire-bouchon corkscrew
tirer to pull
tiret dash (-)
tissu cloth
toilette toilet
toit roof
tomber to fall
tongues flip-flops
tôt early
total total
toucher to touch
toujours always
tour tour; tower
touriste tourist
tournevis screwdriver
tous everything
tous les deux both
tous les jours daily
tousser to cough
tout all
tout le monde everybody
toux cough (n)
tradition tradition
traditionnel traditional
traduire to translate
train train
train de nuit overnight train
train direct express train
traitement treatment (medical)
traiteur delicatessen; caterer

tranche slice (n)
tranquille tranquil
transpirer to sweat
travail work (n)
travailler to work
travaux construction (sign)
travers, à through
trépied tripod
très very
trésorerie treasury
triangle triangle
tri-bande tri-band
triste sad
trois three
trombone paper clip
trop too (much)
trou hole
trouver to find
tu you (informal)
tuba snorkel
tuer to kill
Turquie Turkey
TVA (Taxe sur la Valeur Ajoutée) VAT (Value-Added Tax)

U

un one
une fois once
Union Européenne European Union (EU)
université university
urètre urethra
urgence emergency
urgences, aux emergency room
urgent urgent
usine factory
utérus uterus
utiliser to use

V

vacances vacation
vache cow
vagin vagina
vague wave (water)
valeur value (worth)
valise suitcase
vallée valley
vase vase
végétarien vegetarian (n)
vélo bicycle
vélo tout-terrain (VTT) mountain bike
vélomoteur moped
velours velvet
vendre to sell
vendredi Friday
venir to come
vent wind (n)
venteux windy
ventilateur fan (machine)
ver worm
verglas ice (on roadway)
vérité truth
vernis à ongles nail polish
verre glass
verrue wart
vers toward
vert green
vertige dizziness
vessie bladder
veste jacket
vêtement clothing
veuf widower
veuve widow

V

viande meat
vicieuse (f) / vicieux (m) creepy; vicious
vide empty
vidéo video
vie life
vieille (f) / vieux (m) old
vieille ville old town
vignoble vineyard
VIH HIV
village dans les collines / village perché hill town
ville city
villeneuve new town
vin wine
vin, blanc white wine
vin, rouge red wine
viol rape (n)
violet purple
virage curve
visage face
visite visit (n)
visite guidée guided tour
visiter to visit
vitamine vitamin
vite fast
vitesse speed (n)
vitesses gears
vivant live (adj)
voie track (train)
voile sailing
voilier sailboat
voir to see
voiture car; train car
voiture restaurant dining car (train)
voix voice
vol flight
volaille poultry
volé stolen
voler to fly; to steal
voleur thief; pickpocket
vomir to vomit
votre your
vôtre, le yours
vouloir to want
vous you (formal)
voyage trip
voyager to travel
voyageur traveler
vue view (n)

W

wagon-lit sleeper car (train)
WC toilet
webcam webcam
week-end weekend
Wi-Fi Wi-Fi

Y

yaourt yogurt
yoga yoga
yeux eyes

Z

zéro zero
zone Wi-Fi Wi-Fi hotspot
zoo zoo

ENGLISH / FRENCH

A

aboard à bord
abortion avortement
above au-dessus
abstract abstrait
abuse (v) abuser
accept accepter
access (n) accès
accident accident
accountant comptable
ache (n) mal
adapter, electrical adaptateur électrique
address adresse
address, email adresse email
adult adulte
affordable abordable
(to be) afraid avoir peur
Africa Afrique
after après
afternoon après-midi
aftershave après rasage
afterwards après
again encore
age âge
aggressive agressif
agnostic agnostique
agree être d'accord
AIDS SIDA
air air
air mail par avion
air-conditioned climatisé
airline ligne aérienne
airport aéroport
aisle couloir
alarm clock réveille
alcohol alcool
allergic allergique
allergies allergies
allowed autorisé
alone seul
already déjà
altar autel
always toujours
ambulance (emergencies) SAMU
ambulance (medical transport) ambulance
America Amérique
American football football américain
amount quantité
arm bras
amusement park parc d'amusement
ancestor ancêtre
ancient ancien
and et
angry fâché
animal animal
ankle cheville
anniversary (wedding) anniversaire (de mariage)
announcement annonce
another (a different one) autre
another (more of the same) encore
answer (n) réponse
answer (v) répondre
answering machine répondeur
ant fourmi

A

antacid anti-acide
antibiotic antibiotique
antiques antiquités
antiques shop magasin d'antiquités
anxiety angoisse
anyone n'importe qui
anything n'importe le quel
anytime n'importe quand
anywhere n'importe où
apartment appartement
apology excuses
appetizer entrée
apple pomme
appointment rendez-vous
approximately environ
April avril
aquarium aquarium
area code code régional
around (go around) le tour (faire le tour)
arrivals arrivées
arrive arriver
art art
art gallery gallérie d'art
Art Nouveau art nouveau
arthritis arthrite
artificial artificiel
artist artiste
ashtray cendrier
ask demander
ask for demander pour
asleep endormi
aspirin aspirine
asthma asthme
at à
"at" sign (@) signe arobase
atheist athée
athlete athlète
athlete's foot mycose
ATM distributeur automatique
attend (an event) assister
attractive attirant
audioguide audioguide
August août
aunt tante
Austria Autriche
author auteur
authorize autoriser
automatic automatique
autumn automne
available disponible
avenue avenue

B

baby bébé
baby booster seat rehausseur
baby car seat siège voiture
baby food nourriture pour bébé
baby formula lait pour bébé
babysitter baby-sitter
babysitting service service de babysitting
back (body) dos
back (place) au fond
backpack sac à dos
bad mauvais
bag sac; sachet
bag, plastic sac en plastique
bag, Ziploc sac en plastique à fermeture
baggage bagages
baggage check (left luggage) consigne

baggage check in (for a flight) contrôle; enregistrement des bagages
baggage claim carrousel des bagages
bakery boulangerie
balcony balcon
ball balle
banana banane
band (musical) groupe
bandage pansement
bandage, support pansement élastique
Band-Aid pansement
bangs (hair) frange
bank banque
bar bar
barber coiffeur
barber shop coiffeur pour homme
baseball baseball
basement sous-sol
basket panier
basketball basket
bastard salaud
bath bain
bathrobe peignoir de bain
bathroom salle de bain
bathtub baignoire; bain
battery (car) batterie
battery (electronic) pile
battery (watch) pile de montre
battery charger chargeur de piles
beach plage
beard barbe
beautiful beau (m); belle (f)
beauty salon coiffeur pour dames
because parce que
bed lit
bed, double grand lit
bed, roll-away lit pliant
bed, single petit lit; lit jumeau
bedbugs punaises de lit
bedroom chambre
bedsheet draps
beef boeuf
beer bière
before avant
begin commencer
beginning début
behind derrière
Belgium Belgique
believe (in) croire (en)
bells cloches
below en-dessous
belt ceinture
berth (train) couchette
best le meilleur
better meilleur
between entre
beware of the dog chien méchant
bib bavoir
Bible Bible
bicycle vélo
big grand
bike path piste cyclable
bike ride randonnée à vélo
bill (payment) facture
bill (restaurant only) addition
bills (money) billets
bird oiseau

B

birth control contraceptif
birth control pill la pilule
birthday anniversaire
bitch salope
bitter amer
black noir
bladder vessie
bland fade
blanket couverture
bleeding saignement
blister ampoule
block (street) pâté de maisons
blond blond
blood sang
blood pressure, high hypertension
blouse chemisier
blue bleu
blush (makeup) blush; rouge à joues
board (v) embarquer
boarding (transportation) embarquement
boarding pass carte d'embarquement
boat bateau
body corps
boil bouillir
boiled bouilli
bomb bombe
bone os
book (n) livre
book (v) réserver
book shop librairie
book, telephone bottin; annuaire
booster seat rehausseur
boots bottes
border frontière
boring ennuyeux
born né
borrow emprunter
boss chef
both tous les deux
bother embêter
bottle bouteille
bottle opener décapsuleur
bottom fond
boulevard boulevard
boutique, clothing boutique; magasin de vêtements
bowl bol
box boîte
boy garçon
boyfriend petit ami
bra soutien-gorge
bracelet bracelet
brain cerveau
brakes freins
brass cuivre jaune
bread pain
break (rest) (n) pause
breakdown (car) en panne
breakfast petit déjeuner
breast seins
breastfeeding allaitement maternel
breath haleine
breathe respirer
bridge pont
briefs slip
bring apporter
Britain Grande-Bretagne
broken (damaged) cassé
broken (out of order) en panne

bronze bronze
brooch broche
brother frère
brown brun
brush (n) brosse
bucket seau
bug bite piqure d'insecte
bug insecte
build construire
building bâtiment
bulb, light ampoule
bunk bed lit superposé
burn (n) brûlure
bus bus
bus station gare routière
bus stop arrêt de bus
bus, city bus
bus, long-distance car
business affaires
business card carte de visite
busy occupé
but mais
butcher boucherie
butter beurre
buttocks fesses
button bouton
buy acheter
by (train, car, etc.) en
bypass rocade; périphérique

C

calendar calendrier
call (v) appeler
call (n) appel
calm (adj) calme
calorie calorie
camera appareil photo
camera shop magasin de photo
camping camping
campsite emplacement
can (n) boîte de conserve
can (v) pouvoir
can opener ouvre-boîte
Canada Canada
canal canal
cancel annuler
cancellation policy conditions d'annulation
candle bougie
candy bonbon
cane canne
canoe canoë
cap casquette
captain capitaine
car voiture
car rental agency agence de location de voiture
car seat (baby) siège auto
car, dining (train) voiture restaurant
car, sleeper (train) wagon-lit
carafe carafe
card carte
card, telephone carte téléphonique
cards (deck) jeu de cartes
careful prudent
carpet moquette
carry porter
carry-on luggage bagage de cabine
cash liquide
cash machine distributeur automatique

C

cashier caisse
castle château
cat chat
catch (v) attraper
cathedral cathédrale
Catholic (adj) catholique
caution prudence
cave grotte
CDW (collision damage waiver) garantie dommages collisions
celebrate célébrer
cell phone portable
cell phone shop magasin de portables
cellar cave
center centre
century siècle
ceramic céramique
chain chaîne
chair chaise
championship championnat
chance chance
change (n) monnaie
change (v) modifier; changer
chapel chapelle
charge (amount) (v) facturer
charger chargeur
charming charmant
cheap bon marché
cheaper moins cher
check chèque
check-in (baggage) enregistrement des bagages; contrôle
check-in (hotel) check in
check-out (hotel) libérer la chambre
Cheers! Santé!
cheese fromage
cheese shop fromagerie
chest poitrine
chest pains maux de poitrine
chewing gum chewing-gum
chicken (animal) poule
chicken (meat) poulet
children enfants
children's plate assiette d'enfant
chills frissons
Chinese chinois
chip (electronic) puce
chocolate chocolat
choir choeur
Christian (adj) chrétien
Christmas Noël
church église
church service messe
cigarette cigarette
cinema cinéma
circle cercle
city ville
city (fortified, medieval) cité
class classe
class, first première classe
class, second deuxième classe
classical classique
clean (adj) propre
clear (adj) clair
cliff falaise
clinic, medical clinique médicale
clock horloge
clock, alarm réveille
cloister cloître
close (v) fermer
closed fermé

closet placard
cloth tissu
clothing vêtement
clothes pin pince à linge
clothesline corde à linge
clothing boutique boutique; magasin de vêtements
cloudy nuageux
club (nightclub) boîte de nuit
coast côte
coat manteau
coat hanger cintre
cockroach cafards
coffee café
coffee shop café
coin pièce
cold (adj) froid
cold (n) rhume
cold medicine remède contre le rhume
cologne cologne
color (n) couleur
comb (n) peigne
come venir
comfortable confortable
common ordinaire; fréquent
compact disc disque compact
companion compagnon
complain plaindre
complaint réclamation
complicated compliqué
computer ordinateur
concert concert
conditioner, hair après-shampoing
condom préservatif
conductor conducteur
confirm confirmer
confirmation confirmation
congestion (sinus) congestion
congratulations félicitations
connect (link up) relier
connect (log on) connecter
connection (train) correspondance
conservative (n) droitiste
constipation constipation
construction (sign) travaux
contact lenses lentilles de contact
contact solution, all purpose solution pour lentilles multifonction
contact solution, cleaning solution pour lentilles nettoyante
contact solution, soaking solution pour lentilles trempage
contagious contagieux
container barquette
continue continuer
contraceptive contraceptif
contractions (pregnancy) contractions
control (v) contrôler
convertor (electrical) convertisseur
cook (v) cuisiner
cooked cuit
cookies biscuits; petits gâteaux
cool (slang) sympa
cool (temperature) frais
copper cuivre
copy (n) reproduction

C

copy (v) copier
copy shop magasin de photocopie
cork bouchon
corkscrew tire-bouchon
corner coin
corridor couloir
corruption corruption
cost (n) coût
cost (v) coûter
cot lit de camp
cotton coton
cotton swabs (Q-Tips) coton-tiges
cough (n) toux
cough (v) tousser
cough drop pastille
count (v) compter
country pays
country home rental gîte
countryside compagne
course, first entrée
course, main plat principal
cousin cousin
cover (v) couvrir
cow vache
cozy confortable
crafts arts plastiques
cramp crampe
cramp, stomach crampe d'estomac
cramps, menstrual crampes menstruelles
crazy fou (m); folle (f)
crayon crayon de cire
cream crème
cream, first-aid crème antiseptique
credit card carte de crédit
creep vicieux
crib berceau; lit à barreau
cross croix
crowd (n) foule
cruise ship bateau de croisière
cry (v) pleurer
crypt crypte
cup (n) tasse
curfew couvre-feu
curtains rideaux
curve virage
customs douane
cut (n) coupure
cut (v) couper
cute mignon
Czech Republic République Tchèque

D

dad papa
daily tous les jours; quotidien
dairy products produits laitiers
dance (v) danser
danger danger
dangerous dangereux
dark sombre
dash (-) tiret
date (calendar) date
daughter fille
day jour
day after tomorrow après demain
dead mort

dead end sans issue
deal (good value) bonne affaire
debit card carte bancaire
decaf / decaffeinated déca / décaféiné
December décembre
declare (customs) déclarer
decongestant décongestant
delay (n) retard
delayed en retard
delete supprimer
delicate délicat
delicatessen charcuterie; traiteur
delicious délicieux
democracy démocratie
demonstration (public) manifestation
dental floss fil dentaire
dentist dentiste
deodorant déodorant
depart partir
department store grand magasin
departures départs
deposit caution
depression dépression
desk bureau
desperate désespéré
dessert dessert
destination destination
detergent, laundry lessive
detour (n) déviation
diabetes diabète
diabetic diabétique
diamond diamant
diaper couche
diaper ointment crème pour les fesses
diaper rash érythème fessier
diaper wipe lingette de couche
diarrhea diarrhée
diarrhea medicine médicament pour la diarrhée
dictionary dictionnaire
die mourir
diesel gasoil; gazole; diesel
difficult difficile
digital camera appareil photo numérique
dine (v) dîner
dining car (train) voiture restaurant
dinner (n) dîner
direct (adj) direct
direction direction
directory assistance renseignements
dirty (adj) sale
disaster désastre
discount (n) réduction; remise
discrimination discrimination
discuss discuter
disease maladie
dish plat
disinfectant désinfectant
distance distance
disturb déranger
divorced divorcé
dizziness vertige
dizzy étourdi
do faire
doctor médecin; docteur
dog chien

doll poupée
dome dôme
domestic domestique
done terminé
donkey âne
door porte
dormitory dortoir
dot (computer) point
double double
double bed grand lit
doubt (v) douter
down en bas
downhill descente
download (v) télécharger
downtown centre-ville
dozen douzaine
dream (n) rêve
dream (v) rêver
dress (n) robe
drink (n) boisson
drink (v) boire
drive (v) conduire
driver chauffeur
drug (medicine) médicament
drugstore pharmacie
drunk ivre
dry (adj) sec
dry (v) sécher
dryer machine à sécher
duck canard
duct tape ruban adhésif
dungeon cachot
dust poussière
duty free hors taxe

E

each chaque
ear oreille
earache mal aux oreilles
earbuds écouteurs
early tôt
earplugs boules quiès
earrings boucle d'oreille
earth terre
east est
Easter Pâques
easy facile
eat manger
economical économique
education éducation
effective efficace
egg oeuf
eight huit
elbow coude
electrical adapter adaptateur électrique
electrical outlet prise
elevator ascenseur
email email
email address adresse email
embarrassing gênant
embassy ambassade
emergency urgence
emergency exit sortie de secours
emergency room aux urgences
empty (adj) vide
end (n) fin
engaged fiancé
engine moteur
engineer ingénieur
England Angleterre
English anglais
English Channel la Manche

enjoy apprécier
enough assez
enter entrer
entertainment divertissement
entrance entrée
entry entrée
envelope enveloppe
environment (nature) environnement
epilepsy épilepsie
equal égal
erase effacer
eraser gomme
especially spécialement
Europe Europe
European Union (EU) Union Européenne
evening soir; soirée
every chaque
everybody tout le monde
everything tous
everywhere partout
exact exact
exactly exactement
examine examiner
example exemple
excellent excellent
except sauf
exchange (n) échange
exchange (v) échanger
exchange rate taux de change
excited ravi
excuse me (to get attention) excusez moi
excuse me (to pass) pardon
exercise (v) faire du sport
exhausted épuisé
exhibit / exhibition exposition
exit (n) sortie
exit, emergency sortie de secours
expensive cher
expiration (validity) date limite de validité
explain expliquer
explanation explication
express express
expression (facial, phrase) expression
expressway autoroute
extra en plus
eye / eyes oeil / yeux
eye drops gouttes pour les yeux
eye shadow ombre à paupières
eyebrow sourcil
eyeliner eyeliner; crayon pour les yeux

F

fabric tissu
facade façade
face visage
face cleanser lait nettoyant
face powder fond de teint compact
facial (spa) masque facial
facial tissue kleenex; mouchoirs en papier
factory usine
fair (just) juste
fall (autumn) automne
fall (v) tomber
false faux
familiar familier

family famille
famous fameux
fan (machine) ventilateur
fan belt courroie du ventilateur
fantastic fantastique
far loin
farm (n) ferme
farmer fermier
farmer's market marché alimentaire
fashion mode
fast vite; rapide
fast food restauration rapide
fat (n) matière grasse
fat (adj) gros
father père
father-in-law beau-père
faucet robinet
favor (n) service
favorite favori
fax (n) fax
fear (n) peur
fear (v) craindre
February février
fee frais
feed nourrir
feel (touch) sentir
feet pieds
female femelle
ferry bac; bateau
festival festival; fête
fever fièvre
few peu
field champ
fight (n) lutte
fight (v) combattre
file (computer) fichier
fill (v) remplir
filling copieux
film (camera) pellicule
final finale
finally enfin
find (v) trouver
fine (good) bon
fine (penalty) amende
finger doigt
fingernail ongle
finish (v) finir; terminer
finished terminé
fire feu
fire alarm alarme incendie
fire department les pompiers
fireworks feux d'artifices
first premier
first aid premiers secours
first-aid cream crème antiseptique
first class première classe
first course (meal) entrée
fish (n) poisson
fish (v) pêcher
fit (clothes) taille
five cinq
fix (v) réparer
fizzy pétillant
flag drapeau
flash (camera) flash
flash drive carte mémoire flash
flashlight lampe de poche
flavor (n) parfum
flea puce
flea market marché aux puces
flight vol
flip-flops tongues

floor étage; sol
floss, dental fil dentaire
flower fleur
flower market marché aux fleurs
flu grippe
fly (v) voler
fog brouillard
follow suivre
food nourriture
food poisoning empoisonnement alimentaire
foot pied
football, American football américain
footwear chaussures
for pour
forbidden interdit
foreign étranger
foreigner étranger
forest forêt
forget oublier
fortified wall remparts
fork fourchette
form (document) formulaire
formula (for baby) lait pour bébé
foundation (makeup) fond de teint
fountain fontaine
four quatre
fragile fragile
France France
free (available) libre; disponible
free (no cost) gratuit
freeway autoroute
French français
French State Railways SNCF
frequency fréquence
frequent fréquent
fresh fraîche
Friday vendredi
fried frit
friend ami
friendly amical
friendship amitié
fries frites
Frisbee frisbee
from de
fruit fruit
frustrated frustré
fry (v) frire
fuel essence
full plein; complet
fun amusement
funeral enterrement
funny drôle
furniture meubles
fuse fusible
future avenir

G

gallery galerie
game jeu
game (sports) match
garage garage
garden jardin
gardening jardinage
gas (vapor) gaz
gas station station de service
gas tank réservoir
gasoline essence
gauze gaze
gay gay; homosexuel
gears vitesses

G

gender sexe
generous généreux
gentleman monsieur
genuine authentique
Germany Allemagne
get (obtain) obtenir
gift cadeau
girl fille
girlfriend petite-amie
give donner
glass verre
glasses (eye) lunettes
glasses case étui à lunettes
gloves gants
gluten gluten
go aller
go back (return) rentrer
go through passer
goat chèvre
God Dieu
good bon; bien
gold or
golf golf
good day bonjour
goodbye au revoir
Gothic gothique
government gouvernement
grammar grammaire
grandchildren des petits-enfants
granddaughter petite-fille
grandfather grand-père
grandmother grand-mère
grandson petit-fils
grass (lawn) pelouse
gray gris
greasy graisseux
great (large) grand
great (terrific) super
Great Britain Grande-Bretagne
Greece Grèce
green vert
grilled grillé
grocery store épicerie; supermarché
ground (earth) terre
ground floor rez-de-chaussée
group groupe
guarantee garantie
guest invité
guide (n) guide
guide (v) guider
guidebook guide
guided tour visite guidée
guilty coupable
guitar guitare
gum (mouth) gencive
gun fusil
gymnastics gymnastique
gynecologist gynécologue

H

habit habitude
hair cheveux
hair dryer sèche-cheveux
hair salon salon de coiffure
hairbrush brosse
haircut coupe de cheveux
half demi
half day demi-journée
half portion demi-portion
hall (room) salle
hall (passage) couloir
ham jambon
hammer marteau

hand main
hand lotion crème pour les mains
hand sanitizer désinfectant pour les mains
handicapped handicapé
handicrafts produits artisanaux
handle (n) poignée
handsome beau
hang accrocher
happy heureux; content
happiness bonheur
harbor port
hard dur
hardware store quincaillerie
hash (drug) hachisch
hat chapeau
hate (v) détester
hatred haine
have avoir
hay fever rhume des foins
he il
head tête
headache mal de tête
headlight phare
headphones casque
health santé
health insurance assurance maladie
healthy en bonne santé
hear entendre
heart coeur
heart condition problème cardiaque
heartburn reflux gastrique
heat (n) chauffage
heat (v) chauffer
heaven ciel; paradis
heavy lourd
hello bonjour
helmet casque
help (n) secours
help (v) aider
helpful serviable
hemorrhoids hémorroïdes
hepatitis hépatite
her elle
herb herbe
here ici
hers à elle
hi salut
hidden caché
high haut
high blood pressure hypertension
high chair chaise haute
high-speed train TGV
highway grande route
hike (n) randonnée
(to go) hiking faire de la randonnée
hiking map carte de randonné
hill colline
hill town village dans les collines; village perché
hip (body part) hanche
his à lui
history histoire
hitchhike faire de l'autostop
hobby hobby
hockey hockey
hole trou
holiday jour férié
holy sacré

home page page d'accueil
homemade fait maison
homesickness mal du pays
honest honnête
honeymoon lune de miel
hope (n) espoir
hope (v) espoir
horrible horrible
horse cheval
horse riding équitation
hospital hôpital
hot (spicy) piquant
hot (temperature) chaud
hot flashes bouffées de chaleur
hotel hôtel
hotel, small pension
hour heure
house maison
how comment
how long combien de temps
how many combien
how much combien
human (n) humain
humid humide
hundred cent
(to be) hungry avoir faim
hurried pressé
hurry (v) dépêcher
hurt (adj) blessé
hurt (v) blesser
husband mari
hydrofoil hydroptère

I

I je
ibuprofen ibuprofène
ice (cubes) glaçons
ice (on road) verglas
ice cream glace
idea idée
ideal idéal
if si
ignore ignorer
ill malade
illegal illégal
illness maladie
immediately immédiatement
immigrant immigré
immigration immigration
important important
imported importé
impossible impossible
Impressionist impressionniste
in en; dans
include inclure
included inclus
incorrect incorrect
incredible incroyable
independent indépendant
indigestion indigestion
indoors l'intérieur
industry industrie
inedible immangeable
infant nourrisson
infection infection
infection, urinary tract infection urinaire
inflammation inflammation
inflation inflation
inform informer
information information; renseignements
injured blessé
injury blessure

innocent innocent
insect insecte
insect repellant insectifuge
inside à l'intérieur; dedans
insomnia insomnie
inspect inspecter
instant instant
instead au lieu de
instructions (directions) instructions
insulin insuline
insult (n) insulte
insurance assurance
insurance, health assurance maladie
insured assuré
intelligent intelligent
intend avoir l'intention
interesting intéressant
international international
Internet internet
Internet access accès internet
Internet café café internet
intersection carrefour
intestine intestin
intimates lingerie
into dans
investigation enquête
invitation invitation
invite inviter
iodine teinture d'iode
Ireland Irlande
ironed repassé
is est
Islamic islamique
island île
it's a pity quel dommage
Italy Italie
itch (n) démangeaison
itch reliever crème anti-démangeaison
itchy (it itches) ça démange

J

jacket veste
January janvier
jaw mâchoire
jealous jaloux (m); jalouse (f)
jeans jean
jet lag décalage horaire
jewelry bijoux
jewelry shop bijouterie
Jewish juif
job boulot
jogging jogging; footing
joint (marijuana) joint
joke (n) blague
journey voyage
judge (v) juger
juice jus
July juillet
jump (v) sauter
June juin

K

kayak kayak
keep garder
kettle bouilloire
key clef; clé
kidney stone calcul rénal
kill (v) tuer
kilogram kilo
kilometer kilomètre
kind aimable

K

king roi
kiss (n) bisou
kiss (v) embrasser
kitchen cuisine
kitchenette kitchenette
knee genou
knife couteau
knight chevalier
know savoir
knowledge connaissance
kosher kasher

L

lace dentelle
lactose intolerant intolérant au lactose
ladder échelle
ladies mesdames
lake lac
lamb agneau
lamp lampe
land (earth, soil) terre
language langue
laptop ordinateur portable
large grand
last dernier
late tard
later plus tard
laugh (v) rire
launderette laverie
laundry soap lessive
lawyer avocat
laxative laxatif
lazy paresseux
lead (v) diriger
learn apprendre
least le moins
leather cuir
leave partir
left gauche
leg jambe
legal légal
lend prêter
lens cap bouchon d'objectif
lenses, contact lentilles de contact
lesbian lesbienne
less moins
let (allow) laisser
letter lettre
liberal gauchiste
liberate libérer
library bibliothèque
lice poux
lie (fib) (v) mentir
lie (untruth) mensonge
life vie
lift (v) lever
light (v) allumer
light (n) lumière
light (weight) (adj) léger
light up (illuminate) illuminer
lightbulb ampoule
lighter (n) briquet; feu
lightheaded tête légère
lighthouse phare
like (as) comme
like (v) aimer bien
line (n) ligne
line (queue) queue
linen lin
lip lèvre
lip balm baume pour les lèvres
lipstick rouge à lèvres

liquid liquide
liquor store caviste
list (n) liste
listen écouter
liter litre
little (adj) petit
live (adj) vivant
live (v) habiter
local régional
local train TER (train express régional)
lock (n) serrure
lock (v) fermer à clef
locked (mobile phone) bloqué
locker consigne automatique; casier
long long
look at regarder
look for chercher
lose perdre
lost perdu
lost and found office bureau des objets trouvés
lotion, hand crème pour les mains
lotion, suntan lotion solaire
loud bruyant
love (n) amour
love (v) aimer
lover amant
low bas
lozenge pastille
luck chance
lucky chanceux
luggage bagage
luggage, carry-on bagage de cabine
lukewarm tiède
lunch déjeuner
lungs poumons
luxurious luxueux

M

machine machine
macho macho
mad fâché
magazine magazine
mail (n) courrier
mail (v) poster
mailbox boîte aux lettres
main principal
main course (meal) plat principal
make (v) faire
makeup maquillage
male mâle
mall (shopping) centre commercial
man homme
manage gérer
manager directeur; gérant
manicure manucure
many beaucoup
map carte
marble (material) marbre
March mars
marijuana herbe; marijuana
market (n) marché
market, farmer's marché alimentaire
market, flea marché aux puces
market, flower marché aux fleurs

market, open-air marché en plein air
marriage mariage
married marié
mascara mascara
Mass messe
massage (medical) massage
massage (spa) modelage
match / matchstick allumette
material matière
maximum maximum
May mai
maybe peut-être
McDonald's Mac Do
me moi
meal repas
mean méchant
meat viande
mechanic mécanicien
media médias
medicine médicaments
medicine, cold remède contre le rhume
medicine, pain reliever (ibuprofen) ibuprofène
medieval médiéval
medium moyen
meet (v) rencontrer
member membre
membership card (hostel) carte de membre
memory mémoire; souvenir
memory card carte mémoire
men hommes
menstrual cramps crampes menstruelles
menstruation menstruation
menu carte
message message
metal métal
meter, taxi compteur
method méthode
microwave micro-onde
middle au milieu
midnight minuit
migraine migraine
mild doux
mileage (in kilometers) kilométrage
military militaire
milk lait
mind (brain) tête; cerveau
mine (adj) à moi; le mien
minority minorité
mineral water eau minérale
minimum minimum
minus moins
minute (time) minute
mirror miroir; glace
miscarriage fausse couche
Miss Mademoiselle
miss (long for) manquer
miss (fail to reach) rater
missing (lost) perdu
mistake erreur
misunderstanding malentendu
mix (n) mélange
mix (v) mélanger
mixed mixte
moat fossé
mobile phone portable
mobile-phone shop magasin de portables
modern moderne

moisturizer crème hydratante
mole grain de beauté
moleskin moleskin
moment moment
monastery monastère
Monday lundi
money argent
month mois
monument monument
moon lune
moped mobylette
more encore; plus
morning matin
mosque mosquée
mosquito moustique
most le plus
mother mère
mother-in-law belle-mère
motion sickness mal des transports
motor scooter scooter
motorcycle moto; motocyclette
mountain montagne
mountain bike VTT
mountain pass col
mouse / mice souris
moustache moustache
mouth bouche
mouthwash rince-bouche
move (v) déplacer
movie film
movie theater cinéma
MP3 player baladeur MP3
Mr. Monsieur
Mrs. Madame
much beaucoup
muggy humide
mural mural
muscle muscle
museum musée
music musique
musician musicien
Muslim musulman
my mon; ma

N

nail (screw) clou
nail (finger) ongle
nail clipper pince à ongles
nail file lime à ongles
nail polish vernis à ongles
nail polish remover dissolvant
naked nu
name, first prénom
name, last nom
nap (n) sieste
napkin serviette
narrow étroit
national national
national highway route nationale
nationality nationalité
natural naturel
nature nature
nausea nausée
near près
nearsighted myope
necessary nécessaire
neck cou
necklace collier
need (n) besoin
need (v) avoir besoin de
needle aiguille
neither ni

Neoclassical néoclassique
nephew neveu
nervous nerveux
Netherlands Pays-Bas
network réseau
never jamais
new nouveau
new town villeneuve
news nouvelles
newspaper journal
newsstand kiosque à journaux
next prochain
next to à côté de
nice gentil
nickname surnom
niece nièce
night nuit
nightclub boîte de nuit
nightgown chemise de nuit
nine neuf
no non
no one personne
no parking stationnement interdit
no vacancy complet
nobody personne
noisy bruyant
none aucun
non-smoking non-fumeur
noon midi
normal normale
north nord
nose nez
not pas
note (message) mot
notebook calepin; cahier
nothing rien
November novembre
now maintenant
nowhere nulle part
nude nu
nude beach plage naturiste
numbness engourdissement
nurse infirmière
nuts noix
nylon (material) nylon
nylons (pantyhose) collants

O

occupation emploi
occupied occupé
ocean océan
October octobre
odor odeur
of de
offer (n) offre
offer (v) offrir
office bureau
office supplies store papeterie
official officiel
oil huile
OK d'accord; OK
old vieux (m); vieille (f)
old town vieille ville
Olympics Olympiques
on sur
on time à l'heure
once une fois
one un
one way (street) sens unique
one way (ticket) aller simple
only seulement
open (adj) ouvert
open (v) ouvrir

open-air market marché en plein air
opening hours heures d'ouverture
opera opéra
operation (medical) opération
operator téléphoniste
opinion avis
opportunity occasion
optician opticien
optimistic optimiste
or ou
orange orange
order (v) commander
organ (instrument) orgue
organic biologique
original original
other autre
outdoors dehors
outlet (plug) prise
outside dehors
oven four
over (above) au-dessus
over (finished) fini
overcooked trop cuit
overnight train train de nuit
overweight (fat) en surpoids
overweight (above limit) trop lourd
owner propriétaire

P

pacifier tétine
pack (v) faire le bagage
package colis
paddleboat pédalo
page page
pail seau
pain douleur
pain killer antidouleur
pains, chest maux de poitrine
paint (v) peindre
painting tableau
pair paire
pajamas pyjama
palace palais
panties slip; culotte
pants pantalon
paper papier
paper clip trombone
paradise paradis
parents parents
park (n) parc
park (v) garer
parking lot parking
parking space place
partner conjoint
party soirée; fête
passenger passager
passport passeport
password mot de passé
past passé
paste (v) coller
pastry pâtisserie
pastry shop pâtisserie
path sentier
patient (n, adj) patient
pay (v) payer
pay phone téléphone publique
peace paix
pedestrian piéton
pedicure pédicure
pen stylo
pencil crayon

penicillin pénicilline
penis pénis
people gens
pepper (spice) poivre
percent pourcentage
perfect parfait
perfume parfum
period (time) période
period (menstruation) règles
permanent permanente
person personne
pessimistic pessimiste
pet (n) animal domestique
pewter étain
pharmacy pharmacie
phone booth cabine téléphonique
phone call appel téléphonique
phone, mobile portable
photo photo
photocopy (n) photocopie
photocopy shop magasin de photocopie
pickpocket pickpocket; voleur
picnic pique-nique
piece morceau
pig cochon
pill pilule
pill, birth control la pilule
pillow oreiller
pillow, fluffy coussin
pin épingle
PIN code code PIN
pink rose
pity, it's a quel dommage
pizza pizza
place (position) position
place (site) endroit
place (v) placer
plain (adj) simple; nature
plain (n) plaine
plane avion
plant (n) plante
plastic plastique
plastic bag sac en plastique
plate assiette
platform (train) quai
play (n) pièce de théâtre
play (v) jouer
playground aire de jeux (park); cour de récréation (school)
playpen parc pour bébé
please s'il vous plaît
please (make happy) plaire
pliers pinces
plug (outlet) prise
pneumonia pneumonie
pocket poche
point (n) point
point (reason) objet
point (v) indiquer
police police
policy règle
political politique
politician politicien
pollution pollution
polyester polyester
poop caca
poor pauvre
popular populaire
porcelain porcelaine
pork porc
portion portion
portrait portrait

Portugal Portugal
possible possible
possibly peut-être
postcard carte postale
poster affiche
poultry volaille
powder poudre
power pouvoir
powerful puissant
practical pratique
practice (v) entraîner
precious précieux
prefer préférer
pregnancy grossesse
pregnancy test test de grossesse
pregnant enceinte
prescription ordonnance
present (gift) cadeau
president président
pretty joli
price prix
priest prêtre
prince prince
princess princesse
principle principe
print (computer) (v) imprimer
private privé
problem problème
produce (v) produire
produce stand primeur
product produit
profession profession
prohibited interdit
promise (v) promettre
pronunciation prononciation
prosper prospérer
protect protéger
Protestant protestant
public publique
pull tirer
pulpit chaire
pulse pouls
pump (n) pompe
punctual à l'heure
purple violet
purse sac à main
push (v) pousser
put (v) poser

Q

Q-Tips (cotton swabs) coton-tiges
quad-band quad-bande
quantity quantité
quarter (¼) quart
quay quai
queen reine
question (n) question
quick rapide
quiet silence

R

rabbit lapin
racism racisme
radiator radiateur
radical radical
radio radio
raft radeau
railpass passe Eurail
railway chemin de fer
rain (n) pluie
rain (v) pleuvoir
rainbow arc-en-ciel

R

raincoat imperméable
raisin raisin sec
ramp rampe
rape (n) viol
rash boutons
rash, diaper érythème fessier
raw cru
razor rasoir
read lire
reading glasses lunettes de lecture
ready prêt
realize réaliser
receipt reçu
receive recevoir
recent récent
receptionist réceptionniste
recharge recharger
recipe recette
recommend recommandé
recommendation recommandation
rectum rectum
red rouge
reduced fare tarif réduit
re-enter rentrer
refill (v) remplir de nouveau
refresh (v) rafraîchir
refugee réfugié
refund (n) remboursement
relax (v) reposer
relaxation relaxation
relic relique
religion religion
remember souvenir
remind rappeler
remove retirer
Renaissance renaissance
rent (v) louer
repair (v) réparer
repeat (v) répéter
require exiger
required obligatoire
reservation réservation
reserve réserver
resolve résoudre
respect (n) respect
rest (v) reposer
restaurant restaurant
restored restauré
retired à la retraite
return (go back) rentrer; retourner
return (bring something back) rendre
rich riche
right (correct) correct
right (direction) droite
ring (n) bague
ring road rocade; périphérique
ripe mûr
river rivière
road route
robbed volé
rock (n) rocher
roller skates patins à roulettes
rollerblades roller
Romanesque romanesque
romantic romantique
roof toit
room chambre
room rental (in a private home) chambre d'hôte
rope corde

rotten pourri
round trip aller-retour
roundabout rondpoint
route (n) route
rowboat canot
rude impolis
rug tapis
ruins ruines
rule (n) règle
ruler règle
run (v) courir
run out of épuisé de
rush hour heure de pointe
Russia Russie
R.V. camping-car

S

sad triste
safe en sécurité
safety pin épingle à nourrice
sailboat voilier
sailing voile
saint saint
salad salade
salad bar buffet à salade
sale solde
salt sel
salty salé
same même
sandals sandales
sandwich sandwich
sanitary pads serviettes hygiéniques
Santa Claus Père Noël
Saturday samedi
sausage saucisse
save (money) garder
save (computer) sauver
say dire
scandalous scandaleux
Scandinavia Scandinavie
scarf écharpe; foulard
scenic panoramique; beau
schedule (timetable) horaire
school école
school crossing passage piéton
science science
scientist scientifique
scissors ciseaux
screen (n) écran
screwdriver tournevis
sculptor sculpteur
sculpture sculpture
sea mer
seafood fruits de mer
search (v) chercher
seasick mal de mer
season saison
seat place
second deuxième
second class deuxième classe
secret secret
see voir
seem sembler
self-portrait autoportrait
self-service libre-service
sell vendre
send envoyer
seniors gens âgés
sensible raisonnable
separate (adj) séparé
September septembre
serious sérieux
serve servir

service service
service, church messe
set (schedule) (v) fixer
set (put something down) poser
settings paramètres
seven sept
sew coudre
sex sexe
sexy sexy
shade (n) ombre
shampoo (n) shampooing
share (v) partager
shave (v) raser
shaving cream crème à raser
she elle
sheet drap
shell coquille
shellfish crustacés; coquillages
ship (n) navire
ship (v) envoyer
shirt chemise
shoelaces lacets
shoes chaussures
shoes, tennis baskettes; chaussures de tennis
shop (n) magasin
shop (v) faire du shopping
shop, antique magasin d'antiquités
shop, barber coiffeur des hommes
shop, camera magasin de photo
shop, cell phone magasin de portables
shop, cheese fromagerie
shop, clothing boutique de vêtements
shop, coffee café
shop, jewelry bijouterie
shop, pastry pâtisserie
shop, photocopy magasin de photocopie
shop, souvenir boutique de souvenirs
shop, sweets confiserie
shop, wine marchand de vin; cave
shopping shopping
shopping mall centre commercial
short court
shorts short
shoulder épaule
show (n) spectacle
show (v) montrer
shower (n) douche
shrink rétrécir
shy timide
shuttle bus navette
sick malade
side côté
sign (n) panneau
signature signature
silence silence
silk soie
silver argent
silverware couverts
SIM card carte SIM
similar semblable
simple simple
since depuis
sing chanter
singer chanteur (m); chanteuse (f)

single (unmarried) célibataire
single (for one person) single
sink (n) lavabo
sink stopper bouchon pour le lavabo
sinus problems problèmes de sinus
sir monsieur
sister soeur
sit asseoir
six six
size taille
skating patinage
ski (v) faire du ski
skiing ski
skin peau
skinny maigre
skirt (n) jupe
sky ciel
sleep (n) sommeil
sleep (v) dormir
sleeper (train) compartiment privé
sleeper car (train) wagon-lit
sleeping bag sac de couchage
sleepy avoir sommeil
sleeves manches
slice (n) tranche
slice (v) couper en tranches
slide (photo) diapositive
slip (n) jupon
slippers chaussons
slippery glissant
slow (adj) lent
Slow down! Ralentissez!
small petit
smartphone smartphone
smell (n) odeur
smell (v) sentir
smell bad (v) puer
smile (n, v) sourire
smoke (n) fumée
smoking fumeur
snack snack; casse-croûte
sneeze (v) éternuer
snore ronfler
snorkel tuba
snow (n) neige
snowboarding snowboard
soap savon
soap, laundry lessive
soccer football
socks chaussettes
soft doux
soil (earth, land) terre
sold out complet
soldier soldat
solution solution
some quelques
someone quelqu'un
something quelque chose
somewhere quelque part
son fils
song chanson
soon bientôt
sore avoir les courbatures
sore throat mal à la gorge
sorry désolé
soup soupe
sour aigre
south sud
souvenir shop boutique de souvenirs
soy soja

spa spa
space (room, spot) place
Spain Espagne
sparkplug bougie
speak parler
special spécial
special of the day (restaurant) plat du jour
specialty spécialité
speed (n) vitesse
speed limit limite de vitesse
spend dépenser
spice épice
spicy piquant
spider araignée
splinter (n) écharde
split partager
splurge faire une folie
spoon cuillère
sport sport
spouse époux (m); épouse (f)
spring printemps
square (shape) carré
square (town) place
stain (n) tache
stain remover détachant
stairs escalier
stall (bus station) quai
stamp (n) timbre
stapler agrafeuse
star (in sky) étoile
start (v) commencer
state (n) état
station station
station wagon break
stay (v) rester
STD (sexually transmitted disease) MST (maladie sexuellement transmissible)
steak bifteck; steak
steal (v) voler
stink (v) puer
stinky (it stinks) ça pue
stolen volé
stomach estomac
stomachache mal à l'estomac
stoned défoncé
stop (n) stop; arrêt
stop (v) arrêter
stoplight feu
stopper, sink bouchon pour le lavabo
store (n) magasin
store, department grand magasin
store, hardware quincaillerie
store, office supplies papeterie
store, toy magasin de jouets
storm tempête
story (floor) étage
story (tale) histoire
straight droit
strange bizarre
stranger (person) étranger
straw (drinking) paille
stream (n) ruisseau
street rue
strenuous difficile
strep throat angine
string ficelle
stroll (v) balader; promener
stroller (baby) poussette
strong fort

stuck coincé
student étudiant
stupid stupide
sturdy robuste
style mode
subtitles sous-titres
subway Métro
subway entrance l'entrée du Métro
subway exit sortie du Métro
subway map plan du Métro
subway station station de Métro
subway stop arrêt de Métro
suddenly soudain
suffer souffrir
sufficient suffisant
sugar sucre
suitcase valise
summer été
sun soleil
sunbathe se bronzer
sunburn (n) coup de soleil
Sunday dimanche
sunglasses lunettes de soleil
sunny ensoleillé
sunrise aube
sunscreen crème solaire
sunset coucher de soleil
sunshine soleil
sunstroke insolation
suntan (n) bronzage
suntan lotion crème solaire
supermarket supermarché
supplement (n) supplément
surf (v) surfer
surfboard planche de surf
surfer surfeur
surgery chirurgie
surprise (n) surprise
swallow (v) avaler
sweat (v) transpirer
sweater pull
sweet doux
sweets shop confiserie
swelling (n) gonflement
swim nager
swim trunks maillot de bain pour hommes
swimming natation
swimming pool piscine
swimsuit maillot de bain
Switzerland Suisse
symbol symbole
synagogue synagogue
synthetic synthétique

T

table table
tablet computer tablette
tail queue
taillight feu arrière
take prendre
take out (food) (v) emporter
talcum powder talc
talk parler
tall grand
tampon tampon
tank, gas réservoir d'essence
tape, duct ruban adhésif
tape (Scotch) scotch
taste (n) goût
taste (v) goûter
tasty savoureux
tattoo tatouage

T

tax taxe; impôt
tax refund détaxe
taxi taxi
taxi meter compteur
taxi stand station de taxi
tea thé
teach (v) enseigner
teacher professeur
team équipe
teenager adolescent
teeth dents
teething (baby) poussée des dents
telephone téléphone
telephone card carte téléphonique
telephone number numéro de téléphone
television télévision
tell dire
temperature température
temporary temporaire; spéciale
ten dix
tender tendre
tendinitis tendinite
tennis tennis
tennis shoes baskettes; chaussures de tennis
tent tente
tent pegs piquets de tente
terrace terrasse
terrible terrible
terrorist terroriste
test (v) tester
testicles testicules
text message texto; SMS
thanks merci
that (thing) ça
theater théâtre
their leur
then puis
there là; là-bas
thermometer thermomètre
they ils (m); elles (f)
thick épais
thief voleur
thigh cuisse
thin mince
thing chose
think penser
thirsty soif
this (adj) ce (m); cette (f)
thongs tongues
thousand mille
thread (n) fil
three trois
throat gorge
through à travers
throw (v) jeter
thumb pouce
Thursday jeudi
tick (insect) tique
ticket billet
ticket window guichet
tie (clothing) cravate
tie (v) attacher; nouer
tight serré
time (duration) temps
time (occasion) moment
time (clock) l'heure
time, arrival or check-in l'heure d'arriver
time, departure l'heure de départ

time, on à l'heure
timetable horaire
tip (gratuity) pourboire; service
tired fatigué
tire pneu
tissue, facial kleenex; mouchoirs en papier
to à
toasted grillé
today aujourd'hui
toe orteil
together ensemble
toilet toilette; WC
toilet paper papier hygiénique
token jeton
toll péage
toll-free gratuit
tomorrow demain
tomorrow, day after après demain
tongue (mouth, language) langue
tonight ce soir
too (also) aussi
too (much) trop
tooth dent
toothache mal aux dents
toothbrush brosse à dents
toothpaste dentifrice
toothpick cure-dent
total total
touch (v) toucher
tough dur
tour tour
tour, guided visite guidée
tourist touriste
tow truck dépanneur
toward vers
towel, bath serviette de bain
tower (n) tour
town ville
toy jouet
toy store magasin de jouets
track (train) voie
tracking number numéro de suivi
tradition tradition
traditional traditionnel
traffic circulation
traffic jam embouteillage; bouchon
trail sentier; chemin
train train
train car voiture
train station gare
tranquil tranquille
transfer (transportation) (n) correspondance
transfer (v) prendre une correspondance
translate traduire
transmission fluid liquide de transmission
transmission, automatic boîte automatique
transmission, manual boîte manuelle
trash / trashcan poubelle
travel (v) voyager
travel agency agence de voyage
traveler voyageur
travelers check chèque de voyage
treasury trésorerie

T

treat (v) soigner
treatment (medical) traitement
tree arbre
triangle triangle
tri-band tri-bande
trim (hair) (v) rafraîchir
trip (n) voyage
tripod trépied
trouble trouble
truth vérité
try (attempt) essayer
T-shirt T-shirt
Tuesday mardi
tuna thon
tunnel tunnel
turkey dinde
Turkey Turquie
turn off (lights, devices) éteindre
turn on (lights, devices) allumer
turn signal clignotant
tweezers pince à épiler
twin bed lit jumeau
twins jumeaux
two deux
type (v) taper

U

ugly laid
umbrella parapluie
uncle oncle
unconscious inconscient
under sous
undercooked pas assez cuit
underline (n) soulignement
underpants slip
underscore (_) souligne
understand comprendre
underwear sous-vêtements
unemployment chômage
unfortunate malheureux
unfortunately malheureusement
United States États-Unis
university université
unleaded (gas) sans plomb
unlimited illimité
unlock (a door) déverrouiller
unlock (mobile phone) débloquer
until jusqu'à
up en haut
uphill montée
upside-down à l'envers
upstairs en haut; à l'étage
urethra urètre
urgent urgent
urinary tract infection infection urinaire
urine urine
us nous
USB cable câble USB
use (v) utiliser
uterus utérus

V

vacancy (hotel) chambre libre
vacant libre
vacation vacances
vagina vagin
valid bon
validate composter; valider
valley vallée
value (worth) valeur
van camion

vase vase
Vaseline Vaseline
VAT (Value-Added Tax) TVA (Taxe sur la Valeur Ajoutée)
vegan végétalien
vegetable légume
vegetarian végétarien
velvet velours
very très
vest gilet
video vidéo
video camera caméra vidéo
videogame jeu vidéo
view (n) vue
viewpoint point de vue; panorama
village village
vineyard vignoble
violence violence
virus virus
visit (n) visite
visit (v) visiter
vitamin vitamine
voice voix
voicemail boîte vocale
vomit (v) vomir

W

waist taille
wait (v) attendre
waiter serveur
waiting room salle d'attente
waitress serveuse
wake up se réveiller
walk (v) marcher
walker (for disabled) déambulateur
wall (room) mur
wall, fortified remparts
wallet portefeuille
want (v) vouloir
war guerre
warm (adj) tiède
wart verrue
wash (v) laver
washcloth gant de toilette
washer machine à laver
waste (v) gaspiller
watch (jewelry) montre
watch (v) regarder
watch battery pile de montre
water eau
water, drinkable eau potable
water, mineral eau minérale
water, sparkling eau gazeuse
water, still eau plate
water, tap eau du robinet
water park parc aquatique
waterfall cascade
waterskiing ski nautique
wave (water) vague
wax (spa) (n) épilation à la cire
we nous
weak faible
wear (v) porter
weather temps
weather forecast météo
webcam webcam
website site web
wedding mariage
Wednesday mercredi
week semaine
weekend week-end
weight poids

weight limit poids limite
welcome bienvenue
well (well-being, manner) bien
west ouest
wet mouillé
what quoi
whatever n'importe quoi
wheat blé
wheel roue
wheelchair fauteuil roulant; chaise roulante
wheelchair-accessible accessible à un fauteuil roulant
when quand
where où
whipped cream crème chantilly
white blanc
who qui
why pourquoi
widow veuve
widower veuf
wife femme
Wi-Fi Wi-Fi
Wi-Fi hotspot zone Wi-Fi
wild sauvage
wind vent
windmill moulin
window fenêtre
windshield pare-brise
windshield wiper essuie-glace
windsurfing planche à voile
windy venteux
wine vin
wine, red vin rouge
wine, white vin blanc
wine shop marchand de vin
wing aile
winter hiver
wipe (v) essuyer
wireless sans fil
wise sage
wish (v) souhaiter
with avec
without sans
woman femme; dame (formal)
women femmes; dames (formal)
wood bois
wool laine
word mot
work (n) travail
work (v) travailler
world monde
worms vers
worry (v) inquiéter
worse pire
worst le pire
wrap emballer
wrist poignet
write écrire

X

X-ray radio

Y

year année
yellow jaune
yes oui
yesterday hier
yield céder le passage
yoga yoga
yogurt yaourt

you vous (formal); tu (informal)
young jeune
your votre
yours à vous; le vôtre
youth hostel auberge de jeunesse
youths jeunes

Z

zero zéro
zip code code postal
Ziploc bag sac en plastique à fermeture
zipper fermeture éclair
zoo zoo

TIPS FOR HURDLING THE LANGUAGE BARRIER

A fear of the language barrier keeps many people (read: English speakers) out of Europe, but the "barrier" is getting smaller every day. English has arrived as Europe's second language, but you'll win the respect of locals by starting conversations in French—ask ***Parlez-vous anglais?*** (Do you speak English?). And if you need help speaking French, remember that you're surrounded by expert tutors.

Creative Communication

Speak slowly, clearly, and with carefully chosen words. When speaking English, choose easy words and clearly pronounce each syllable (fried po-ta-toes). Avoid contractions. Be patient—speaking louder and tossing in a few extra words doesn't help.

Keep your messages grunt-simple. Make single nouns work as entire sentences. A one-word question ("Photo?") is just as effective as something grammatically correct ("May I take your picture, sir?"). Things go even easier if you include the local "please" (e.g., "Toilet, ***s'il vous plaît?***").

Can the slang. Someone who learned English in a classroom will be stumped by American expressions such as "sort of like," "pretty bad," or "Howzit goin'?"

Risk looking goofy. Butcher the language if you must, but communicate. I'll never forget the clerk in the French post office who flapped her arms and asked, "Tweet, tweet, tweet?" I answered with a nod, and she gave me the airmail stamps I needed.

Be melodramatic. Exaggerate the native accent. The locals won't be insulted; they'll be impressed. English spoken with an over-the-top sexy French accent makes more sense to the French ear.

A notepad works wonders. Written words and numbers are much easier to understand than their mispronounced counterparts. Bring a notepad. To repeatedly communicate something difficult or important (such as medical instructions, "I'm a strict vegetarian," etc.), write it in the local language.

Assume you understand and go with your gut. Treat most problems as multiple-choice questions, make an educated guess at the meaning, and proceed confidently. I'm correct about 80 percent of the time—and even when I'm wrong, I usually never know it. I only blow it about 10 percent of the time. My trip becomes easier—and occasionally much more interesting.

Navigating France (and the French)

When you talk to someone who just returned from France and ask their impressions, they almost always say, "The people were so much nicer than I expected!"

The easily misunderstood French have an unfairly negative reputation. While it's dangerous to generalize about any group of people, it helps to try to tune into the uniquely French way of looking at things. I asked some of my French friends what they perceive as the biggest cultural gaps between American visitors and the Frenchman on the street. Here's what they told me:

It's difficult to sufficiently emphasize the importance of formality to the French. In the US, rules are made to be broken. We find it roguish, even a bit charming, when someone has the nerve to deftly defy our social mores. But in France, these rules—for respect and courtesy—are sacrosanct. For example, when interacting with someone, simply behave as if you've been invited into the home of someone you respect. (Maybe your boss invited you to dinner with her family.) You don't have to tiptoe around them, but you want to make a good impression.

Shop clerks take pride in their work. It's their personal and professional space, and you're being invited into it. Greet them kindly, don't touch display items without asking first, and don't bring outside food or drinks in with you. You wouldn't do that if you visited a stranger in their house.

The French are insulted by any insinuation that your money talks. Play by their rules and don't try to buy yourself into their favor—it won't work.

French people are very conscious of accents. From the way people speak French, they can tell what part of the country they're from, which class they belong to, and so on. They are painfully aware that they speak English less than perfectly, which makes them particularly self-conscious. That's why you might find them reluctant to speak English.

Most French people don't multitask. Drinking a Starbucks latte while munching a crêpe while window shopping doesn't allow you to fully enjoy any of those activities. Do things one at a time and live in the moment. French culture respects the subtleties in life.

I know you're on vacation. But look at it this way: Making an effort to adapt to French customs won't take much effort at all, and the payoff is huge in the way your respect will be reciprocated. You'll see a France of warm, welcoming people that other visitors miss. Or you could defiantly stick to your casual ways, dare the people you meet to accept you on your own standards, and go home hating the French.

It's all part of ***l'art de vivre***—the art of living, the uniquely French approach to life.

French Gestures

Here are a few common French gestures and their meanings:

The Fingertips Kiss: Gently bring the fingers and thumb of your right hand together, raise to your lips, kiss lightly, and toss your fingers and thumb into the air. Be careful: Tourists look silly when they over-emphasize this subtle action. It can mean sexy, delicious, divine, or wonderful.

The Eyelid Pull: Place your extended forefinger below the center of your eye, and pull the skin downward. This means: "I'm alert. I'm looking. You can't fool me."

The Roto-Wrist: Hold your forearm out from your waist with your open palm down, and pivot your wrist clockwise and counter-clockwise like you're opening a doorknob. When a Frenchman uses this gesture while explaining something to you, he isn't sure of the information or it's complete B.S. He'll usually say ***Bof!*** or ***Comme ci, comme ça.***

The Hand Shave: Move the back of your hand gently up and down the side of your face as if checking a clean shave. This denotes a boring person, show, talk, or whatever, and is often accompanied by the expression ***La barbe*** (the beard).

The Shoulder Shrug: Move your shoulders up towards your ears and slightly lift your arms with palms up. This basically means, "I don't know and I don't care."

The Nose-Grab-and-Twist: Wrap your hand around your nose and twist it down. If someone does this to you, put down your wine glass—it means you're drunk.

The French Puff: Fill your cheeks with air and slowly release your breath. This indicates that you are unsure and buys you time to come up with something clever to say. It can also be a response in and of itself, saying simply that you don't know.

To beckon someone in northern Europe, you bring your palm up. But in France and the south, you wave it down. To Americans, this looks like "go away"—not the invitation it actually is.

International Words

As our world shrinks, more and more words leap their linguistic boundaries and become international. Sensitive travelers choose words most likely to be universally understood ("auto" instead of "car"; "holiday" for "vacation"; "kaput" for "broken"; "photo" for "picture"). They also internationalize their pronunciation: "University," if you play around with its sound (oo-nee-vehr-see-tay), can be understood anywhere.

Here are a few internationally understood words. Remember, cut out the Yankee accent and give each word a pan-European sound ("autobooooos," "Engleesh").

Hello	**Rock 'n' roll**	**Bank**
No	**Mamma mia**	**Hotel**
Stop	**No problem**	**Post (office)**
Kaput	**Super**	**Camping**
Ciao	**Sex/Sexy**	**Auto**
Bye-bye	**Oh la la**	**Autobus**
OK	**Moment**	**Taxi**
Mañana	**Bon voyage**	**Tourist**
Pardon	**Restaurant**	**Beer**

International Words *(cont.)*

Coke, Coca-Cola	Toilet	Central
Tea	Police	Information
Coffee	English	University
Vino	Telephone	Passport
Chocolate	Photo	Holiday (vacation)
Picnic	Photocopy	Gratis (free)
Self-service	Computer	America's favorite four-letter words
Yankee, Americano	Sport	
Amigo	Internet	

French Verbs

These conjugated verbs will help you assemble a caveman sentence in a pinch.

TO BE	ÊTRE	eh-truh
I am	je suis	zhuh swee
you are (formal, singular or plural)	vous êtes	vooz eht
you are (singular, informal)	tu es	tew ay
he / she / one is ("one"—or in French, "on"—is colloquial for "we")	il / elle / on est	eel / ehl / ohn̲ ay
we are	nous sommes	noo suhm
they (m / f) are	ils / elles sont	eel / ehl sohn̲
TO HAVE	**AVOIR**	**ah-vwahr**
I have	j'ai	zhay
you have (formal, singular or plural)	vous avez	vooz ah-vay
you have (singular, informal)	tu as	tew ah
he / she / one has	il / elle / on a	eel / ehl / ohn̲ ah

we have	nous avons	nooz ah-vohn
they (m / f) have	ils / elles ont	eelz / ehlz ohn
TO SPEAK	**PARLER**	**par-lay**
I speak	je parle	zhuh parl
you speak (formal, singular or plural)	vous parlez	voo par-lay
you speak (singular, informal)	tu parles	tew parl
he / she / one speaks	il / elle / on parle	eel / ehl / ohn parl
we speak	nous parlons	noo par-lohn
they (m / f) speak	ils / elles parlent	eel / ehl parl
TO WALK	**MARCHER**	**mar-shay**
I walk	je marche	zhuh marsh
you walk (formal, singular or plural)	vous marchez	voo mar-shay
you walk (singular, informal)	tu marches	tew marsh
he / she / one walks	il / elle / on marche	eel / ehl / ohn marsh
we walk	nous marchons	noo mar-shohn
they (m / f) walk	ils / elles marchent	eel / ehl marsh
TO LIKE	**AIMER**	**ehm-ay**
I like	j'aime	zhehm
you like (formal, singular or plural)	vous aimez	vooz eh-may
you like (singular, informal)	tu aimes	tew ehm
he / she / one likes	il / elle / on aime	eel / ehl / ohn ehm
we like	nous aimons	nooz eh-mohn
they (m / f) like	ils / elles aiment	eelz / ehlz ehm

TO GO	ALLER	ah-lay
I go	je vais	zhuh vay
you go (formal, singular or plural)	vous allez	vooz ah-lay
you go (singular, informal)	tu vas	tew vah
he / she / one goes	il / elle / on va	eel / ehl / ohn vah
we go	nous allons	nooz ah-lohn
they (m / f) go	ils / elles vont	eel / ehl vohn

TO DO / MAKE	FAIRE	fair
I do	je fais	zhuh fay
you do (formal, singular or plural)	vous faîtes	voo feht
you do (singular, informal)	tu fais	tew fay
he / she / one does	il / elle / on fait	eel / ehl / ohn fay
we do	nous faisons	noo fuh-sohn
they (m / f) do	ils / elles font	eel / ehl fohn

TO SEE	VOIR	vwahr
I see	je vois	zhuh vwah
you see (formal, singular or plural)	vous voyez	voo vwah-yay
you see (singular, informal)	tu vois	tew vwah
he / she / one sees	il / elle / on voit	eel / ehl / ohn vwah
we see	nous voyons	noo vwah-yohn
they (m / f) see	ils / elles voient	eel / ehl vwah

TO BE ABLE	POUVOIR	poo-vwahr
I can	je peux	zhuh puh
you can (formal, singular or plural)	vous pouvez	voo poo-vay
you can (singular, informal)	tu peux	tew puh
he / she / one can	il / elle / on peut	eel / ehl / ohn puh
we can	nous pouvons	noo poo-vohn
they (m / f) can	ils / elles peuvent	eel / ehl puhv

TO WANT	VOULOIR	vool-wahr
I want	je veux	zhuh vuh
you want (formal, singular or plural)	vous voulez	voo voo-lay
you want (singular, informal)	tu veux	tew vuh
he / she / one wants	il / elle / on veut	eel / ehl / ohn vuh
we want	nous voulons	noo voo-lohn
they (m / f) want	ils / elles veulent	eel / ehl vuhl

TO NEED	AVOIR BESOIN DE	ah-vwahr buh-swan duh
I need	j'ai besoin de	zhay buh-swan duh
you need (formal, singular or plural)	vous avez besoin de	vooz ah-vay buh-swan duh
you need (singular, informal)	tu as besoin de	tew ah buh-swan duh
he / she / one needs	il / elle / on a besoin de	eel / ehl / ohn ah buh-swan duh
we need	nous avons besoin de	nooz ah-vohn buh-swan duh
they (m / f) need	ils / elles ont besoin de	eelz / ehlz ohn buh-swan duh

TIPS

French Tongue Twisters

Tongue twisters are a great way to practice a language and break the ice with local Europeans. Here are a few French tongue twisters that are sure to challenge you and amuse your hosts.

Bonjour madame la saucissonière!	Hello, madame sausage-seller!
Combien sont ces six saucissons-ci?	How much are these six sausages?
Ces six saucissons-ci sont six sous.	These six sausages are six cents.
Si ces saucissons-ci sont six sous, ces six saucissons-ci sont trop chers.	If these are six cents, these six sausages are too expensive.
Je veux et j'exige qu'un chasseur sachant chasser sans ses èchasses sache chasser sans son chien de chasse.	I want and demand that a hunter who knows how to hunt without his stilts knows how to hunt without his hunting dog.
Ce sont seize cent jacynthes sèches dans seize cent sachets secs.	These are 600 dry hyacinths in 600 dry sachets.
Ce sont trois très gros rats dans trois très gros trous roulant trois gros rats gris morts.	These are three very fat rats in three very fat rat-holes rolling three fat gray dead rats.

English Tongue Twisters

After your French friends have laughed at you, let them try these tongue twisters in English:

If neither he sells seashells, nor she sells seashells, who shall sell seashells? Shall seashells be sold?	Si ni lui ni elle ne vendent de coquillages, qui les vendra? Les coquillages seront-ils vendus?
Peter Piper picked a peck of pickled peppers.	Pierre Pipant a choisi un picotin de cornichons.
Rugged rubber baby buggy bumpers.	Des pare-chocs solides en caoutchoue pour les voitures d'enfants.
The sixth sick sheik's sixth sheep's sick.	Le sixième mouton du sixième sheik est malade.
Red bug's blood and black bug's blood.	Sang d'insecte rouge, sang d'insecte noir.
Soldiers' shoulders.	Epaules de soldats.
Thieves seize skis.	Les voleurs s'emparent de skis.
I'm a pleasant mother pheasant plucker. I pluck mother pheasants. I'm the most pleasant mother pheasant plucker that ever plucked a mother pheasant.	Je suis une plaisant plumeur de faisanes. Je plume les faisanes. Je suis le plumeur de faisanes le plus plaisant qui ait jamais plumé de faisanes.

APPENDIX

LET'S TALK TELEPHONES

Smart travelers use the telephone to reserve or reconfirm rooms, get tourist information, reserve restaurants, confirm tour times, and phone home.

Dialing Within France

France has a direct-dial phone system (without area codes). All of France's phone numbers are 10 digits long and can be dialed direct throughout the country. For example, the number of one of my recommended hotels in Nice is 04 97 03 10 70. That's exactly what you dial, whether you're calling it from across the street or across the country. Understand the various prefixes. Any number beginning with 06 or 07 is a mobile phone and costs more to dial. France's toll-free numbers start with 0800, but any 08 number that does not have a 00 directly following is a toll call. Directory assistance is also pricey (tel. 12).

For more information, see www.ricksteves.com/phoning.

Dialing Internationally

If you want to make an international call, follow these steps:

- Dial the international access code (00 if you're calling from Europe, 011 from the US or Canada). If you're dialing from a mobile phone, you can replace the international access code with +, which works regardless of where you're calling from. (On many mobile phones, you can insert a + by pressing and holding the 0 key.)
- Dial the country code ***(code du pays)*** of the country you're calling (for example, 33 for France, or 1 for the US or Canada).
- Dial the area code ***(code de zone)***—if the country uses area codes—and the local number, keeping in mind that calling many countries requires dropping the initial zero of the phone number (this applies to France). The European calling chart in this chapter lists specifics per country.

Calling from the US to France: Dial 011 (the US international access code), 33 (France's country code), then the French number without its initial zero. For example, if you're calling the Nice hotel cited earlier, you'd dial 011-33-4-97-03-10-70.

Calling from any European country to the US: To call my office in Edmonds, Washington, from anywhere in Europe, I dial 00 (Europe's international access code), 1 (the US country code), 425 (Edmonds' area code), and 771-8303.

Embassies

US Embassy/Consulate: Tel. 01 43 12 22 22; 4 avenue Gabriel, Paris (Métro stop: Concorde); http://france.usembassy.gov
Canadian Embassy/Consulate: Tel. 01 44 43 29 00; 35 avenue Montaigne, Paris (Métro stop: Franklin-Roosevelt); www.amb-canada.fr

NUMBERS AND STUMBLERS

Here are a few things to keep in mind:

- Europeans write a few of their numbers differently than we do. 1=1, 4=4, 7=7.
- In Europe, dates appear as day/month/year.
- Commas are decimal points, and decimal points are commas. A dollar and a half is $1,50, one thousand is 1.000, and there are 5.280 feet in a mile.
- When counting with fingers, start with your thumb. If you hold up your first finger to request one item, you'll probably get two.
- What Americans call the second floor of a building is the first floor in Europe.
- On escalators and moving sidewalks, Europeans keep the left "lane" open for passing. Keep to the right.

Metric Conversions

A kilogram is 2.2 pounds, and l liter is about a quart, or almost four to a gallon. A kilometer is six-tenths of a mile. I figure kilometers to miles by cutting the kilometers in half and adding back 10 percent of the original (120 km: 60 + 12 = 72 miles, 300 km: 150 + 30 = 180 miles).

European Calling Chart

Just smile and dial, using this key:
AC = Area Code, LN = Local Number.

European Country	Calling long distance within...	Calling from the US or Canada to...	Calling from a European country to...
Austria	AC + LN	011 + 43 + AC (without the initial zero) + LN	00 + 43 + AC (without the initial zero) + LN
Belgium	LN	011 + 32 + LN (without initial zero)	00 + 32 + LN (without initial zero)
Britain	AC + LN	011 + 44 + AC (without initial zero) + LN	00 + 44 + AC (without initial zero) + LN
France	LN	011 + 33 + LN (without initial zero)	00 + 33 + LN (without initial zero)
Germany	AC + LN	011 + 49 + AC (without initial zero) + LN	00 + 49 + AC (without initial zero) + LN
Gibraltar	LN	011 + 350 + LN	00 + 350 + LN
Ireland	AC + LN	011 + 353 + AC (without initial zero) + LN	00 + 353 + AC (without initial zero) + LN
Italy	LN	011 + 39 + LN	00 + 39 + LN

European Country	Calling long distance within...	Calling from the US or Canada to...	Calling from a European country to...
Morocco	LN	011 + 212 + LN (without initial zero)	00 + 212 + LN (without initial zero)
Netherlands	AC + LN	011 + 31 + AC (without initial zero) + LN	00 + 31 + AC (without initial zero) + LN
Portugal	LN	011 + 351 + LN	00 + 351 + LN
Spain	LN	011 + 34 + LN	00 + 34 + LN
Switzerland	LN	011 + 41 + LN (without initial zero)	00 + 41 + LN (without initial zero)

- The instructions above apply whether you're calling to or from a European landline or mobile phone.
- If calling from any mobile phone, you can replace the international access code with "+" (press and hold 0 to insert it).
- The international access code is 011 if you're calling from the US or Canada.
- To call the US or Canada from Europe, dial 00, then 1 (country code for US and Canada), then the area code and number. In short, 00 + 1 + AC + LN = Hi, Mom!

Temperature Conversion

For a rough conversion from Celsius to Fahrenheit, double the number and add 30. For weather, remember that 28°C is 82°F—perfect. For health, 37°C is just right.

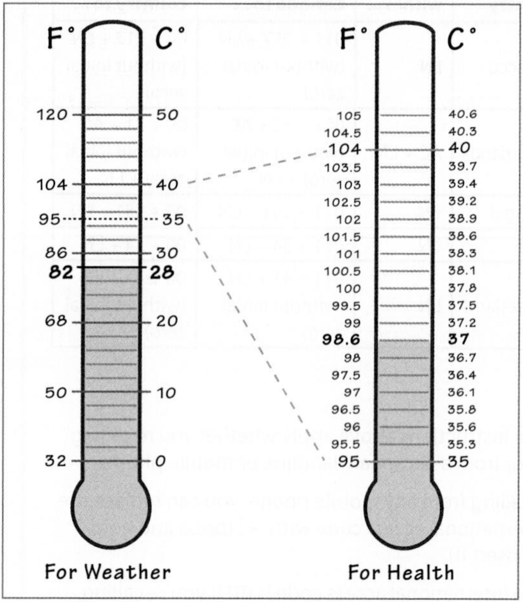

FILLING OUT FORMS

If you need to decipher paperwork or forms, the following can help.

Monsieur	Mr.
Madame	Mrs.
Mademoiselle	Miss
prénom	first name
nom	name
adresse	address
lieu de domicile	address
rue	street
ville	city
état	state
pays	country
nationalité	nationality
originaire de	origin
destination	destination
âge	age
date de naissance	date of birth
lieu de naissance	place of birth
sexe	sex
mâle / femelle	male / female
marié (m) / mariée (f)	married
célibataire	single
divorcé (m) / divorcée (f)	divorced
veuf (m) / veuve (f)	widowed
profession	profession
adulte	adult
enfant / garçon / fille	child / boy / girl
enfants	children
famille	family
signature	signature
date	date

When filling out dates, do it European-style: day/month/year.

TEAR-OUT CHEAT SHEETS

Basics

Tear out this sheet of French survival phrases and keep it in your pocket to use in case you're caught without your phrase book.

Good day.	Bonjour. bohn-zhoor
Mr.	Monsieur muhs-yuh
Mrs.	Madame mah-dahm
Miss	Mademoiselle mahd-mwah-zehl
Do you speak English?	Parlez-vous anglais? par-lay-voo ahn-glay
Yes. / No.	Oui. / Non. wee / nohn
I don't speak French.	Je ne parle pas français. zhuh nuh parl pah frahn-say
I'm sorry.	Désolé. day-zoh-lay
Please.	S'il vous plaît. see voo play
Thank you.	Merci. mehr-see
You're welcome.	De rien. duh ree-an
Excuse me. (to get attention)	Excusez-moi. ehk-skew-zay-mwah
Excuse me. (to pass)	Pardon. par-dohn
OK?	Ça va? sah vah
No problem.	Pas de problème. pah duh proh-blehm
Very good.	Très bien. treh bee-an
Goodbye.	Au revoir. oh ruh-vwahr
How much is it?	Combien? kohn-bee-an
Write it?	Ecrivez? ay-kree-vay
euro (€)	euro uh-roh
zero	zéro zay-roh
one / two	un / deux uhn / duh
three / four	trois / quatre trwah / kah-truh
five / six	cinq / six sank / sees

seven / eight	sept / huit seht / weet
nine / ten	neuf / dix nuhf / dees
Can you help me?	Vous pouvez m'aider? voo poo-vay meh-day
I'd like...	Je voudrais... zhuh voo-dray
We'd like...	Nous voudrions... noo voo-dree-ohn
...this.	...ceci. suh-see
...a ticket.	...un billet. uhn bee-yay
...the bill.	...l'addition. lah-dee-see-ohn
Where is a cash machine?	Où est un distributeur? oo ay uhn dee-stree-bew-tur
Where are the toilets?	Où sont les toilettes? oo sohn lay twah-leht
men / women	hommes / dames ohm / dahm
Is it free?	C'est gratuit? say grah-twee
Included?	Inclus? an-klew
Is it possible?	C'est possible? say poh-see-bluh
entrance / exit	entrée / sortie ahn-tray / sor-tee
At what time does this open / close?	À quelle heure c'est ouvert / fermé? ah kehl ur say oo-vehr / fehr-may
Just a moment.	Un moment. uhn moh-mahn
now	maintenant man-tuh-nahn
soon / later	bientôt / plus tard bee-an-toh / plew tar
today	aujourd'hui oh-zhoor-dwee
tomorrow	demain duh-man
Sunday	dimanche dee-mahnsh
Monday	lundi luhn-dee
Tuesday	mardi mar-dee
Wednesday	mercredi mehr-kruh-dee
Thursday	jeudi zhuh-dee
Friday	vendredi vahn-druh-dee
Saturday	samedi sahm-dee

Restaurants

I'd like / We'd like...	Je voudrais / Nous voudrions... zhuh voo-dray / noo voo-dree-ohn
...to reserve...	...réserver... ray-zehr-vay
...a table for one / two.	...une table pour un / deux. ewn tah-bluh poor uhn / duh
Is this table free?	Cette table est libre? seht tah-bluh ay lee-bruh
How long is the wait?	Combien de temps faut-il attendre? kohn-bee-an duh tahn foh-teel ah-tahn-druh
The menu (in English), please.	La carte (en anglais), s'il vous plaît. lah kart (ahn ahn-glay) see voo play
breakfast	petit déjeuner puh-tee day-zhuh-nay
lunch	déjeuner day-zhuh-nay
dinner	dîner dee-nay
service (not) included	service (non) compris sehr-vees (nohn) kohn-pree
to go	à emporter ah ahn-por-tay
with / without	avec / sans ah-vehk / sahn
and / or	et / ou ay / oo
fixed-price meal	menu / prix fixe muh-new / pree feeks
special of the day	plat du jour plah dew zhoor
specialty of the house	spécialité de la maison spay-see-ah-lee-tay duh lah may-zohn
appetizers	hors-d'oeuvres or-duh-vruh
What do you recommend?	Qu'est-ce que vous recommandez? kehs kuh voo ruh-koh-mahn-day
first course (soup, salad)	entrée ahn-tray
main course (meat, fish)	plat principal plah pran-see-pahl
bread	pain pan

cheese	fromage froh-mahzh
sandwich	sandwich sahnd-weech
soup	soupe soop
salad	salade sah-lahd
meat	viande vee-ahnd
chicken	poulet poo-lay
fish	poisson pwah-sohn
seafood	fruits de mer frwee duh mehr
fruit	fruit frwee
vegetables	légumes lay-gewm
dessert	dessert duh-sehr
mineral water	eau minérale oh mee-nay-rahl
carafe of tap water	une carafe d'eau ewn kah-rahf doh
milk	lait lay
(orange) juice	jus (d'orange) zhew (doh-rahnzh)
coffee	café kah-fay
tea	thé tay
wine	vin van
red / white	rouge / blanc roozh / blahn
glass / bottle	verre / bouteille vehr / boo-teh-ee
beer	bière bee-ehr
Cheers!	Santé! sahn-tay
More. / Another.	Plus. / Un autre. plew / uhn oh-truh
The same.	La même chose. lah mehm shohz
Finished.	Terminé. tehr-mee-nay
The bill, please.	L'addition, s'il vous plaît. lah-dee-see-ohn see voo play
Do you accept credit cards?	Vous prenez les cartes? voo pruh-nay lay kart
tip	pourboire poor-bwahr
Delicious!	Délicieux! day-lee-see-uh

The perfect complement to your phrase book

Travel with Rick Steves' candid, up-to-date advice on the best places to eat and sleep, the must-see sights, getting off the beaten path—and getting the most out of every day and every dollar while you're in Europe.

Audio Europe™

RICK STEVES AUDIO EUROPE

Rick's Free Travel App

Get your FREE **Rick Steves Audio Europe**™ app to enjoy…

- Dozens of self-guided tours of Europe's top museums, sights and historic walks
- Hundreds of tracks filled with cultural insights and sightseeing tips from Rick's radio interviews
- All organized into handy geographic playlists
- For iPhone, iPad, iPod Touch, Android

With Rick whispering in your ear, Europe gets even better.

Find out more at ricksteves.com

Join a
Rick Steves
tour
Enjoy Europe's
warmest welcome...
with the flexibility and
friendship of a small group
getting to know Rick's
favorite places and people.
It all starts with our free
tour catalog and DVD.
Great guides, small
groups, no grumps.
See more than three dozen itineraries throughout Europe
ricksteves.com

Start your trip at

Free information and great gear to

▸ Plan Your Trip

Browse thousands of articles and a wealth of money-saving tips for planning your dream trip. You'll find up-to-date information on Europe's best destinations, packing smart, getting around, finding rooms, staying healthy, avoiding scams and more.

▸ Travel News

Subscribe to our free Travel News e-newsletter, and get monthly updates from Rick on what's happening in Europe.

▸ Graffiti Wall & Travelers Helpline

Learn, ask, share—our online community of savvy travelers is a great resource for first-time travelers to Europe, as well as seasoned pros.

Rick Steves' Europe Through the Back Door, Inc.

ricksteves.com

turn your travel dreams into affordable reality

▸ Rick's Free Audio Europe™ App

The Rick Steves Audio Europe™ app brings history and art to life. Enjoy Rick's audio tours of Europe's top museums, sights and neighborhood walks—plus 200 tracks of travel tips and cultural insights from Rick's radio show—all organized into geographic playlists. Learn more at ricksteves.com.

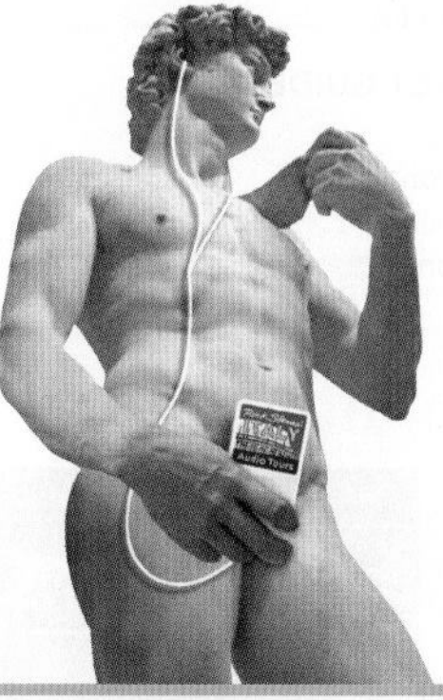

▸ Great Gear from Rick's Travel Store

Pack light and right—on a budget—with Rick's custom-designed carry-on bags, wheeled bags, day packs, travel accessories, guidebooks, journals, maps and DVDs of his TV shows.

130 Fourth Avenue North, PO Box 2009 • Edmonds, WA 98020 USA
Phone: (425) 771-8303 • Fax: (425) 771-0833 • www.ricksteves.com

Rick Steves® www.ricksteves.com

EUROPE GUIDES
Best of Europe
Eastern Europe
Europe Through the Back Door
Mediterranean Cruise Ports
Northern European Cruise Ports

COUNTRY GUIDES
Croatia & Slovenia
England
France
Germany
Great Britain
Ireland
Italy
Portugal
Scandinavia
Spain
Switzerland

CITY & REGIONAL GUIDES
Amsterdam, Bruges & Brussels
Barcelona
Budapest
Florence & Tuscany
Greece: Athens & the Peloponnese
Istanbul
London
Paris
Prague & the Czech Republic
Provence & the French Riviera
Rome
Venice
Vienna, Salzburg & Tirol

SNAPSHOT GUIDES
Berlin
Bruges & Brussels
Copenhagen & the Best of Denmark
Dublin
Dubrovnik
Hill Towns of Central Italy
Italy's Cinque Terre
Krakow, Warsaw & Gdansk
Lisbon
Madrid & Toledo
Munich, Bavaria & Salzburg
Naples & the Amalfi Coast
Northern Ireland
Norway
Scotland
Sevilla, Granada & Southern Spain
Stockholm

POCKET GUIDES
Athens
Barcelona
Florence
London
Paris
Rome
Venice

NOW AVAILABLE: eBOOKS, DVD & BLU-RAY

TRAVEL CULTURE

Europe 101
European Christmas
Postcards from Europe
Travel as a Political Act

eBOOKS

Nearly all Rick Steves guides are available as eBooks. Check with your favorite bookseller.

RICK STEVES' EUROPE DVDs

11 New Shows 2013–2014
Austria & the Alps
Eastern Europe
England & Wales
European Christmas
European Travel Skills & Specials
France
Germany, BeNeLux & More
Greece, Turkey & Portugal
Iran
Ireland & Scotland
Italy's Cities
Italy's Countryside
Scandinavia
Spain
Travel Extras

BLU-RAY

Celtic Charms
Eastern Europe Favorites
European Christmas
Italy Through the Back Door
Mediterranean Mosaic
Surprising Cities of Europe

PHRASE BOOKS & DICTIONARIES

French
French, Italian & German
German
Italian
Portuguese
Spanish

JOURNALS

Rick Steves' Pocket Travel Journal
Rick Steves' Travel Journal

PLANNING MAPS

Britain, Ireland & London
Europe
France & Paris
Germany, Austria & Switzerland
Ireland
Italy
Spain & Portugal

Rick Steves guidebooks are published by Avalon Travel, a member of the Perseus Books Group.
Rick Steves books and DVDs are available at bookstores and through online booksellers.

Avalon Travel
a member of the Perseus Books Group
1700 Fourth Street, Berkeley, CA 94710, USA

Text © 2013, 2008 by Rick Steves. All rights reserved.
Cover © 2013 by Avalon Travel.
All rights reserved.
Maps © 2013 , 2008 by Europe Through the Back Door.
All rights reserved.

Printed in China by RR Donnelley.

Seventh edition. First printing January 2014.

ISBN-13: 978-1-61238-202-9

For the latest on Rick's lectures, guidebooks, tours, and public television series, contact Europe Through the Back Door, P.O. Box 2009, Edmonds, WA 98020, tel. 425/771-8303, fax 425/771-0833, www.ricksteves.com, rick@ricksteves.com.

Europe Through The Back Door
Managing Editor: Risa Laib
Series Manager: Cathy Lu
Project Editor: Tom Griffin
Editors: Jennifer Madison Davis, Glenn Eriksen, Cameron Hewitt, Suzanne Kotz, Carrie Shepherd, Gretchen Strauch
Editorial Assistant: Jessica Shaw
Editorial Interns: Caitlin Fjelsted, Valerie Gilmore, Samantha Oberholzer, Rebekka Shattuck
Translation: Scott Bernhard, Mary Campbell Bouron, Paul Desloover, Sabine Leteinturier, Michelle Martin, Arnaud Servignat, Steve Smith